Thought and Poetry

Bloomsbury Studies in Philosophy and Poetry

Series Editors:
Rick Anthony Furtak and James D. Reid

Bloomsbury Studies in Philosophy and Poetry explores ancient, modern, and contemporary texts in ways that are sensitive to philosophical themes and problems that can be fruitfully addressed through poetic modes of writing, and focused on questions of style, the relations between form and content, and the conduciveness of literary modes of expression to philosophical inquiry. With a keen interest in the intertwining of poetry and philosophy in all forms, the series will cover the philosophical register of poetry, the poetics of philosophical writing, and the literary strategies of philosophers.

The series provides a home for work on figures across geographical landscapes, with contributions that employ a wide range of methods across academic disciplines, and without regard for divisions within philosophy, between analytic and continental, for example, that have outworn their usefulness. Featuring single-authored works and edited collections, curated by an international editorial board, the series aims to redefine how we read and discuss philosophy and poetry today.

Editorial Board: Daniel Brown, University of Southampton, UK; Kristen Case, University of Maine Farmington, USA; Hannah Vandegrift Eldridge, University of Wisconsin–Madison, USA; Cassandra Falke, University of Tromsø, Norway; Luke Fischer, University of Sydney, Australia; John Gibson, University of Louisville, USA; James Haile III, University of Rhode Island, USA; Kevin Hart, University of Virginia, USA; Eileen John, University of Warwick, UK; Troy Jollimore, California State University, USA; David Kleinberg-Levin, Northwestern University, USA; John Koethe, University of Wisconsin–Milwaukee, USA; John T. Lysaker, Emory University, USA; Karmen MacKendrick, Le Moyne College, USA; Rukmini Bhaya Nair, Indian Institute of Technology, India; Kamiyo Ogawa, Sophia University, Japan; Kaz Oishi, University of Tokyo, Japan; Yi-Ping Ong, Johns Hopkins University, USA; Anna Christina Soy Ribeiro, Texas Tech University, USA; Karen Simecek, University of Warwick, UK; Ruth Rebecca Tietjen, University of Copenhagen, Denmark; Íngrid Vendrell Ferran, Goethe University Frankfurt, Germany

Forthcoming Titles:
Philosophical Fragments and the Poetry of Thinking, by Luke Fischer
A Philosophy of Lyric Voice, by Karen Simecek
Skepticism and Impersonality in Modern Poetry, by Joshua Adams
A Black Poetics of the Everyday, by James Haile III

Thought and Poetry

*Essays on Romanticism,
Subjectivity, and Truth*

John Koethe

BLOOMSBURY ACADEMIC
LONDON • NEW YORK • OXFORD • NEW DELHI • SYDNEY

BLOOMSBURY ACADEMIC
Bloomsbury Publishing Plc
50 Bedford Square, London, WC1B 3DP, UK
1385 Broadway, New York, NY 10018, USA
29 Earlsfort Terrace, Dublin 2, Ireland

BLOOMSBURY, BLOOMSBURY ACADEMIC and the Diana logo are
trademarks of Bloomsbury Publishing Plc

First published in Great Britain 2022
This paperback edition published 2023

Copyright © John Koethe, 2022

John Koethe has asserted his right under the Copyright, Designs and
Patents Act, 1988, to be identified as Author of this work.

For legal purposes the Acknowledgments on p. vi constitute an
extension of this copyright page.

Series design by Ben Anslow
Cover image: Mount Sainte-Victoire (1904), Paul Cezanne
(© PAINTING / Alamy Stock Photo)

All rights reserved. No part of this publication may be reproduced or transmitted in
any form or by any means, electronic or mechanical, including photocopying,
recording, or any information storage or retrieval system, without prior
permission in writing from the publishers.

Bloomsbury Publishing Plc does not have any control over, or responsibility for, any
third-party websites referred to or in this book. All internet addresses given in this
book were correct at the time of going to press. The author and publisher regret any
inconvenience caused if addresses have changed or sites have ceased to exist, but
can accept no responsibility for any such changes.

A catalogue record for this book is available from the British Library.

A catalog record for this book is available from the Library of Congress.

ISBN: HB: 978-1-3502-6244-7
PB: 978-1-3502-6248-5
ePDF: 978-1-3502-6245-4
eBook: 978-1-3502-6246-1

Series: Bloomsbury Studies in Philosophy and Poetry

Typeset by Newgen KnowledgeWorks Pvt. Ltd., Chennai, India

To find out more about our authors and books visit www.bloomsbury.com
and sign up for our newsletters.

Contents

Acknowledgments	vi
Introduction	1
1 The Metaphysical Subject of John Ashbery's Poetry (1978)	9
2 Contrary Impulses: The Tension between Poetry and Theory (1990)	21
3 Poetry and the Experience of Experience (1993)	33
4 The Romance of Realism (1996)	49
5 Poetry at One Remove (1998)	63
6 Thought and Poetry (2000)	73
7 Styles of Temptation and Refusal in Wittgenstein and Stevens (2003)	81
8 On John Ashbery's "Definition of Blue" (2007)	91
9 Wittgenstein and Lyric Subjectivity (2007)	93
10 Comments on Susan Wolf's *Meaning in Life* and *Why It Matters* (2007)	101
11 Poetry and Truth (2009)	107
12 Poetry, Philosophy, and the Syntax of Reflection (2012)	117
13 On John Ashbery's "Clepsydra" (2013)	129
14 Perplexity and Plausibility: On Philosophy, Lyrical and Discursive (2013)	133
15 On Helen Vendler's Wallace Stevens (2014)	141
16 The Microcosm: Poetry and Humanism (2016)	143
17 On *Wordsworth's Fun* (2021)	147
18 Philosophical Reflection on Poetry (2021)	155
Appendix: Metaphysics and the Mind–Body Problem (2019)	163
Notes	183
Bibliography	193
Index	195

Acknowledgments

The following are the original venues of publication (or presentation) of these essays, arranged in chronological order. Some of them were also previously published in book form in Koethe, John, *Poetry at One Remove* (PAOR), Ann Arbor: University of Michigan Press, 2000.

"The Metaphysical Subject of John Ashbery's Poetry," PAOR; Lehman, David, ed., *Beyond Amazement: New Essays on John Ashbery*, Ithaca, NY: Cornell University Press, 1980.

"Contrary Impulses: The Tension between Poetry and Theory," PAOR; *Critical Inquiry*, Autumn 1980.

"Poetry and the Experience of Experience," PAOR.

"The Romance of Realism," PAOR; *New Literary History*, Autumn 1997.

"Poetry at One Remove," PAOR; *New Literary History*, Winter 1999.

"Thought and Poetry," *Midwest Studies in Philosophy*, 2002.

"Styles of Temptation and Refusal in Wittgenstein and Stevens," *Fulcrum*, Summer 2003.

"On John Ashbery's 'Definition of Blue,'" LIT, Spring 2007.

"Wittgenstein and Lyric Subjectivity," *Literary Imagination*, 2007.

"Comments of Susan Wolf's *Meaning in Life and Why It Matters*," Wolf, Susan, et al., *Meaning in Life and Why It Matters*, Princeton, NJ: Princeton University Press, 2010.

"Poetry and Truth," *Midwest Studies in Philosophy*, 2009.

"Poetry, Philosophy and the Syntax of Reflection," Invited Symposium, American Philosophical Association, Pacific Division meeting, 2012.

"On John Ashbery's 'Clepsydra,'" *At Length*, 2013.

"Perplexity and Plausibility: On Philosophy, Lyrical and Discursive," *Common Knowledge*, Winter 2014.

"On Helen Vendler's Wallace Stevens," Invited Symposium, Modern Language Association, 2014.

"The Microcosm: Poetry and Humanism," *FSG Work in Progress*, 2017.

"On *Wordsworth's Fun*," *Raritan*, Spring 2021.

Introduction

As a poet who is also a philosopher, I've long had a sense that some sort of kinship, however indirect, exists between these two forms of activity in which the mind becomes engaged through the medium of language. But at the same time, I've also been unsure, and continue to be unsure, exactly what that kinship might be. The essays in this book don't attempt to offer a settled account of the relationship between poetry and philosophy (assuming there is one). Rather, they manifest an evolving sense that some of the themes, perplexities, and habits of thought that inform the latter discipline can find a home in the former as well. Since most of them were occasional or invited pieces, it's inevitable that there are repetitions and redundancies, as well as changes of view or emphases and even inconsistencies. Nevertheless, I present them in chronological order as originally written in order to give a sense of how the themes and concerns they wrestle with arose and evolved, something I'll try to convey in this introduction.

Plato famously denied poetry a place in his ideal city, a denial made all the more poignant by the fact that he had written poetry in his youth and, through his philosophical writings, ranks as one of the Western canon's greatest literary stylists (surely Socrates's death scene in the *Phaedo* is one of the most moving depictions to be found in imaginative literature). But his reasons for banning poetry from the republic are actually indicative of a certain affinity between poetry and philosophy, at least at the level of content if not of purpose. Plato feared that poetry's rhythmic and metrical qualities—or more broadly, its affective dimensions—might lead it to rival or displace philosophy as the basis on which the city would be governed, even though the poet's relation to his subject matter was not one of knowledge or even informed opinion. Yet this fear indicates that Plato thought that poetry and philosophy could at least appear to share certain themes and ideas—for otherwise, how could poetry's ill-founded pronouncements threaten the authority of philosophy's properly grounded claims? Plato's opposition to poetry is thus based on a grudging respect for it and a recognition that poetry and philosophy have enough in common for there to be a danger of one being mistaken for the other.

My initial sense of what philosophy and poetry have in common, which I continue to believe in some form, but which I've come to find increasingly problematic over the years (especially recently), is something like this. Both poetry and philosophy are speculative activities, in that both involve the entertainment of propositions (in a broad sense) in the absence of certainty about their truth and often in the absence of any means of even establishing their truth. And if one rejects the narrow view of poetry that limits it to the concrete and personal, the propositions they involve may be, in a broad sense, similar in kind, often concerning the character and nature of the world and the self and the relation between them; the nature and experience of time and memory; the differences and relations between reality, imagination, and illusion; the character of consciousness, thought, sensation, and feeling; and the relations between one's own self and experiences and those of others. But the speculation about matters like these that philosophy involves is essentially constrained in the way it develops and proceeds. It is typically initiated by the recognition of a *problem*, usually not a problem first formulated by the philosopher himself, but one that has been raised and discussed previously by others, who have ventured various solutions to it. One proceeds to canvass these solutions, to defend one or to offer objections that render them untenable, and then perhaps to put forward a new proposal, to be critically examined in turn. The process is constrained both in its inception and its development: positions have to be offered in response to recognized problems, and once objections to a position have been adduced, one can't continue to maintain the position until those objections have been rebutted or at least acknowledged. And the whole procedure is subject to requirements of consistency, coherence, and plausibility, and its ultimate goal is truth.

Speculation in poetry is, by contrast, unconstrained, or at least not subject to the same kinds of constraints, and the way it is initiated and proceeds seems to me to have a very different structure. Coleridge's remark about "the willing suspension of disbelief that constitutes poetic faith" is directed to the reader of the poem and posits a more or less passive abandonment of ordinary standards of plausibility. But I think that a more active form of this relation holds between the *poet* and the poem, where the aim is the creation, through an act of will, of an extraordinary construction, which may be personal or impersonal, abstract or concrete. The occasion is typically a heightened awareness of a situation or oneself, and in the course of the poem's elaboration one may entertain or assay notions of whose untenability one is perfectly aware—an untenability one may even acknowledge—without being led to abandon them. Indeed, the awareness of the futility of a conception may lead to an even greater insistence on it, because the animating force of poetic speculation is usually *desire*, rather than an ideal of impersonal accuracy. Theses and concepts, explanations and hypotheses, seem to me to enter into poetry more as possibilities to be explored and inhabited, as opposed to being assessed and evaluated; and the poet, if he finds the habitation congenial, isn't likely to abandon them simply because the property has been declared condemned.

I still think that this idea that philosophy and poetry can arise from shared areas of common concern is basically correct, at least for certain forms of concern that can be pursued either philosophically or in poetry. But recently I've become less sure of what those areas are, and have begun to suspect that some seemingly philosophical matters of human importance aren't really amenable to philosophical treatment at all, but find their genuine expression in poetry. As many of these essays indicate, Wittgenstein is a philosopher important to me, though I've never had as much sympathy for his anti-philosophical tendencies as some other philosophers I respect have. Heidegger, on the other hand, is someone I have little knowledge of or sympathy for, and I tend to share the positivists' disdain for what he took to be the central question of philosophy, "Why is there something rather than nothing?" as an unintelligible pseudoquestion, largely because it's hard to see how anything could count as an answer to it. Wittgenstein has almost nothing to say about Heidegger, but I was surprised to learn that in remarks made around 1929, he expresses sympathy for Heidegger's obsession with this question, while at the same time rejecting the idea that it's a genuine question capable of philosophical treatment and resolution. What he suggests is that the feeling that it is arises from a mistaken attempt to conceptualize and articulate a sense of puzzlement and awe at the existence of the world, but that a failure to feel this sense of puzzlement and awe amounts to a kind of spiritual deficiency. While the attempt to treat it as a theoretical question is indeed productive of nonsense, it isn't nonsense to be ridiculed and deplored as the positivists did, but almost to be reveled in as an expression, however misguided, of a matter or deep human astonishment and concern. And it's tempting to see poetry not as an alternative way of exploring this concern that can also be pursued philosophically, but as the proper way of giving voice to something that can't be articulated philosophically at all. Of course, this is only one example, and it isn't clear to me that something similar should be said of other questions and issues that poetry and philosophy may seem to share. But it makes me suspect that my initial idea that philosophy and poetry offer alternative responses to a shared set of issues may be overly tidy.

A second set of qualms I've begun to have has to do with the status of philosophical writing about poetry. I've noted that the pieces gathered here were mostly occasional or invited, and as such are somewhat off the cuff and not as carefully formulated as philosophical writing usually aspires to be. But lately I've begun to wonder whether it's really possible to talk about the nature, character, and goals of poetry with the degree of rigor that's supposed to be characteristic of philosophy. Certainly the state of the orthodox philosophical literature on poetry isn't reassuring. The literature on metaphor, for instance, is fairly extensive, but seems to me to be of almost no interest to anyone with a serious involvement with poetry. I'll turn in a moment to some of the themes and concerns that inform these essays and that engage me in poetry, but the idea that they're somehow inherent in the nature of poetry seems to me overly essentialist and increasingly dubious. Poetry is, in a broad sense, a linguistic activity, but beyond this it's difficult to say much about what it is or what its goals are. The themes and concerns that preoccupy me in poetry are ones I find compelling, but the idea that they're inevitable is hard to reconcile with the range of preoccupations other people associate with poetry; and it may be that the speculative and associative character of these pieces, which I'd tended to attribute to their impromptu origins, may be the form philosophical writing about poetry ought to take, a suggestion I expand on in the last essay in this collection, "Philosophical Reflection on Poetry."

But let me put aside these qualms and try to indicate some of the recurring themes and concerns that informed these essays as they were being written. Though I just indicated a degree of skepticism as to whether a substantial characterization of the nature and character of poetry is possible, there are certainly conceptions of poetry that I find congenial and compelling and that underlie the way I think of its relation to philosophy. The poetry that interests me is basically humanistic, in that it's open to and reflects the full range of human experience, including self-conscious reflective experience. I'm engaged by much of the poetry and many of the poets Harold Bloom emphasizes (though not always by what he says about them), and one reason he subtitled his long book on Shakespeare *The Invention of the Human* is that he believes that the kind of reflexive self-conscious subjectivity enacted by the Shakespearean soliloquy is fundamental to our humanity, and that at its most basic poetry is a form of talking to one's self—a conception of poetry I very much agree with (which isn't to say that I think that poetry is essentially solipsistic, since one can talk to one's self about anything, including other people, politics, and society). The poetic outlook that engages me is romantic in a very broad sense, in that it's preoccupied with the relation between the subjective self and the natural world in which it's situated, a relation which is often problematic. Wordsworth is the first modern poet, in that he's the first to make subjectivity itself the subject of the poem, and I think that modernism is best understood not as a repudiation of romanticism but as a continuation of it, not in the unified and affirmative form it took in high romanticism, but in the fragmentary and pessimistic form it evolved into in the twentieth century. Of course, not everyone would share this outlook, including some who share my preoccupations with romanticism and modernism. Bloom's early antipathy to T. S. Eliot was largely based on the latter's rejection of the excesses of romanticism, though to me Eliot is, in his meditative individualism, a deeply romantic poet. And while I see the line of romanticism's continuation in modernism as running through poets like Eliot, Wallace Stevens, W. H. Auden, and John Ashbery, others have an almost classical conception of modernism that sees it running through poets like Ezra Pound, William Carlos Williams, Louis Zukofsky, and Charles Olson, and characterized by an emphasis on the concrete and the objective and an avoidance of individual subjectivity. Nevertheless, this basically humanistic conception of poetry, which originates in its modern form with Shakespeare (though its roots lie in Greek tragedy) and runs through high romanticism, high modernism, and postmodernism (as I see them), is the one that underlies the essays gathered in this book and informs the way I think about the relationship between poetry and philosophy.

Some of the topics discussed in the individual essays include the conceptions of the self to be found in the works of various poets; the tension between poetry and theoretical forms of thought; the relation between romanticism and philosophical realism; how poetry renders life meaningful and significant; the role of truth in philosophy and poetry; stylistic and syntactic differences between poetry and philosophy; and poetry and humanism. But two themes in particular emerge repeatedly in many of the essays, and they're the main subjects of one of them, "Poetry and the Experience of Experience" (the title alludes to a line in Ashbery's prose sequence *Three Poems*). I've indicated that poetry as I conceive it is basically romantic in the broad sense of being centered on individual subjective experience, and the first theme is the nature and character of such experience and what it encompasses. I've mentioned the familiar prejudice about poetry that tries to limit it to the concrete and the personal and insists on an avoidance of the abstract and the theoretical; and against this I try to argue that what might be called abstract meditation and reflection is not only an essential part of human subjective conscious experience but also a part poetry is uniquely capable of capturing and conveying, as well as the ultimate basis of human importance and value. And the second theme is a particular kind of conscious experience that lies at the heart of romanticism, one that Kant calls the experience of the sublime. In the original form of it Kant describes, it involves the self's feeling of being threatened or overwhelmed by some powerful physical enormity—a vast, raging sea, a towering mountain—followed by its realization that however great this enormity may be, it's finite and bounded, and that the mind is capable of containing it in thought and conceiving of an unbounded magnitude, and finally by the realization of the self's transcendence of the natural world. In its pure form, this experience of the sublime is central to high romanticism and seems to occur repeatedly in, say, Wordsworth's poetry (though one of the late pieces questions the extent to which this is really true), but even in more frustrated, attenuated forms it continues to inform the continuation of romanticism in modernism. What I try to suggest in "Poetry and the Experience of Experience" is that the movement of the Kantian sublime is simply a particular instance of a more general interplay between two basic perspectives on the self and the world, the interplay or oscillation between what Thomas Nagel calls the subjective perspective of the individual conscious viewpoint and the objective "view from nowhere" of natural science, in which people and their thoughts and feelings are simply part of the natural order, not fundamentally different in kind from other parts of it. And it's this sense of the tension between these two irreducible viewpoints that underlies the kind of poetry I find compelling and try to address in these essays, as well as the tension between poetry and philosophy as they pursue their shared subjects of human concern.

While most of them are concerned with broad thematic relations between poetry and philosophy, some of these essays are concerned with the works of particular poets who I think exemplify these relations. Some of the poets I talk about in varying amounts of detail include Wordsworth, Eliot, Stevens, Ashbery, Marianne Moore, and Elizabeth Bishop. Some of what I say about them is close to literary criticism of a familiar kind, though I've tried to focus on aspects of their work that make them relevant to an understanding of the interplay between poetry and philosophy that is the broad subject of these essays. Ashbery in particular is a poet I discuss quite a few times, as the poetry of his middle period perhaps best exhibits the tendencies of language and thought that I believe underlie the similarities and differences that link the two disciplines. I touch on these similarities and differences in a short piece on Helen Vendler's reading of Stevens, and it seems worth giving a brief summary of my view of philosophically interesting poets like Ashbery, Stevens, and Eliot here. If by "philosophical poetry" one means poetry in which the poet engages in philosophy in the literal sense, then none of them, and especially Ashbery, write philosophical poetry at all, and indeed it's hard to think of an important poet who does—which is, to my mind, a good thing. Neither Stevens nor Ashbery had any formal training in philosophy, and while Stevens at times expressed philosophical aspirations, Ashbery certainly never did. And while Eliot was trained in philosophy and wrote a dissertation on F. H. Bradley, I would insist that his poetry doesn't exhibit the systematic preoccupation with truth characteristic of philosophy either. What Ashbery, Stevens, and Eliot are in their philosophically most interesting moments are *meditative* poets, in the sense that while they're often drawn to some of the abstract issues and perplexities that underlie both philosophy and much poetry, what compels them isn't a disinterested ambition to resolve them but (as Vendler suggests of Stevens) the experience of feeling them, and the expression that desire tries to find in language. I earlier described poetry as a way of talking to yourself, but that you can talk to yourself about almost anything. What these poets often find themselves talking to themselves about are the kinds of perplexities about the self, time, reality, and the imagination that preoccupy philosophers too, but it's usually because they're immersed in the experience of momentarily inhabiting them, rather than a determination to see them through and bring them to a conclusion. This doesn't make them philosophical poets, in the sense that in writing poetry they're doing philosophy—which is, as I said, a good thing. But it does make them philosophically relevant or significant poets, in the sense that they share some of the same conceptual and linguistic predilections that could, when differently pursued, lead to philosophy.

In the course of these reflections, I often allude to issues in the philosophy of mind, particularly ones having to do with the mind–body problem. For instance, discussing romanticism and the experience of the sublime involves talking about the sense of a distinction between the self or mind on the one hand and the material or physical world on the other, and this is tantamount to a form of philosophical dualism. And several times I suggest that we might think of dualism as a kind of inescapable illusion we know to be false and that few philosophers would accept, but that this doesn't vitiate poems that embody it, since the poet's aim isn't to defend the truth of dualism, but to convey a sense of what it's like to look at the self and the world from its perspective. I still think this is true, but I thought it would be helpful if readers had a sense of what my own views actually are on some of these issues in the philosophy of mind, since they're somewhat qualified and unusual, and so I've included as an appendix a straightforward philosophy paper, "Metaphysics and the Mind–Body Problem," that makes no reference to poetry at all but is perhaps more sympathetic to conceptions of the self and conscious experience that inform some of the poems and poets I discuss than many philosophers would be. What I argue in this paper is that the kind of experience one has of the self and of the qualitative and perspectival character of conscious experience does indeed lead to a kind of dualism that holds that the mind and its experiences are real but immaterial; but that this dualism doesn't threaten an overall materialism about the world and human beings—for while a broadly Quinean criterion of ontological commitment requires us to affirm the existence of minds and mental phenomena, they're "metaphysically thin" in a way that makes their existence, properly understood, no more a threat to an overall scientific conception of the world than are the truths of mathematics. And while this paper makes no reference to poetry and isn't meant to obscure the differences I've tried to draw throughout these essays between philosophy and poetry, I hope it might reinforce the sense I've always had that it's possible to respect and engage in both of these deeply human forms of activity without being haunted by the fear that they're ultimately incompatible.

1

The Metaphysical Subject of John Ashbery's Poetry (1978)

A conception of the self can inform a poet's work in a variety of ways. Perhaps the most familiar is through its possession of a distinctive "voice," which basically amounts to a projection of a personality—either the poet's actual personality or one he assumes. There can be as many voices as there are personalities, but it does not follow that differences between two poets' voices reflect a difference in the *conception* of the self that informs their work. For example, Robert Lowell's characteristic voice is quite different from John Berryman's and the personalities their poems project are correspondingly different. But it strikes me that these distinctive personalities represent selves of essentially the same *kind*: they *are* personalities, that is, they are or are to be regarded as actual psychological egos as much a part of the real world as the historical circumstances, incidents, feelings, and relationships with which they become engaged. Poetry that is characterized primarily by its voice embodies, it seems to me, a psychological conception of the self: the self is a real entity among other real entities, maybe more important than most of them, but, like them, a part of the world it is trying to tell us about.

But poetry can also involve conceptions of the self not so directly tied to the poet's own distinctive personality or voice. It can force us to consider the *position* of the "speaker"—or what I would prefer to call the "subject"—of the poetry with respect to the incidents, objects, thoughts, and personalities (including the poet's own) it describes. And sometimes this position seems drastically different from the vantage point in the world that the poem presents and that is occupied by the psychological subject of the poem. In reading poetry informed primarily by the psychological notion of the self embodied in the poet's voice, we are struck by questions like "How does he sound?" or "Whose voice is it?" (and a sense that the answers to these questions are indeterminate tells against the poetry). But for poetry involving a less psychological conception of the self or subject, the important question is not so much what the voice sounds like as *where it comes from*; and a mark of the success of this sort of poetry is that this question seems to have a determinate answer, even when we find ourselves unable to formulate it.

Remembrance of Things Past serves to illustrate the difference between the conceptions of a psychological ego and a nonpsychological subject. The character Marcel has a particular personality and lives in time and in tension between Swann's way of domesticity and the Guermantes' way of social circulation. And we can think of the novel as Marcel's autobiography, whose theme is the fusing of the two ways over the course of time. But the vantage point of the narrator is an atemporal one from which the moments in his life do not succeed one another but coexist simultaneously. We are supposed to read the novel twice, the second time not as autobiography but as the narrator's attempt to circumscribe the atemporal position Marcel comes to occupy at the end. Had someone other than Proust written a novel to this point, the personality of the protagonist and the incidents of his life would have been different: the psychological ego embodied in the work would not have been Marcel's. Yet the *subject* of this hypothetical novel could have been the same: a *different* voice could have emanated from the same durationless position occupied by Proust's narrator.

Now it seems to me that a distinctive quality of John Ashbery's poetry, a source of much of its power, is that the conception of the self it embodies is not primarily a psychological one. I say not *primarily* psychological, because his work is possessed of an authentic individual voice, gently reticent, delighting equally in the abstract, the literal, and the silly, and usually heard through a haze of humor:

> And so we to
> Came where the others came: nights of physical endurance,
> Or if, by day, our behavior was anarchically
> Correct, at least by New Brutalism standards, all then
> Grew taciturn by previous agreement. We were spirited
> Away *en bateau*, under the cover of fudge dark.
> It's not the incomplete importunes, but the spookiness
> Of the finished product.
>
> ("Daffy Duck in Hollywood")[1]

This passage captures some of Ashbery's characteristic "twang." He does actually something like this in conversation, and one reason his imitators are usually unconvincing is that this tone, however cool and detached, works to project a genuine human voice and personality, in whose absence it seems (like any strong poet's style in someone else's mouth) willed, mannered, and depersonalized.

But even though Ashbery's work embodies the presence of a particular psychological ego, it is almost unique in the degree to which it is informed by a nonpsychological conception of the self or subject: a unitary consciousness from which his voice originates, positioned outside the temporal flux of thought and experience his poetry manages to monitor and record (*almost* unique in this respect: I sometimes feel something similar to be true of Elizabeth Bishop's work, though—and this is part of the point—her *voice* is decidedly different from his). The sense of the presence of a unified subject that conceives these poems is very strong, almost palpable. Among the stylistic indications that this subject is not a particular personality are Ashbery's characteristic use of pronouns: it seems a matter of indifference whether the subject is referred to as "I," "you," "he," "she," "it," or "we,"[2] shifts between which often occur rapidly within the course of the same poem:

SHE

But now always from your plaint I
Relive, revive, springing up careless,
Dust geyser in city absentmindedness,
And all day it is writ and said:
We round women like corners. They are the friends
We were always saying goodbye to and then
Bumping into the next day. School has closed
Its doors on a few. Saddened, she rose up
And untwined the gears of that blank, blossoming day,
"So much for Paris, and the living in this world."
But I was going to say
It differently, about the way
Time is sorting us all out, keeping you and her
Together yet apart, in a give-and-take, push-pull
Kind of environment. And then, packed like sardines,
Our wit arises, survives automatically. We imbibe it.

This from "Fantasia on 'The Nut-Brown Maid,'"[3] a long poem written in the form of a dialogue between HE and SHE, two identities that are not really differentiated by the poem at all. The references of HE and SHE, the pronouns within the previous passage, and Ashbery's pronouns generally, are anaphoric. But these references are never given *in* the poem: they seem to belong to a world outside it, and there is a strong sense that any distinctions between them would be basically arbitrary.

"Time is sorting us all out." Another stylistic clue to the nature of Ashbery's subject is the pervasive sense of temporal dislocation that characterizes his work: the grammatical past tense is often used to indicate the present of the poem, even when the present is the moment of writing itself (as David Kalstone has observed, "Tense will shift while the poem refers to itself as part of the past").[4] Another passage from "Fantasia" both illustrates and offhandedly tries to explain this tendency:

> HE
>
> To him, the holiday-making crowds were
> Energies of a parallel disaster, the fulfilling
> Of all prophecies between now and the day of
> Judgment. Spiraling like fish.
> Toward a distant, unperceived surface, was all
> The reflection there was. Somewhere it had its opaque
> Momentary existence.
>
>   But if each act
> Is reflexive, concerned with itself on another level
> As well as with us, the strangers who live here,
> Can one advance one step further without sinking equally
> Far back into the past? There was always something to see,
> Something going on, for the historical past owed it
> To itself, our historical present. Another month a huge
> Used-car sale on the lawn shredded the sense of much
> Of the sun coming through the wires, or a cape
> Would be rounded by a slim white sail almost
> Invisible in the specific design, or children would come
> Clattering down fire escapes until the margin
> Exploded into an ear of sky. Today the hospitals
> Are light, airy places, tented clouds, and the weeping
> In corridors is like autumn showers. It's beginning.

Time's job of "sorting us all out" is always in progress but never gets completed, for the subject cannot "advance one step further without sinking equally / Far back into the past." Ashbery's subject seems possessed by an impulse, which it knows has to be frustrated, to *reify* itself, to find or create some *thing* with which it can identify totally:

> I shall use my anger to build a bridge like that
> Of Avignon, on which people may dance for the feeling
> Of dancing on a bridge. I shall at last see my complete face
> Reflected not in the water but in the worn stone floor of my
>   bridge.
>
> ("Wet Casements")[5]

"I shall at last see"—the tone is wistful and resigned. The attempt at reification yields only a personality or image that is "other," "A portrait, smooth as glass … built up out of multiple corrections / [which] has no relation to the space or time in which it was lived" ("Definition of Blue").[6] The subject inhabits "the sigh of our present" ("Blue Sonata")[7] and is timeless, while any representative of it in the real world is timebound, part of "The present past of which our features, / Our opinions are made." It can only be a *surface*:

> But your eyes proclaim
> That everything is surface. The surface is what's there
> And nothing can exist except what's there.
>
> ("Self-Portrait in a Convex Mirror")[8]

The note of desperation in the poetry that attends the subject's impulse to reify itself does not arise because the surface representation leaves out something real:

> there are no words for the surface, that is,
> No words to say what it really is, that it is not
> Superficial but a visible core.

This "Wooden and external representation / Returns the full echo of what you meant / With nothing left over" ("Clepsydra").[9] Rather, the trouble is that the subject and its "Wooden and external representation" occupy fundamentally different *positions*. The latter, like the psychological ego or self, *is* a thing, existing in the real world of past, present, and future; whereas the subject of Ashbery's poems—what I shall call the "metaphysical subject"—seems to inhabit a durationless "now," existing in a condition of "drifting … toward a surface which can never be approached, / Never pierced through into the timeless energy of a present" ("Wet Casements"). And what both drives and frustrates his poetry is the attempt to fuse the two positions, an attempt conducted in the full knowledge that it cannot possibly succeed: "Why, after all, were we not destroyed in the conflagration of the moment our real and imaginary lives coincided, unless it was because we never had a separate existence beyond those two static and highly artificial concepts whose fusion was nevertheless the cause of death and destruction not only for ourselves but in the world around us?" ("The Recital").[10]

At this point we might be tempted to conclude that the moral of Ashbery's work is that the whole concept of the self is delusory. This would be a mistake. It is true only to the extent that by "I" one understands an individual psychological ego or personality: the referential and temporal vagaries of his poetry are simply incompatible with the speaker's being a real person in the world, with a particular, individual biography. What is striking about Ashbery's work is that, despite these distortions and pressures to which his "self" is subjected, surely sufficient to dismantle any *personality*, one never loses the sense that a perfectly definite point of consciousness is behind the whole enterprise. Later I want to compare the concepts of the self that inform Ashbery's work and Frank O'Hara's: both of them try to undermine the notion of the self as a permanent and objective personality, but I think one (among many) of the significant differences between them involves the different philosophical conceptions of the self alternative to that of the psychological ego to which their works have affinities.

The reification of the self as the psychological ego represents what might be called a Cartesian conception of the self. According to this conception, the self *is* an object in the world among other objects (Descartes identifies it with the mind, a *res cogitans* or "thinking thing"); and as an object in the world we can experience it (introspectively), hold beliefs about it, and frame descriptions of it—at least as much as we can for any object in the world (e.g., the sun). Of course, for Descartes the mind or self is a spiritual or mental substance, unlike, say, the sun, which is a physical or material substance; but this just means that our world of acquaintance and experience contains substances of two sorts, mental and material, and does not affect the main point of this conception of the self—that it *is* a substance or thing and part of the world of substantial things.

Descartes's is not the only view of the self found in the Western philosophical tradition. Hume's critique of the Cartesian conception boils down to the idea that experience simply fails to acquaint us with any single persisting thing we might mean by "I" but, rather, discloses only the various sensations and passions we mistakenly ascribe to a persisting self whose experiences we take them to be:

> But self or person is not any one impression, but that to which our several impressions and ideas are supposed to have reference. If any impression gives rise to the idea of self, that impression must continue invariably the same, thro' the whole course of our lives; since self is supposed to continue to exist after that manner. But there is no impression constant and invariable. Pain and pleasure, grief and joy, passions and sensations succeed each other, and never

> all exist at the same time ... For my part, when I enter most intimately into what I call myself, I always stumble on some particular perception or other, of heat or cold, light or shade, love or hatred, pain or pleasure. I can never catch *myself* at any time without a perception, and never can observe anything but the perception ... I may venture to affirm of ... mankind, that they are nothing but a bundle or collection of different perceptions, which succeed each other with an inconceivable rapidity, and are in perpetual flux and movement.[11]

According to Hume's conception, there is literally *no such thing* as the self. The illusion that there is is partly grammatical and partly due to resemblances between the perceptions comprising the bundle. What is real are the perceptions themselves; but what is illusory is the persisting Cartesian ego whose perceptions we take them to be.

A third conception of the self derives from Kant and emerges in a somewhat modified form in Schopenhauer and Wittgenstein. Consciousness, Hume's "bundle of perceptions," possesses a unity that cannot be reduced to relations of resemblance among its constituents; but Descartes's error, according to Kant, consists in confusing this unity of conscious experience with the experience of a unitary substance, a self, or subject. We can have no *concept* of such an ego, for to us it is "nothing more than the feeling of an existence without the least concept ... only the representation of that to which all thinking stands in relation":[12]

> We do not have, and cannot have, any knowledge whatsoever of any such subject. Consciousness is, indeed, that which alone makes all representations to be thoughts, and in it, therefore, as the transcendental subject, all our perceptions must be found; but beyond this logical meaning of the word "I," we have no knowledge of the subject in itself, which as substratum underlies this "I," as it does all thoughts.[13]

Schopenhauer's modification was to reify this purely logical notion of the transcendental ego yet to construe it not as a substantial thing in the world but "as an indivisible point" outside space and time,[14] on whose existence the world or experience and representation rests. And it is this somewhat murky conception of the self that lies behind Wittgenstein's obscure remarks towards the end of the *Tractatus*:

> I am my world. (the microcosm.)
> There is no such thing as the subject that thinks or entertains ideas.
> If I wrote a book called *The World as I found it*, I should have to include a report

on my body, and should have to say what parts were subordinate to my will, and which were not, etc., this being a method of isolating the subject, or rather of showing that in an important sense there is no subject; for it alone could *not* be mentioned in the book.—

> The subject does not belong to the world; rather, it is a limit of the world.
> Where *in* the world is a metaphysical subject to be found?
> You will say that this is exactly like the case of the eye and the visual field. But really you do *not* see the eye.
> And nothing *in the visual field* allows you to infer that it is seen by an eye…
> The philosophical self is not the human being, not the human body, or the human soul, with which psychology deals, but rather the metaphysical subject, the limit of the world—not a part of it.[15]

I am not going to try to assess these three philosophical approaches to the notion of the self or subject. But I do think they provide useful devices for making sense of different poets' bodies of work, since the conception of the self that informs the work of a particular poet usually has stronger affinities with one among these three traditional views than with the others. The most familiar conception of the self is that of the Cartesian ego; it is this conception that, I think grounds any poetry introspective to a significant extent and characterized by a distinctive sense of personality or voice. While there is usually a degree of alienation of the self from the world, that self is still seen as *part* of the world, a part to which the poet has a privileged means of introspective access, and a part whose experiences and nature the poetry ventures to depict (even though the expression may involve a variety of voices and personae—e.g., Berryman's Henry).

The conception of the self-underlying Ashbery's poetry is, I believe, that of the transcendental or metaphysical subject; and I think this helps account for the radical difference between his poetry and most other poets for whom the self is a main theme, including ones who have managed to capture some of his characteristic tone and voice. I have already noted some of the reasons for this way of looking at this work: the extreme referential, temporal, and spatial dislocations and transitions in his poems, which make it impossible to read them as an autobiographical record of the experiences of a time-bound, self-identical Cartesian ego; his subject's characteristic impulse to identify or produce an adequate representation of itself while simultaneously distancing itself from every such image, which all become "other" as soon as they become concrete or clear enough (and in this connection note David Kalstone's observation that "Alive in its present, and determined as a Jack-in-the-Box, that self pops up when any moment of poetic condition threatens to obliterate it");[16] and, most important, the fact that despite these tendencies we are aware, reading his poems, of an undeniable "feeling of existence without the least concept [of it]"[17] (to use Kant's characterization of the transcendental subject), together with the impression that it is from the vantage point of this ineffable existence, that his poetry monitors the details of the world, among which is his own personality:

> Each detail was startlingly clear, as though seen through a magnifying glass,
> Or would have been to an ideal observer, namely yourself—
> For only you could watch yourself so patiently from afar
> The way God watches a sinner on the path to redemption,
> Sometimes disappearing into valleys, but always *on the way.*
>
> ("The Bungalows")[18]

Of course Ashbery's is not the only poetry infused with a conception of the self different from the traditional Cartesian one. Frank O'Hara's is another. In the course of discussing O'Hara's poem "Music," Marjorie Perloff observes that

> the pronoun "I" and its cognates appear ten times in the space of twenty-one lines.
> Yet, unlike the typical autobiographical poem with its circular structure (present-past-return to present with renewed insight), "Music" does not explore the speaker's past so as to determine what has made him the person he is; it does not, for that matter "confess" or "reveal" anything about his inner psychic life. The role of the "I" is to respond rather than to confess ... As in Pasternak's *Safe Conduct*, one of O'Hara's favorite books, the "I" fragments into the surfaces it contemplates. Hence the poet can only tell us what he does ... how he *responds* to external stimuli ... and what he *recalls* ... But he makes no attempt to reflect upon the larger human condition, or to make judgments upon his former self, as Robert Lowell does in the *Life Studies* poems ... It is a matter of reifying a feeling rather than remembering another person or a particular event; in so doing, that feeling becomes part of the poet's present.[19]

This strongly recalls Hume's statement that "when I enter most intimately into what I call *myself*, I always stumble on some particular perception of other, of heat or cold, light or shade, love or hatred, pain or pleasure. I can never catch *myself* at any time without a perception, and can never observe anything but the perception."[20] Many critics have remarked on the diversity among the poets who constitute what used to be called "the New York School"; and certainly in O'Hara and Ashbery the differences in form, voice, and projected personality alone are enormous. But I think the deeper distinction between them involves a difference between the views of the self their works embody. Neither's poetry offers an autobiographical record of the history of a Cartesian mind; but O'Hara's affinity is with Hume's "no self" view, on which the very notion of a self is delusory, corresponds to no reified perception of passion encountered in experience, and has to be dismantled:

> I could not change it into history
> and so remember it,
>   and I have lost what is always and everywhere
> present, the scene of my selves, the occasion of these ruses,
> which I myself and singly must now kill
>   and save the serpent in their midst.
>
>   ("In Memory of My Feelings")[21]

The vantage point of O'Hara's voice is always situated in real time, in fact, at the moment of writing. But Ashbery's vantage point is an atemporal one from which even the moment of actual utterance seems remote (here compare Kalstone on Ashbery: "Tense will shift while the poem refers to itself as part of the past,"[22] with Perloff on O'Hara: "It is a matter of reifying a feeling … in so doing, that feeling becomes part of the poet's present").[23] Ashbery's impulse is not so much to dismantle the various emblems with which the self might mistakenly try to identify as to try to see them, from the vantage point of the metaphysical subject, as what they really are, things among other things, and so to transcend them:

> So that now in order to avoid extinction it again became necessary to invoke the idea of oneness, only this time if possible on a higher plane, in order for the similarities in your various lives to cancel each other out and the differences to remain, but under the aegis of singleness, separateness, so that each difference might be taken as the type of all the others and yet remain intrinsically itself, unlike anything in the world. Which brings me to the scene in the little restaurant. You are still there, far above me like the polestar and enclosing me like the dome of the heavens; your singularity has become oneness, that is your various traits and distinguishing works have flattened out into a cloudlike protective covering whose irregularities are all functions of its uniformity, and which constitutes an arbitrary but definitive boundary line between the new informal, almost haphazard way of life that is to be mine permanently and the monolithic sameness of the world that exists to be shut out. For it has been measured once and for all. It would be wrong to look back at it, and luckily we are so constructed that the urge to do so can never waken in us. We are both alive and free.
>
>   ("The System")[24]

There is a curious and exhilarating sense of liberty in Ashbery's work, quite independent of his penchant for syntactic license (which occasionally serves to strain the more genuine sense of freedom his poems convey). I think it is significant, in this connection, that the idea of the transcendental or metaphysical subject was originally invoked by Kant in an effort to reconcile our awareness of that freedom we conceive ourselves as possessing with the fact that any merely psychological ego or personality must, as an object in the natural world, be constrained by the natural laws that govern this world. Writing of an artwork by Owen Morrel called *Asylum*, which he characterizes as a "private and transcendental experience,"[25] Ashbery quotes with evident sympathy the artist's own description of the piece: "If the room/cell becomes the confines of the light/energy of the mind, the open wall points to the future beyond the self—to no mind or one mind. *Asylum* becomes a gateway to a specific kind of freedom available to those who open the right door."[26]

In the last analysis the conception of the metaphysical subject merely serves to make palpable that "specific kind of freedom," that sense that "We are both alive and free," which is one of Ashbery's poetry's most distinctive characteristics and the one that makes it so valuable.

2

Contrary Impulses: The Tension between Poetry and Theory (1990)

A striking fact of our current literary culture is the estrangement between poets and critics and reviewers of contemporary poetry on the one hand, and proponents of that loosely defined set of doctrines, methodologies, and interests that goes by the name of "theory," on the other. There are individual exceptions to this on both sides, and one can find counterexamples to every generalization I shall suggest here. Nevertheless, anyone familiar with the climates of opinion to be found in English and philosophy departments, poetry workshops and critical symposia, creative writing and cultural studies programs, and the (dwindling) nonacademic counterparts of these, especially among people in their twenties and thirties, has to acknowledge the lack of acquaintance and interest—and often even the disdain and contempt—that characterizes the relations between poets and those engaged in the kind of high-level, quasiphilosophical reflective activity that literature, and poetry in particular, used to occasion. Illustrations are easy to come by. References to modern poetry by younger theorists are typically confined to the high modernists and to poets canonized twenty or thirty years ago in books like Donald Allen's *New American Poetry* or Richard Howard's *Alone with America*; and their rare allusions to the poetry of their contemporaries often betray a striking lack of familiarity and taste. Conversely, the fact that, eighty years after Pound called for the breaking of everything breakable, a poet as intelligent and conceptually ambitious as Jorie Graham should title a book *The End of Beauty*, and have the theoretical outlook evoked by the title hailed as radical by as informed a critic as Helen Vendler, surely suggests that the level of reflective awareness in the poetry community is not what it might be.[1]

This estrangement is a recent phenomenon. *Theory* currently has a fairly specific sense—or, rather, a number of senses—but in its broadest sense it refers to the kind of reflective activity that aims to articulate and criticize the general principles and assumptions underlying artifacts, practices, and forms of expression taken to have cultural (and, in particular, aesthetic) significance. Theory in this sense was an integral part of the development of modernist poetry, with Eliot's essays, for example, constituting a critique of the enervated poetry of turn-of-the-century England and the culture against which modernist work was to be read; a revision of the canon of Western literature; and an argument for certain principles regarding objectivity, expression, feeling, and knowledge in poetry. And following the establishment of modernism, New Criticism, taken as a whole, provided a sustained theoretical legitimation of the preeminent place poetry had come to occupy in literary culture, in part by endowing it with a distinctive epistemological status as a source of "presentational" (as opposed to "discursive") knowledge of human experience. (New Criticism's insistence on poetry's "fidelity to its own nature" tends to obscure this;[2] but the real point was that poetry's epistemological status is unique to it, rather than the result of features it shares with psychology, history, or science.) Given then that poetry and theoretical reflection, at least in some forms, are not inherently inimical to each other, how might their recent estrangement be explained?

I think it is useful to distinguish here between what might be called "institutional" and "intrinsic" explanations. The former emphasize differences between the cultural and academic settings in which poetry and theory are practiced, while the latter try to identify conceptual tensions between poetry and theory themselves. The distinction is too simple—for surely the ways in which poetry and theory are institutionalized reflect some of their underlying principles, and their institutional settings influence how those principles get articulated and developed—but at least it helps identify the kinds of tensions I want to explore. My interest is in intrinsic or inherent tensions between poetry and theory in their current forms; but I want to look briefly at some of the institutional factors at work (for these may be, in the end, the more important). Contemporary theory, especially in the United States, began as a reaction against New Criticism and has tended ever since to define itself by contrast with the latter's characteristic preoccupations and associations, of which poetry was preeminent. Its rise has also been accompanied by the emergence of cultural and film studies and canon revision as central components of academic literary culture—tendencies that sit uneasily with poetry, whose status as a "high" art form seems difficult to subvert (despite perennial attempts to do so). For its part, the single most striking institutional fact about poetry in the last twenty years has been its incorporation into academic writing programs and workshops, situated (often uneasily) within English departments. Not only has the resultant commodification of poetry tended to preclude (if only for practical reasons) the kind of anxious self-consciousness about writing characteristic of current theory; but also the need for academic legitimation has led most writing programs to require a certain level of familiarity with the kinds of historical and critical texts and outlooks that have been so insistently called into question in literary studies at large.

Theory in its current form comprises a number of disparate doctrines and methodologies, which include deconstruction, critical theory, cultural studies, psychoanalysis, Marxist analysis, feminist criticism, and reception theory. I am going to concentrate on the first of these and try to identity some possible sources of intrinsic tension between poetry and deconstruction. There are several reasons for this limitation. Deconstruction's predecessor, New Criticism, had an intimate conceptual relation to poetry, whereas most of the other current theoretical tendencies had no particular historical association with it. Thus any tensions between deconstruction and poetry are more likely to be intrinsic, and therefore more interesting, than in the cases of the other theoretical tendencies. In addition, deconstruction's obsessions with the possibilities and limitations of the expression of thought and experience, and with the status of the subjective self, are ones it shares with most of the poetry that I think merits being taken seriously.

Deconstruction is not an easy view to characterize. As a philosophical position in the strict sense, as originally formulated by Derrida, I take it to be something like the view that there is nothing either in the circumstances of the employment of tokens of repeatable signs or signifiers, or in the intentions or conscious mental states of language users that fixes their meanings or symbolic contents or associates with them determinate concepts. Rather, they are subject to multiple, shifting interpretations based on past and future instances of employment that are never "present." This philosophical view has interesting similarities to those of such mainstream philosophers of language as W. V. Quine, Donald Davidson, and Wittgenstein (particularly on Saul Kripke's reading of him), though there are significant differences too (especially over the appropriate constraints on interpretation).[3]

Whether or not there are tensions between poetry and deconstruction in its purely philosophical form seems to me a moot question, as it isn't in this form that it usually impinges on literary studies and practice. Moreover, philosophical deconstruction isn't really a body of doctrines or claims at all but an attempt to break the hold of certain illusions about the source or ground of linguistic meaning. It would only be at odds then with conceptions of poetry that essentially subscribed to those illusions, and few do (though what I term below the "instrumental" conception of poetry may be one that does).

Yet philosophical deconstruction is often invoked by those engaged in deconstructive criticism of specifically literary texts; and that critical practice is in turn often taken to illustrate or support certain general claims about language and mentality that may be at some remove from the philosophical original. In *The Linguistic Moment*, for instance, J. Hillis Miller gives a reading of Stevens in which three conceptions of poetry—as depiction, as discovery, and as creation—are simultaneously in play, though the poet's commitment to them is irresolvably indeterminate. The "linguistic moment" at which this indeterminacy emerges exemplifies "the effacement of extra-linguistic reference initiated by the apparent act of self-reference."[4] And this effacement or indeterminacy is said by Miller to be due neither to any peculiarity of the literacy text, nor the author's confusion, nor to limitations of the reader's interpretative powers; it arises, rather, "as an intrinsic necessity of language," that "airy and spacious prison" in which Western literature has resided for twenty-five hundred years.[5] Thus over and above deconstruction in the strict philosophical sense there is deconstruction as it figures in the discussion of specifically literary texts, as it informs theoretical speculation within literary studies, and as it tends to be perceived by writers and critics of poetry. And it is deconstruction in this form—a debased form, if you will—that I think is important in the present context.

The central claim of this more widely received version of deconstruction is that all forms of linguistic or symbolic representation are marked by radical indeterminacy. The notions that terms possess determinate meanings and references, that assertions have well-defined contents, that statements possess objective truth-conditions, and that texts have uniquely correct interpretations are to be rejected as illusory. Moreover, since there is no such thing as the unmediated expression of thought or feeling, all such expression being mediated by inherently indeterminate symbolic systems or texts, the idea of determinate, prelinguistic cognitive and emotional states, fidelity to whose contents is the criterion of a text's accuracy and authenticity is illusory as well. More generally, the whole notion of an objectively existing Cartesian self or subject possessing a privileged introspective access to its own thoughts, feelings, and intentions is an illusory one. Nevertheless, these illusions are powerful and pervasive, engendered by systems of interpersonal, social, and political arrangements and institutions that they in turn help justify and maintain. It thus becomes an important task of deconstructive criticism to make this inherent indeterminacy manifest, particularly in the kinds of literary texts whose hallmarks are commonly taken to be genuineness and authenticity.

The merits of the case for this outlook are really beside the point here; what matters is that it is widespread and influential. What I do think is important to recognize is that the *impulse* behind the outlook, is, in a certain sense, a philosophical one. This may sound odd, especially in light of the antiphilosophical rhetoric of deconstruction's attack on "logocentrism" and the "Western metaphysics of presence" and its preference for strategies of verbal play over those of rational argumentation. But in suggesting that its fundamental impulse is philosophical, I am alluding to the fact that its basic gesture is one of *unmasking*: the illusory nature of commonly accepted ideas of language and the self is to be made apparent, and the arbitrariness of the assumptions governing expression and interpretation is to be revealed. It thus manifests the impulse with which the pre-Socratics inaugurated Western philosophy, namely, the refusal to acquiesce in what thereby comes to be regarded as the realm of appearance, and which opens the way for the introduction of *some* version of the distinction between appearance and reality. This needs qualification. In saying that deconstruction's impulse is philosophical, I am not claiming that the product of that impulse is a body of philosophical texts. Philosophical texts presuppose criteria of response, assessment, and disagreement; and the strategy of deconstructive writing is usually to distance itself from these sorts of criteria. Also, deconstruction's critique of metaphysics is essentially a rejection of "realist" notions of objectivity and truth and of the foundationalist epistemologies that have traditionally accompanied them; and I am not suggesting that it seeks to introduce different versions of the appearance/reality distinction, or different epistemologies, in their stead. Yet the underlying impulse—the refusal of what, by that very refusal, comes to be seen as appearance—is, I believe, a protophilosophical one. The fact that this movement of unmasking is to be continued indefinitely, with the removal of each mask revealing a further one, should not be allowed to obscure the fundamental character of the gesture.

Now I think that much of the intrinsic tension between deconstructive theory and poetry is due to the fact that a contrary impulse is at work in poetry. But before turning to this, I want to note a much more obvious incompatibility between deconstruction and one familiar conception of poetry, a conception that might be called the "instrumental" one. According to this conception, poems are instruments or vehicles for the public expression of something conceptually independent of and prior to themselves—actual or imaginary historical or personal events, individual experiences, or states of perception, thought, and feeling. Successful poems create a sense of authenticity or fidelity to this "prepoetic given" and convey its character in a manner that is vivid, engaging, clear, or affecting. And just as poems themselves are mere instruments for achieving these ends, so the rhetorical and semantic possibilities of language are themselves only instruments for helping them achieve them.

It is obvious that this conception of poetry is at odds with deconstruction's emphasis on the radical indeterminacy of thought and expression, and on the illusory nature of the notions of the prelinguistic given and the subjective self. Yet one may wonder how widespread this conception of poetry actually is. Shouldn't it have been a casualty of New Criticism's insistence on a poem's organic unity and unparaphrasability and confined by now to examples of the primitively confessional sorts of poems Randall Jarrell likened to severed limbs? But I think its influence is more pervasive than this description of it may suggest. To take a random example that comes to hand, in a recent symposium on kitsch Charles Molesworth adduced Rupert Brooke's "The Soldier" as an example of the genre.[6] While there was disagreement among the participants as to whether the poem actually fell under that concept, there was virtual unanimity in the judgment that it was a "bad poem," for the reasons summarized by Irving Howe: its "overblown language" is "inflated, false, stale, etc."[7] Yet the poem is not without interest. Instead of emphasizing the "overblown" and false character of the language, one could as well note the pleasurable ease with which the perspective of the poem's subject moves from the personal to the transcendental. True, the movement is not an unfamiliar one, however deftly accomplished, and the poem's failure to acknowledge this is a limitation. But I think it is symptomatic of the appeal of the instrumental conception of poetry that the symposium participants' shared perception of the poem was not one of limitation but of falsehood and a failure of authenticity.

Now as I hope to make clear in a moment, I am not simply identifying this conception of poetry—which obviously I regard as a retrograde one—with the adoption of the rhetorical strategy of truthfulness. In fact, my main complaint about current theoretical perspectives on poetry is that they tend to regard the fact that a certain poetic mode or stance is a linguistic or social construction (rather than something natural or inevitable) as a reason to disown it. My point is that the prevalence of the identification of "good poems" with truthful ones indicates the widespread acceptance of an idea of poetry that presupposes, to adapt Wittgenstein's phrase, "a criterion which gives us a conception of [poetic] 'truth' as distinct from 'truthfulness.'"[8]

The institutionalization of poetry in writing programs has, in an indirect way, helped reinforce the instrumental conception. This is not because, as is often claimed, writing programs instill a formulaic approach to the writing of verse. Just the opposite is more likely to be the case. Most writing programs are free—too free—of any sort of theoretical orientation that sanctions some forms of writing and excludes others. The fact is that it is institutionalizations of poetry that include a large theoretical component that tend to be exclusionary—the Black Mountain and St. Mark's schools come to mind and, more recently, the Language poets. Writing programs are not usually "schools" in this sense. But this tolerance is not, to my mind, a virtue. In the absence of explicitly articulated theoretical principles regarding the nature and purpose of poetry, they inculcate, by default, a poetics of the "individual voice" that valorizes authenticity and fidelity to its origins in prepoetic experience or emotion. The avoidance of any over theoretical orientation thus reinforces, in the institutionalized setting of the writing program, the particular theoretical conception of poetry I have been calling the instrumental one.

Yet I think there is a deeper source of tension between deconstructive theory and poetic practice that is independent of this conception of poetry. By way of approaching it, I want to remark briefly on the most conspicuous exception to the current estrangement between poetry and theory, the school of Language writers. These poets share with deconstructionists a rejection of the idea that poetic language provides a natural, transparent medium for the transmission of a psychological content or meaning that is constituted independently of its expression; and much of their theoretical writings constitute a sustained polemic against the forms of poetry they take to embody it. To this extent, their influence is salutary (though their characterization of the tainted forms as "officially sanctioned verse"—which usually seems to include everything other than Language poetry—is not particularly illuminating). Against this naturalistic idea of language and content, they argue that our ordinary notions of meaning, which we take to be inevitable, are really social constructions constituted by contingent conventions. The most important aim of poetry is to make this manifest, both by deploying words in ways that focus attention on them and dispel the aura of transparency with which poems usually invest them and by disrupting the conventions that shape our ordinary expectations in reading poems. This requires the scrupulous avoidance of the rhetorical strategies they associate with what they think of as conventional poetry, including the use of the first person (with its implications of reportage and communication), narrative voice (with its suggestions of causal and temporal coherence), and the heightening of affect at closure.

This is an awfully restrictive and didactic view of the function of poetry. The important point, though, is that none of it really follows from the premise that meaning, including meaning in poetry, is socially constructed via conventions of which we are not usually aware. The fact that what we call "the expression of feeling," for example, is a social construction resting on contingent practices and conventions, rather than a natural concomitant of human nature, does not imply that there isn't such thing or that its practice is the result of an arbitrary decision that we might just as well refuse to make. This is related to my earlier reservation about identifying the instrumental conception of poetry with the rhetorical quality of truthfulness. The use of certain rhetorical modes may signal a commitment to a particular theoretical view of language and meaning, but it is never equivalent to it. Rejecting naturalistic conceptions of expression and Cartesian accounts of the self in favor of views that argue for the social constitution of these notions may involve a reorientation of one's attitude towards them but should not prevent one from exploring and exploiting all the expressive possibilities afforded by language, however socially constituted these may be. Just *how* this reorientation might be made manifest is another question, and a difficult one. But the important thing to see—a point that Stanley Cavell has stressed repeatedly and on which he parts company with deconstruction—is that locating the source of our notions of language, thought, and the mind in contingent human practices does not automatically render them illusory.[9]

I think that a deep source of tension between theory and poetry, at least as I conceive it, lies in a difference in their attitudes towards the fact of the contingent basis of human communicative practices. I realize of course that my conception of poetry isn't universally shared and that other conceptions would locate the source of tension differently or even deny it altogether. Still, I hesitate to think of this account of the resistance of poetry to theory as an entirely personal one, since it seems to me to be related to tensions that pervade thought and experience generally, regardless of the particular poetics to which one might happen to subscribe. I tend to share Harold Bloom's view that the context in which poetry has to locate itself—and this includes high modernism as well as its contemporary descendants—is one essentially grounded in romanticism. Romanticism's characteristic impulse, to put it very generally, is subjectivity's contestation of its objective situation, which is ultimately one of anonymity or soullessness or nonexistence and death. The tension is grounded in the conviction—which Thomas Nagel has articulated quite forcefully—that many of the most important aspects of experience can only be apprehended from a "subjective" viewpoint, that they cannot be reduced to or rendered in factual or objective terms, are in some sense not communicable in language, and indeed in some sense are not factually real at all.[10] And by the impulse of contestation

I mean the impulse to appropriate (or, perhaps more accurately, misappropriate) language and other forms of communication either in a misconceived attempt to reify these aspects of experience or (more poignantly) to try to demonstrate the limitations of an entirely objective view of the world. And I take this impulse to be characteristic of romanticism in some very broad sense.

Now the particular form this impulse is going to take depends on how the objective situation is perceived. This is complicated for us (as it has been for some time) by the fact that this setting not only includes the literary heritage of romanticism itself but also, I would argue, a theoretical component constituted in large part by modernist and deconstructive readings of the texts that make up that heritage. Thus our version of the romantic impulse of contestation seems almost bound to have the self-reflexive, oedipal character Bloom describes, marked by an intense awareness both of the natural and temporal situation against which it is directed and of that setting's historical, social, and textual constitution; and marked also by a certain blindness, or at least indifference, towards its own participation in that situation.

I would not want to call this context in which poetry is located a "postromantic" one, for that would imply that there was at one time an unselfconscious attitude called "romanticism" that has now been superseded; and the point about the romantic impulse of subjectivity's contestation of its objective setting is that the form it takes alters as the perception of that setting is altered by the awareness of its historical and textual antecedents. Perhaps it is too essentialistic to say that poetry *has to* locate itself in this context. But it does seem to me that for poetry to remove itself from it entirely is for it to abandon the realm of enactment for the realm of illustration, as in the case of the instrumental poetry of the authentic voice, which I think merely exemplifies an untenable conception of thought and expression; and, in the case of Language poetry, which is too content to merely illustrate the ways in which meaning is conventionally constructed.

Now the contestation that poetry enacts is almost bound to embody such characteristic movements as desire, expansiveness, regret, disappointment, despondency, consolation, and resignation; for it is in terms like these that subjectivity defines itself against its objective setting. The ways in which these movements manifest themselves within the poetic field of the imagination are never (one would hope) straightforward and ingenuous; yet it is difficult to envisage a poetic imagination from which they are entirely absent. Moreover, these movements are realized in poems by rhetorical devices and strategies that are, let us grant, textual and social constructions; and poems that fail to acknowledge this, and which deploy them in a completely unselfconscious manner, enact at best a limited and weak version of romantic contestation (recall the Brooke poem). Yet despite all this, contestation is an active and assertoric gesture (even when its major movements are ones like resignation and regret); and this requires, at *some* level of theoretical self-awareness, a kind of *acquiescence* in the affective movements by which it is constituted and the rhetorical conventions by which these movements are realized.

Earlier I suggested that the impulse behind deconstruction is the protophilosophical one of unmasking, an impulse that attempts to demonstrate that interpretations and forms of expression that would ordinarily be regarded as natural are actually the products of contingent human conventions and practices, that alternatives to them are conceivable, and that therefore (sic) attributions of thought and meaning are to be consigned to the realm of appearance. Its basic gesture is one of *refusal*, since it insists on disassociating itself from any conventions and practices—and from the units of significance they help create—which it is not, in some sense, "logically compelled" to accept. But this gesture is in sharp contrast to the one produced by the impulse of romantic contestation that I believe to be central to poetry; for that impulse requires (again, at *some* level) an acquiescence in the affective movements and rhetorical strategies by which it is enacted—that is to say, an acquiescence in what, from the vantage point of deconstruction, amounts to mere appearance. It isn't that the romantic impulse is entirely incompatible with the sort of theoretical awareness that gives rise to deconstruction—indeed, that awareness ought to be expected to help shape the perception of the objective situation against which the impulse is directed. It is, rather, that deconstruction holds (wrongly, in my view) that this awareness dictates an attitude towards human communicative practices generally and poetic practice in particular that is at odds with the stance towards language and expression poetic practice demands. This isn't to say that deconstructionist views of language and thought are somehow "mistaken"; and I think it is important to acknowledge that the poetic impulse I have been trying to characterize involves a considerable degree of theoretical bad faith—not the gratuitous kind of bad faith exemplified by the poetry of authenticity but, rather, the ineliminable kind manifested in, say, Wittgenstein's writing the *Tractatus* in the full certainty of his belief in its unintelligibility or by the defiant assurance that "I sing alway" with which John Ashbery concludes "Fantasia on 'The Nut-Brown Maid.'"[11]

It may seem odd to assimilate deconstructive theory to the impulse towards the refusal of appearance that is characteristic of philosophical realism; yet I think that this assimilation not only helps locate a fundamental source of tension between poetry and that theoretical perspective but also provides some sense of what a poetics informed by theoretical reflection in a broader sense might be like. Such a poetics would neither reject the domain of subjectivity, as deconstruction does, nor try to incorporate it into the domain of the objective, as the poetics of authenticity tries to do. Unfortunately, this kind of poetics remains largely unformulated, and, given the institutional factors I described earlier, I am not terribly optimistic about its prospects. One conspicuous exception to this bleak outlook is furnished by Allen Grossman's writings, whose "speculative poetics" make up a sustained body of thought about the nature and possibilities of poetry informed by theoretical reflection of a very high order.[12] He takes the function of poetry to be the preservation of the image of a person against the eroding forces of society and time. But he also insists on distinguishing what he means by a "person" from the familiar psychological notion of the self—the subject of social relationships, autobiography, and the kind of poetry that would ordinarily be called personal or confessional. "Preserving the image of a person" seems to come to something like enacting the demands of subjectivity, of demonstrating that there is something that it is actually *like* to be alive, against the eradicating forces of the impersonal and the real. I think that it is significant that the presiding philosophical figure in Grossman's poetics is Emmanuel Levinas (rather than Derrida), for whom the human face stands not only as a nonrepresentational (and nondeconstructible) emblem of alterity or radical metaphysical otherness but also as a moral injunction not to kill, or as the demand for the preservation of something literally inconceivable. For I think that if poetry is going to recover our attention and respect, it has to reconceive itself as the mind's acknowledgment of this injunction and begin to see itself as one effort among others to maintain the demands of subjectivity and the imagination against the inexorable encroachments of the real.

3

Poetry and the Experience of Experience (1993)

It used to be a truism that in the wake of romanticism poetry bore an essential relation, however vexed and problematic, to individual experience. If this is no longer quite the truism it once was, it is in part because of a general distaste for essentialism and in part because the idea that works of art are constituted by their creation has been replaced, at least in some quarters, by the idea that they are constituted by the social processes governing their reception and recognition. Yet even if one is sympathetic to this outlook, it seems to me to remain obviously true that subjective experience plays a central and irreducible role in how poems come into existence and in what they are taken to be. Just why this "obvious" truth should be so important is a question that deserves attention, and I shall turn to it later. But the more immediate problem, I think, is that the conception of experience employed by many of those who take it as dogma that poetry aims at its presentation—as well as by many who regard this as simply another version of "the naïve vision of the individual creator"[1]—is such an attenuated and impoverished one that it is hardly surprising that it tends to be either sentimentally embraced or knowingly dismissed.

Another late truism is that poetry aims at a *representation* of experience. While some of the skepticism that this claim now evokes stems from the anxiety that has come to surround the very idea of representation, mimetic conceptions of art have always occasioned a certain unease. Johnson's famous pronouncement, in the *Preface to Shakespeare*, that poetry ought to furnish "just representations of general nature" is followed shortly by his admission that Shakespeare's adherence to general nature has exposed him to the censure of critics who form their judgements upon narrower principles"; and he goes on to mention Voltaire and several others as examples of critics who fault his depiction of royal subjects for incorporating elements of the comic and the vulgar.[2] It seems to me that one's attitude towards the claim that the representation of experience, or "general nature," is central to the poetic enterprise depends, to a great extent, on what one takes representation and experience to be. And here again, I think that much of the current distrust of this claim derives from narrow and simplistic conceptions of both.

There isn't a single explanation for the impoverished notion of experience that informs so much contemporary poetics and theory and no single form that its attenuation takes. Poetry, in its current state, is itself inhospitable to the discursive and the reflective, in part because of the widespread acceptance of what Mary Kinzie calls "the rhapsodic fallacy"—the assumption, which stems from certain strands in romanticism (though I think only *certain* strands), that poetry aims at "an ecstatic and unmediated self-consumption in the moment of perception and feeling."[3] Neopragmatism is another and more theoretical source of bias against the abstract and reflective aspects of subjective consciousness, since in its aversion to anything that hints at the transcendental it tends to discount the dimensions of experience that encourage certain traditional conceptions of representation and objectivity. Of course there are many more theoretical tendencies working *against* notions of subjectivity that emphasize its phenomenological or qualitative aspects—for not only are these difficult to fit into even the most plausible functionalist or structuralist accounts of mentality and agency; worse, ways of thinking about art that treat such aspects as central are often regarded as naïve or ideologically suspect (though whether this is because of the theoretical recalcitrance of the phenomenological or because of the social significance these views actually have is something usually left unclear). And the culminative effect of these conflicting assumptions, allegiances, and suspicions is to foster the idea—an idea that is seldom made explicit—that many of the most familiar elements of human experience are unimportant or illusory or unreal.

What *does* experience actually encompass, and why should its representation matter? I shall try next to describe what I take to be the range of the subjective and what I think are some of the motives behind the many forms of its denial. I shall then indulge in some speculation about its importance and value and about the importance and value of its depiction. And I'll end by proposing that one way poetry seeks to capture it is through the enactment of a version of the Kantian experience of the sublime.

The Scope of Experience

Early in the *Second Meditation* Descartes frames the question "What then am I?" and he immediately answers, "A conscious being ... that doubts, understands, asserts, denies, is willing, is unwilling; [and] has sense and imagination." The experience enjoyed by such a being is the awareness of what the seventeenth century called "ideas," which Locke characterized as "whatsoever the mind perceives in itself, or is the immediate object of perception, thought or understanding."[4] One doesn't have to follow Descartes in separating the experiencing subject from the body, or follow the theory of ideas in reifying the contents of consciousness, in order to equate experience with subjective awareness and to identify its range with whatever that awareness can include.

Its range includes sensation and emotion. While part of my reason for surveying it is to combat the appeal of the rhapsodic fallacy of reducing experience to perception and feeling, one can hardly deny the vividness with which these can occupy and even dominate the field of consciousness or the defining links they bear to such other modes of experience as desire, belief, and intention. Vivid as they are, though, neither sensations nor emotions are subjectively simple. Perception used to be thought of as a passive process, unadulterated by conceptualization or inference, in which a variety of "sensible qualities" were made directly available to the mind.[5] But with the demise of this "myth of the given," or "myth of presence," the relation between perception and the more abstract or reflective forms of cognition has become increasingly problematic. And since there is also a complementary tendency to locate sensation in its relation to the satisfaction of desire, it is important to remember as well the disinterested forms of perception involved in what Kant called judgments of taste, or in the invasion of sensation by memory—the perception of an "autumnal" slant of light, or the experience of Proustian recollection, when a current sensation awakens the bodily traces of an earlier one and brings about an awareness of the gulf of time that separates them.

Affective experience too is less tidy than it was once taken to be. Descartes thought of emotions as passive and took these "passions" to be a species of perception—namely, the soul's perception of certain "commotions" taking place in the body.[6] Yet as with perception, it has become commonplace to ascribe a cognitive dimension to the emotions and to see the distinction between them and nonaffective states like belief and imagination as less crisp than it once appeared. And while there is still a tendency to link emotions to thoughts about the kinds of concrete situations that impinge more or less directly on our appetites and desires, Eliot's suggestion "that what is often held to be a capacity for abstract thought, in a poet, is a capacity for abstract feeling" is one I have long found intriguing, and I want to come back to later.[7]

Since visceral emotions such as excitement and fear are often associated with the gratification or frustration of desire by sensation, or the experience of bodily pleasure or pain, it is salutary to remember that the range of desire extends well beyond those satisfiable by sensation, or perceptions of the passive sort, to include desires concerning virtually every aspect of experience—the wish that idle curiosity be satisfied or that inquiry broaden the scope and coherence of one's beliefs about the natural order or that various designs involving oneself and others be realized. Even more general are desires occasioned by the Socratic question "How should I live?"—desires that one's life go a certain way or that one's experience as a whole have a certain character. These desires are informed by self-awareness and a conception of oneself as a person, and among the most important of them are those higher-order desires—which Harry Frankfurt has done so much to illuminate—about our own wants and preferences: for instance, that they be different than they are or that they become ineffective or that they maintain themselves and shape our conduct.[8] I think that Frankfurt is right to suggest that that most central and puzzling aspect of experience—the conception and experience of oneself as a "free" agent—has less to do with a belief in one's exemption from the natural order than with a delicate equilibrium between the higher-order desires about the kind of person one would like to be and the desires one would like to have, on the one hand, and the wants and preferences that actually prompt one to act, on the other.

Desires prompt actions in conjunction with beliefs, and beliefs and the concepts they involve are parts of subjective experience too. Crude empiricist models tie beliefs tightly to perception—for Hume, for example, a belief is a particularly vivid idea, an idea that itself is just the trace of an earlier sense-impression—and tend to treat as illusory beliefs and concepts that can't be easily retraced to perception. Yet although beliefs produced and sustained by the experience of the senses have an obvious force, and while the concepts they embody are ones of which our grasp often seems especially sure, it seems undeniable that the scope of our opinions and of our ability to form concepts ranges far beyond them. I am thinking here not just of beliefs about the unobservable and the abstract but also, as in the case of desire, of higher-order thoughts that take beliefs and concepts themselves as objects of experience and reflection. For we don't merely *have* sensations, thoughts, and the other forms of experience; we have also the capacity for an awareness or experience *of* them and for conceiving of them as constituting a single field of awareness. Hume, in a well-known passage, confessed that "when I enter most intimately into what I call *myself*, I always stumble on some particular perception or other, of heat or cold, light or shade, love or hatred, pain or pleasure"; but that "I can never catch *myself*."[9] He concluded that the notion of the self was in some sense illusory. But I think that Hume was misguided in searching for the self among the objects of experience and that Kant was more nearly correct in tracing the notion to the awareness of the unity of experience, to "the representation of that to which all thinking stands in relation."[10] For somehow we *do* manage to form a conception of a self comprising a single field of awareness and to think of it as standing in some sort of relation, however problematic, to a larger context—to the "world" if you like—which includes but isn't exhausted by the experiences through which that field of awareness is constituted.

It is this sort of self-consciousness that gives rise, I believe, to notions like representation, truth, and objectivity. For it is our awareness *of* our sensations, thoughts, and desires, together with our capacity to conceive of them as aspects of a self embedded in some broader context, that allows us to frame the question of their relation to that world. And to try to situate experience in this way is to start to think of it as, in a very broad sense, representational—as leading us to form conceptions of its surrounding context that can be accurate or inaccurate, or as satisfied or frustrated, by that context. It is sometimes suggested that representational conceptions of thought are merely a stage in the development of a Western philosophical tradition that has pretty much exhausted its usefulness. It is true that most attempts to systematically articulate exactly what the representation of the world involves have turned out to be artifacts of particular intellectual moments—Wittgenstein's "picture theory" of the *Tractatus* being one of the more notorious examples. But it strikes me as just perverse to suppose that the roots of the idea that thought can be about the world, and is capable of representing it with varying degrees of accuracy, are to be found in the philosophy section of the local university library, rather than in that conception of subjective experience as embedded in a larger context to which our capacity for self-awareness gives rise.

It is also this conception that allows us to think of ourselves and our experiences in two different and perhaps irreconcilable ways—from what Thomas Nagel calls a "subjective" or "internal" perspective and from an "external" or "objective" one (even though *thinking* of experience in either of these ways is itself part of subjective experience).[11] To think of experience subjectively is to be aware of its "qualitative" aspect—of "what it's like" to *have* a sensation, to *experience* a strong emotion or desire, or to engage in conscious reflection about the range of thought. Calling this perspective internal suggests that it's available only to those whose experiences they are. Yet given that we can form a conception of ourselves and our experience as part of a larger context whose nature is independent of experience and thought, we can also attempt to think of these in the way we seem able to think of other aspects of that world—as they are in themselves, apart from how they are presented to our awareness. Of course we can't actually *adopt* this "view from Nowhere"—for to think of the world at all is to think of it from whatever position we happen to occupy. Talk of a view from Nowhere is simply a vivid way of describing the fact that it is part of our experience itself that we can form an imaginative conception of a world whose nature is independent of our thought and to which we belong. And the expansion of our knowledge of the world has been basically a matter of filling in the details of this conception.

Yet when we try to think of ourselves in this way, the effort seems to remain incomplete. The qualitative dimensions of experience that appear so vivid from an internal perspective, and the importance and significance with which we invest our feelings and desires, seem to evaporate when we try to think of ourselves objectively, as part of the natural order. This appearance of incompleteness could of course be illusory, and we could become convinced that the intuition that certain important aspects of experience defy inclusion in an objective conception of the world is simply mistaken. Or it may be, as Nagel thinks, that the subjective and objective conceptions of ourselves and the world are both necessary and necessarily partial. I'm inclined to believe that Nagel is right, though I have no idea how to argue the point. In either case, though, it does seem a feature of subjective experience as presently constituted that it allows us to form compelling but radically different conceptions of its character and significance.

This survey is partial. The notion of experience that informs contemporary poetry seems so hostile to abstraction that I've concentrated on its conceptual (as opposed to what might be called its Dionysian) aspects. But I want to turn now to some of the impulses that encourage restricted notions of experience in literary and philosophical studies generally.

The survey I have given consists of characterizations of various varieties of conscious thought. There is a widespread tendency to treat descriptions like these as parts of a *theory*, a theory subject to interpretation, revision, or outright rejection. In literary studies this usually means regarding the concepts such descriptions involve—concepts like belief, desire, emotion, the self, and representation—as historically conditioned social constructions or as manifestations of underlying psychoanalytic structures and mechanisms. In cognitive studies it amounts to regarding them as hypotheses—parts of "folk psychology," or what Daniel Dennett calls "heterophenomenology"[12]—to be accepted to the extent that they can be instantiated by neurophysiological processes and states that mirror their causal structure. Yet all this is to transform the field of awareness into a kind of *text* and to treat one's relation to experience on the model of reading, or of having certain propositional attitudes. And it seems to me that none of these approaches is able to accommodate what makes conscious experience interesting in the first place—its qualitative character, or the fact that there is something that it's *like* to have it. This, of course, is a matter of ongoing controversy and isn't going to be resolved soon. But I think that one of the motives for downplaying certain aspects of subjective experience is a commitment to theoretical models of mentality that, to my mind at least, remain largely speculative.

The impulses combined in certain forms of neopragmatism—particularly the form articulated by Richard Rorty—supply another motive for circumscribing the domain of experience.[13] Pragmatists urge us to think of the formation and revision of our beliefs, concepts, and values not as a matter of assessing them with regard to a priori standards of rationality but, rather, as an ongoing effort to adapt them to our interests and experience broadly construed; and to discard as idle those concepts and distinctions that play no role in this effort. Now surely there is something right about this. "Coherence with experience," broadly construed, *must* be our ultimate standard of assessment, since it is our *only* standard of assessment—for to think about anything at all is to think about it from whatever position we happen to occupy as subjects of experience. Yet Rorty combines pragmatism in this broad sense with an antipathy to philosophical traditions that incorporate certain conceptions of knowledge, representation, truth, and objectivity, or a sharp distinction between the world and our representations of it. I suggested earlier that these notions themselves arise from our experience of self-consciousness and from our ability to form an imaginative idea of ourselves and of our experience as parts of a world that is independent of them. But if so, a sweeping dismissal of these notions is bound to lead to a denigration of those aspects of subjective experience that give rise to them—in particular, the experience of forming a self-image that incorporates the idea of a view from Nowhere. This is not, of course, the rhapsodic fallacy's simple-minded self-extinction in a swoon of sensation. Nevertheless, it seems to me that Rorty's pragmatic allegiance to experience, combined with his hostility to a certain theoretical stance, encourages a conception of experience that works to validate that antipathy.

Rorty's considered view is more subtle. It isn't that the familiar concepts and questions of philosophy have no roots at all in subjective experience—for how could they fail to?—but that we'd be *better off* without them or if our experience were somehow reshaped to eliminate them.[14] Better off in what way, though? Well, less fretful or less anxious or less prone to waste our intellectual and emotional resources on "fruitless, irresolvable disagreements on dead-end issues"—or, in a word, happier. Yet what an odd conception of happiness! Whatever it is, happiness surely has more to do with a view of one's life as a whole, and the development and exercise of the capacities one has in the course of that life— what Aristotle called *eudaimonia*, or "flourishing"—than with a mere absence of anxiety and the restriction of one's desires and interests to the most readily satisfied. If the capacity for reflective self-awareness leads us to think of ourselves in irreconcilable ways, why are we better off for ceasing to exercise it? This is the question of the value of experience and its representation, to which I now turn.

Why It Matters What It's Like

Why is subjective experience so important? Perhaps the peculiarity of the question is mitigated by the reflection that the subjective has assumed the mantle of contemporary theory's Other, a specter to be exorcised as "a mere residuum along side the desiring machines," or as a by-product of "the opposition of the forces of attraction and repulsion."[15] The merits of these structuralist deflations, and their functionalist counterparts, strike me as less important than their place in that vast cloud of anxiety and allegiance that has come to surround the whole notion of subjectivity. And this raises the question of why it should have seemed to matter so much in the first place—matter in its own right, or as an object of representation generally or as an object of poetic representation.

I think the answer lies in its connection with moral value. Attempts to distinguish the loose set of judgments, injunctions, and prohibitions that constitute the domain of the ethical from mere customs and patterns of behavior invariably connect it in one way or another with the subjective. The significance of this connection depends, of course, on one's attitude towards the moral. And just as there are deflationary attitudes towards subjectivity, there are strains of thought that are dismissive of moral notions too. Yet just as with subjectivity—perhaps even more so—tendencies like these strike me as theoretical fantasies, fantasies in which one tries to float free of one's actual experience and behavior. For I think that the whole idea of importance, or "mattering," is finally a moral one, central to our self-image, that rests on the notion of a subjective life.

Different conceptions of the moral appeal to subjectivity in different ways. The crudest forms of utilitarianism take ethical injunctions and prohibitions to rest on the relation of conduct to sensations like pleasure and pain. Subtler forms take moral conduct to aim at the promotion of welfare, or the satisfaction of interests—where interests are something like considered desires that one identifies as one's own. Hume thought that morality rested on the experience of sympathy for the experience of others, while Kantian conceptions are based on a respect for persons as intrinsically valuable and an idea of reciprocity—for since each person is worthy of respect, to act morally is to act in ways that would be acceptable from the other's point of view. Here the appeal to subjectivity lies in the thought that people *have* points of view—subjective ones—from which courses of conduct can be appraised. But all these conceptions assume that human conduct impinges on people's experience and that it makes a difference to what life is like *for* them. Without this assumption, the idea that people *have* interests—let alone the idea of considering the world from another person's viewpoint—makes no more sense than the notion of ascribing interests to a fire hydrant or of considering the world from its particular perspective. This isn't to say that all that matters morally is subjective experience, since people have interests ranging well beyond it. But without subjective viewpoints, could there even be interests at all? Could a desiring machine's desires actually matter, if they made no difference from anyone's perspective? A landscape can't have interests, though it can be an interest of *mine*. But this is only because it can matter to me.

So far I've been speaking of the subjective too ingenuously, for it is, I think, problematic in ways that lead to the issue of its representation. Representation is a notion that lends itself to caricature, and I want to caution against models that limit it to description or resemblance while leaving open for now the question of how poetry might accomplish a representation of experience. What seems so problematic about subjectivity is its *tenuous* character—or, since that way of putting it sounds oxymoronic, its *lack* of an objective nature. Sometimes this lack is emblematized by its evanescence—certainly one of its arresting characteristics and one that leads to a complementary view of art as an attempt to preserve the ephemeral. Yet the deeper aspect of its tenuousness isn't the perishability it shares with wildflowers and mayflies but what might be called its "viewpoint dependence."

I said earlier that experience includes the ability to form an objective conception of the world and of one's place in it—where *objective* here means something like "as it really is, apart from how it appears to us or how we conceive of it." The development of natural science can be seen as the elaboration of this conception; and what Nagel has made so vivid is the difficulty—even, one begins to suspect, the impossibility—of incorporating the subjective within it. For while it seems easy to speculate about the nature of regions of time and space remote from our experience, it seems hard, if not impossible, to make sense of wondering what the "nature" of one's experience might actually be—what it really is, apart from how it strikes one or apart from one's apprehension of it. The conspicuous features of interiority are difficult to locate in the landscape of the objective, and if we equate that landscape with the real, we might be tempted to say that such aspects don't literally exist; or be tempted by the "false objectification" of simply expanding our inventory of the world's furniture to include the recalcitrant features of consciousness.[16] I think the right course, though, is to resist both of these temptations and to try to think of the "reality" of the subjective as something constituted by its apprehension, or by its status as a focus of awareness. And since to speak about apprehension or awareness is to speak, in a very broad way, about representation, the point could also be put by saying that subjective experience only exists insofar as it can be represented; or that, apart from our representations of it, this central aspect of our self-image isn't real at all.

Allen Grossman, whom I think of as poetry's most fertile current theoretician, has described poetry's central function as "the keeping of the image of persons as precious in the world" and has characterized poetic speech as a "portrait of the inner and invisible (intuitional) person." While I'm not entirely comfortable with the categorical tone, I believe that the substantive view of the relation between poetry and experience contained in these remarks is basically the same as the one I am trying to develop here. What Grossman means by *person* is a Kantian subject of experience and a rational will, a "being whose existence in itself is an end"; and it seems to me that to say that experience, in the sense I have tried to capture, matters is simply to say that persons—whom Grossman also describes as art's "underlying term or value"—matter. Where I have spoken of the importance of poetry's representation of experience, he locates its value in the preservation of the human image, in its ability to present a portrait of the "inner and invisible," and in its "ontological affirmation …: Here is a person." But the question now is how poetry might manage to accomplish this.[17]

Revisiting the Sublime

Representation is a broad and unruly notion, tied in various ways to such other notions as reference, resemblance, causation, simulation, expression, metaphor, metonomy, evocation, depiction, and performance. One of our century's important philosophical lessons, I believe, is the negative one that questions about the essential nature of representation are misconceived—which is one reason why discussions of cultural, aesthetic, and philosophical issues that turn on critiques of representation so often seem to attack a series of straw men. Attempts to delimit the scope of genuine representation almost invariably wind up acknowledging a complementary domain that undercuts the "real" one, as with Wittgenstein's distinction between what can be said and what can only be shown; or the logical positivists' distinction between language that is cognitively meaningful and that which is merely emotive or expressive; or New Criticism's distinction between the semantic properties intrinsic to a literary text and those that are irrelevant interpolations into it.

All this is by way of disavowing anything resembling a systematic theory of the poetic representation of experience. Reading a poem (and here I use *reading* advisedly, since the dimension of poetry I am trying to characterize emerges more clearly in reading poems than in hearing them) is itself an experience; and to speak of poetry's "representation" of experience, in the broad sense I have in mind, is to speak of an experience of a certain sort that can be induced by reading a poem. The particular sort of experience I mean is a higher-order one involving the thought or awareness—the experience, if you like—of the range of subjectivity as such, and of its precarious relation to the world in which it is situated, which it nevertheless manages to reflect.

In the third *Critique* Kant introduces the notion of what he calls the "dynamical sublime" to describe a particular train of thought or experience that occurs in the presence of natural phenomena of gigantic scale or magnitude. Confronted with a vast physical presence—in the eighteenth century the experience was associated with the Alps, tours of which had recently become fashionable; though something like the Grand Canyon or the St. Louis Arch would do as well—one first feels overwhelmed at the thought of the disparity between one's own physical stature and the natural immensity before one. Yet this very thought of a vast magnitude, by comparison with which one seems limited to the point of insignificance, leads to the thought of an *unbounded* or *infinite* magnitude. And "since in contrast to this standard everything in nature is small"—including the overpowering Alp—the mind is led to an awareness of its "superiority over nature itself in its immensity."[18] For the ability to form a conception of an unbounded magnitude, which isn't to be found in nature, enables us to think of all of nature as "small" and to conceive of ourselves, the subjects of that conception, as distinct from and "above" it. Kant is quick to remark that on the surface "this principle seems far-fetched and the result of some subtle reasoning"; nevertheless, he thinks that "even the commonest judging can be based on [it], even though we are not always conscious of it." Moreover, I think that the oscillations of thought and self-awareness that he describes in characterizing the dynamical sublime can be abstracted from his overt concern with physical immensity and the mind's superiority to nature to characterize the kind of experience involved in the poetic representation of subjectivity.

In an early essay Nagel tried to characterize the sense in which human life might be thought to be "absurd" along the following lines.[19] Each of us has a "personal" perspective on his or her own life, from which we can't help but regard that life and its interests and concerns with tremendous seriousness; and which invests then with an importance informing almost every aspect of our deliberation and practical reasoning. Yet, each of us is also capable of self-awareness and of mentally "stepping back" and regarding that life and its concerns from an impersonal perspective, *sub specie aeternitatis*—a perspective from which those concerns seem to have no real importance or significance at all. And since this is true no matter what our interests may be, there is a ridiculous but inescapable discrepancy between the importance with which we invest our lives and our projects and the importance we realize them to actually possess. One possible response—a response Nagel associates with Camus and dismisses as romantic—would be the affirmative one of adopting an attitude of defiance towards a world one knows to be indifferent to one's life. Nagel's own response, which strikes me as equally romantic and redemptive (though none the worse for that), is to think of our appreciation of life's absurdity as a manifestation of our most "advanced and interesting characteristic," "the capacity to transcend ourselves in thought."[20]

Leaving aside the issues of superiority, affirmation, and redemption, the important thing to notice is the structural similarity between Kant's characterization of the experience of the sublime and Nagel's description of the apprehension of the absurd. Both share a characteristic trajectory of experience, which starts with an unreflective conception of oneself and attitude towards one's experience; followed by an awareness of something inhuman or impersonal (a vast physical presence, a conception of the world *sub specie aeternitatis*), by contrast with which the self and its experiences are rendered problematic and radically diminished; followed finally by the higher-order reflection that this whole chain of apprehension and realization is itself part of the range of subjectivity. There is of course a difference between Kant's optimistic attitude towards this trajectory and Nagel's pessimistic one. But what strikes me as significant isn't so much the outcome of the sequence of shifts between viewpoints—from the subjective to the impersonal and back to the subjective again—as the oscillation itself, "the rhythm of the series of repeated jumps" (in John Ashbery's words from "The Skaters"),[21] "from abstract into positive and back to a slightly less diluted abstract."

For what seems most characteristic of subjectivity—and what allows for the possibility of its poetic representation—isn't the content of any particular state of awareness but, rather, the transitions from instant to instant between perspectives, from an awareness of the objects of thought to an awareness of thought itself, in an unbounded sequence of reflexive movements. The poetry of subjectivity is sometimes associated with privileged conditions of consciousness, simple or elevated. Yet both the rhapsodic fallacy's unselfconscious phenomenology as well as the Kantian sublime's transcendent perception of nature as "small" (which coincides, incidentally, with what Wittgenstein termed "the mystical"— "feeling the world as a limited whole")[22] are just as much theoretical fantasies as the deflationary attitudes towards subjectivity and morality I touched on earlier. What isn't a fantasy, however, is something poetry is especially suited to engender in a heightened way—the vacillation in viewpoints from moment to moment, along with the larger movement between a personal perspective on the objects of one's attention and an objective view of oneself as part of an impersonal natural world.

Poetry has the resources (which it doesn't always draw on) to enact these oscillations: the imagistic and metaphoric potential to evoke perception and sensation; the discursive capacity of language to express states of propositional awareness and reflexive consciousness; the rhythmic ability to simulate the movement of thought across time; and a lyric density that can tolerate abrupt shifts in perspective and tone without losing coherence. This certainly isn't to say that poetry is *uniquely* capable of accomplishing this sort of enactment. Yet music, for instance, while it possesses the dynamical resources to follow the ebb and flow of subjectivity, lacks the discursive capacity to capture its content. Reflexivity and shifts in viewpoint are harder to achieve in painting, though not impossible. And while prose is also a medium well suited for the representation of the subjective, the movements and transitions characteristic of the conventional prose narrative are more gradual and extended than those of poetry, producing less an awareness of the shifts in perspective themselves than of how the novel's world appears from those different vantage points.

The arc of experience of the Kantian sublime comes to rest in the mind's realization of its transcendence of nature; while in Nagel's apprehension of the absurd it falters at the level of the impersonal surround. Yet another model that informs many poems defers the apotheosis, prolonging the oscillation between the subjective and the transcendent indefinitely. The trajectory of Wordsworth's *Prelude*, for example, is close to the Kantian one.[23] Early in book 2 the self becomes objectified in the recognition of

> The vacancy between me and those days
> Which yet have such self-presence in my mind,
> That, sometimes, when I think of it, I seem
> Two consciousnesses, conscious of myself
> And of some other Being.

In book 7 the self is dispersed by its immersion in the urban spectacle of London and Bartholomew Fair, culminating in the confrontation with the Blind Beggar, whose life is externalized in a written label pinned to his chest:

> and it seemed
> To me that in this Label was a type,
> Or emblem, of the utmost that we know,
> Both of ourselves and of the universe;
> And, on the shape of the unmoving man,
> His fixed face and sightless eyes, I look'd
> As if admonished from another world.

Yet the soul is recoverable, for the self's dispersal "is not wholly so to him who looks / In steadiness"; and the poem presses confidently on towards its closure in the soul's transcendence of nature through its perception of the world as a totality:

> The universal spectacle throughout
> Was shaped for admiration and delight,
> Grand in itself alone, but in that breach
> Through which the homeless voice of waters rose,
> That dark deep thoroughfare, had Nature lodged
> The soul, the imagination of the whole.

Contrast the trajectory of Wordsworth's poem with that of John Ashbery's "Self-Portrait in a Convex Mirror."[24] Here the self's confrontation with its externalization consists of a series of approaches and withdrawals taking place in the urban context of New York, "a logarithm / Of other cities." But the movement towards identification is never completed, and at the poem's end the image of the self's double falls back and flattens into inertness, leaving it stranded in the city—"the gibbous / Mirrored eye of an insect"—with the movement remaining only as a never-to-be-realized possibility, a "diagram still sketched on the wind."

Or contrast Stevens's "Auroras of Autumn" with "An Ordinary Evening in New Haven." "Auroras of Autumn" is our century's great poem of the completed Kantian sublime, moving from a series of domestic interiors to an encounter with nature on the scale of the northern lights, to an apotheosis in

> This contrivance of the spectre of the spheres,
>
> Contriving balance to contrive a whole,
> The vital, the never-failing genius,
> Fulfilling his meditations great and small.

How different the cosmic stability of this resolution seems from the endless vacillations of "An Ordinary Evening in New Haven" (the last of Stevens's major long poems), as the mind roams back and forth between "The eye's plain version" and "A recent imagining of reality," the "second giant [that] kills the first." In canto 9 the attention shifts from what is seen to the seeing "eye made clear of uncertainty," in an effort to incorporate "Everything, the spirit's alchemicana / Included." But the effort remains problematic, and one of the poem's final celebrations is of the movement of subjectivity itself, "a visibility of thought / In which hundreds of eyes, in one mind, see at once."

There are endless variations on this trajectory. Its completion can take a self-referentially aesthetic form, as in Marianne Moore's "An Octopus." Or the deflation of the familiar can be abrupt, as in the sudden and disorienting realization, in Elizabeth Bishop's "Over 2,000 Illustrations and a Complete Concordance," of "Everything only connected by 'and' and 'and' "; or it can take the form of a gradual withdrawal from the particularities of the individual life, as in Robert Pinsky's "At Pleasure Bay." But I find that the enactment of such movements takes place most convincingly in poems of a certain scale, which is one reason I associate it with, say, Ashbery's longer works—the prose of *Three Poems* or the lineated "Self-Portrait: and "Flow Chart"—and poems of James Schuyler's like "Hymn to Life" and "The Morning of the Poem," rather than with poems of a relatively brief round.

Yet the question still lingers of why one should care so much about poetry constructed on this model. A complaint often heard about contemporary verse is that it is excessively diffuse and subjective; and certainly there is something right about this complaint as it applies to the almost generic poem (usually short) distinguished by a vapid and unreflective self-absorption. Of course the subjectivity I have been concerned with here is richer and more complex; but one may reasonably wonder why poems embodying it should be more interesting on that account.

I said earlier that the importance of subjectivity and its poetic representation lies in its link with moral value. I still think that this answer is ultimately the right one, yet in a way it seems too remote from the experience of poetry to explain why certain poems seem engaging and moving. What is needed is an explanation at the affective level, and I want to return finally to that intriguing remark of Eliot's I mentioned a while ago—"that what is often held to be a capacity for abstract thought, in a poet, is a capacity for abstract feeling." What in the world could an "abstract feeling" be? For while I've always found the phrase an apt way of characterizing something about certain poems that draws me towards them, this isn't the same as understanding what that feature is.

The most widespread current model of feeling is a cognitive one that assimilates emotions to propositional attitudes. I suppose that on such a model an abstract emotion would simply be an emotion whose content was appropriately "abstract"—like, for instance, feeling elation at the proof of Fermat's Last Theorem. But I think that what Eliot had in mind was an "abstractness" intrinsic to the feeling itself and not merely to whatever it happened to be about; and here I find Descartes's picture of the passions, for all its shortcomings, more suggestive. Descartes thought of emotions as *internal* perceptions, as the awareness of various bodily "commotions"—the flow of "animal spirits" through the nerves, the constriction of the vessels about the heart, a tightening of the muscles—occasioned by external situations that have been found to give rise to such upheavals. Perhaps we can think of abstract feelings in much the same way—as the awareness of the subjective commotions of the reflexive movements of experience and of thought's oscillations between viewpoints, occasioned by situations that are themselves partially subjective. Surely this more nearly captures the experience of the Kantian sublime, which actually feels not so much like a metaphysical apprehension of the self's independence from the natural order, as like an affective transformation of the world. Or if one thinks, as I do, that our notions of freedom and autonomy ultimately derive from our capacity for higher-order reflection, one might call it *both* a metaphysical intuition and an affective transport. In any case, I think that what draws us to poetry that enacts the kind of representation of experience I have tried to describe is its ability to engender those powerful yet abstract feelings of which Eliot spoke; or, better, that this sort of poetry, like the experience on which it draws and which it helps sustain, matters because it moves.

4

The Romance of Realism (1996)

In the *Crito* Socrates, his death imminent, asks of a piece of reasoning "whether this argument will appear in any way different to me in my present circumstances, or whether it remains the same"; and the clear implication of the question is that if a piece of reasoning is valid its force must remain unaffected by alterations in mood or outlook occasioned by changing circumstances. The pretension of philosophy to a passion for truth is traditionally taken to bar the influence of the passions on the way in which truth is pursued: a rational person's assessment of a philosophical argument or thesis must, so the tradition holds, be a disinterested one, in which considerations of temperament, inclination, and intuition have no proper role. On the whole, the effect of this tradition is salutary, bequeathing to philosophy a kind of integrity increasingly absent in other humanistic disciplines, an integrity perhaps purchased at the cost of a certain intellectual marginality.

Yet for a long time it has struck me that in practice philosophers depart considerably from this ideal, in that their attractions and aversions to particular views, problems, and arguments often seem inexplicable on rational (in some narrow sense of that term) grounds alone. When Wittgenstein spoke of philosopher's suffering from a "loss of problems" he seemed to suggest an affective dimension to one's relation to philosophical issues, a suggestion that is certainly true to my experience of the discipline. Some issues that I find profoundly problematic and engaging—skepticism and the mind/body problem, for instance—others regard as quaint academic curiosities; and nowhere, it seems to me, do considerations of temperament play a greater role than in philosophers' attitudes towards the host of issues involved in the problem of philosophical realism. To some (including myself) *some* view that deserves the name *realism* seems obviously correct and beyond serious argument; to others the very word provokes something akin to an allergic reaction. This is all the more striking because the question of what realism and its denial actually involve is a rather subtle one, and it is often not at all clear, when someone passionately defends or denies it, just what is being passionately defended or denied.

Plato's opposition of philosophy to poetry was rooted in the conviction that poetry, whose persuasiveness derives from the vagaries of the passions rather than the force of impersonal argument, was an unfit vehicle for knowledge. I think that the popular idea that poetry ought to remain untainted by the discursive and the conceptual is an insidious one and that it has had a deleterious effect on the recent development of American poetry. Poetry can and should, I believe, approach experience and the world in full generality and embody stances or attitudes towards them that can only be called theoretical. Yet it is true that conceptualization in poetry does not call for impersonal rational justification; rather, it derives its force from the brute fact that the poet has found a particular way of situating himself and his experience in relation to the world compelling.

I want to suggest that something like this occurs in philosophy too and that there are affinities between certain positions or views that are properly thought of as philosophical and certain attitudes or outlooks that inform poetry at its most ambitious and powerful. What I want to suggest is a relation between realism and romanticism.

I. A. Richards, in *Coleridge on Imagination*, raised something like this issue but, because of a certain philosophical view about meaning that he held, declined to pursue it. Richards identified two doctrines and then raised the question of which of them Coleridge held and which was Wordsworth's:

> In the first doctrine Man, through Nature, is linked with something other than himself which he perceives through her. In the second, he makes of her, as with a mirror, a transformed image of his own being.[1]

What Richards meant by the first doctrine is a form of realism (as I shall characterize it in a moment), in that it insists on a discontinuity between the world (what he calls "Nature") and ourselves. The second, which emphasizes the continuity between nature and ourselves, is akin to philosophical idealism. But rather than identity Wordsworth or Coleridge with either of these views, he held that their apparent incompatibility was illusory and that both could be seen as formulations of the same underlying "fact of mind."[2]

Richards wrote at the height of the influence of logical positivism, and his claim that the two doctrines are in some deep sense equivalent directly reflects that influence. Logical positivism, at the time Richards was writing, was promulgated in England by A. J. Ayer, who maintained that the traditional metaphysical dispute between realism and idealism—as to whether, for instance, a table one perceives has a nature and existence independent of perception or whether it is a construction out of our sensory experiences—wasn't a substantive dispute but, rather, a matter of a "choice" between two different vocabularies, both of which could be used to describe the same underlying facts (which is essentially what Richards maintained). But the principles about language and meaning on which claims like Richard's and Ayer's were based are no longer widely accepted; and my own experience, both in poetry and philosophy, suggests to me that there *is* a question as to whether the impulses central to romanticism have a greater affinity with realism or with its denial. But of course one's understanding of this question depends on what one takes those impulses to be and on what philosophical realism amounts to.

What I take realism, in its basic sense, to be is a thesis to the effect that the world has a determinate character and nature that are independent of our beliefs and thoughts about it, our experience of it, and the concepts with which we seek to describe it. Realism thus insists on a sharp distinction between experience and thought, on the one hand, and the world in which our experience and thought are situated, on the other. At times this distinction can seem to take the form of an estrangement, for, while realism doesn't strictly imply skepticism regarding our knowledge of this independent reality, it is a problem for realism to account for how we are able to arrive at a knowledge of that reality, given its independence from our conception of it. The specter of skepticism is historically one of the principal motivations for denying realism, for by eliminating or blurring the distinction between thought and the world, by refiguring it as in some sense a projection of, or construction out of, our experience, the appearance of a gulf to be bridged between the world and our knowledge of it is erased. This characterization of realism as a view whose central tenet is the mind's independence of or estrangement from the world is, I think, the basic one. Philosophical discussions often frame the issue somewhat differently, as a question of how notions like meaning and truth should be understood—for example, whether a statement's truth depends on the objects (and their properties) to which it refers, regardless of our knowledge of those objects, or whether its truth is ultimately a matter of our rational acceptance of it. There are good reasons, in a technical philosophical context, for reformulating the issue of realism as a semantic one. Here, though, where the question is one of the affinities between realism or its denial and a certain poetic impulse or perspective, I think the original ontological conception of realism is the appropriate one, and this is how I shall understand it. Similarly, though in contemporary philosophical debates the term *antirealism* is often used to refer to specific positive semantic doctrines. I shall use it here simply to refer to any denial of realism as I have characterized it.

The central impulse of romanticism is, I take it, the affirmation of subjectivity. While this affirmation may, in concrete instances, be embodied in or disguised by a championing of individualism, the presentation of the heroic, the picturesque, or the languorous, or the celebration of nature, the underlying movement of romanticism is a contestatory one, in which subjective consciousness seeks to ward off the annihilating effect of its objective setting, a context that is lifeless and inert.

The strategy by which this affirmation is to be achieved is problematic. A straightforward celebration of subjectivity risks collapsing into posturing and vapidity—especially since the contrast between consciousness and its objective setting in the world is liable to make the former appear illusory and a too vigorous insistence upon it an act of delusion. The more likely strategies are indirect, involving a projection through the imagination in which the subjective self is reified or identified with something other or external. This may take the form of personification or the investment of abstractions with subjectivity, as in Milton's allegory of Sin and Death in *Paradise Lost*. It may take the form of animism or the pathetic fallacy, in which nature becomes a mirror for subjective consciousness. It may involve the positing of a quest-object, whose attainment would constitute the self's realization. Or it may take the more complicated form of the sequence of interior movements that Kant called the dynamical sublime, in which the subjective self first feels overwhelmed to the point of extinction by some vast natural presence but is then led, by the realization that it is able to comprehend a presence of this magnitude and to conceive of an even greater and unbounded magnitude not to be found in nature, to posit and identify with a self transcending the natural order.

All these strategies are subject to their own difficulties. Personification risks degenerating into hollow symbolism if the abstractions are rendered too figuratively and into an amorphous vagueness if they are not. The investment of nature with the qualities of consciousness quickly becomes unconvincing and sentimental, while, on the other hand, the object of a quest-romance is liable to appear too external, too lacking in interiority. And the self's identification, in the course of the movements of the sublime, with the transcendental ego posited by the imagination, produces, as Steven Knapp notes, "a mad or comical inflation of the self" that Kant called "fanaticism" or a condition of rational raving."[3]

Both the issue of realism and the issue of the form romanticism's affirmation of subjectivity should take are thus concerned with the question of how subjective consciousness is seen to be situated in the world, or of what one takes its relation to its objective setting to be. And what I want to consider is whether romanticism's underlying impulse is best implemented in ways that suggest an affinity with the distinction between consciousness and the world posited by realism, on the one hand, or with the blurring of the distinction between them posited by antirealism, on the other.

Stanley Cavell is one of the few philosophers to explore the relationship between philosophical positions and outlooks that would more likely be deemed literary. His main concern is with epistemological skepticism, which he regards as a condition of "despair of the world,"[4] an estrangement that threatens to be a consequence of realism's insistence on the independence of thought and reality. Cavell personifies skepticism in the figure of "the sceptic" and attempts to diagnose the skeptic's rejection of ordinary standards and claims to knowledge. This approach is based on the idea that skeptical arguments are no different in form from arguments we usually find unobjectionable and thus are not open to refutation in any straightforward sense; but that nothing in the concept of knowledge requires that the standards for it be set so high that none of our ordinary beliefs can satisfy them. And this leads us to ask just what attitude towards or relation to the world might be involved in accepting the skeptic's claims:

> My idea is that what in philosophy is known as skepticism ... is a relation to the world, and to others, and to myself, that is known to what you might call literature, or anyway responded to in literature, in uncounted other guises.[5]

And he takes this relation to be what he calls a refusal of "acknowledgment"—which means, in part, a withdrawal from the everyday forms of life and social practices on which, following Wittgenstein, he takes communication and knowledge to rest.[6]

Responding to skepticism, according to Cavell, involves overcoming an "anxiety about our human capacities as knowers" by recovering what he calls "the prize of the ordinary"—that is, achieving a sense of an "ordinariness [that] speaks of an intimacy with existence."[7] Such a response is furnished, he maintains, by ordinary language philosophy as practiced by J. L. Austin and others, by American transcendentalism, and by the romanticism of Coleridge and Wordsworth. He takes the fundamental romantic quest to be for the installation of the self *in* the world and the romantic "calling for poetry" to be the attempt to "give the world back, to bring it back, as if to life"—even if that means becoming entangled in the "mysteries of animism" and the pathetic fallacy.[8]

The bases on which Cavell enlists romanticism in this project of the recovery of the ordinary are Wordsworth's professed aim, in the preface to the *Lyrical Ballads*, of rendering "the incidents of common life interesting" and his reading of the Immortality ode. He takes the ode's speaker's address to nature to be a replacement for the more blatant pantheism of the opening stanzas but still a form of expression of an impulse towards the incorporation of the self into the world, or the world into the self. And he regards as an *affirmation* Wordsworth's acknowledgment that the "vision splendid of The Soul that rises with us" and that "Hath had elsewhere its setting / And cometh from afar" must ultimately "fade into the light of common day."

This seems to me to confuse the originating impulse of romanticism, which is towards a condition of transcendent subjectivity, with the inevitable recognition that this condition is unsustainable and that it can be achieved, if at all, only in glimpses or intimations. While the child's "exterior semblance doth belle / [The] Soul's immensity," too soon that "Soul shall have her earthly freight / ... / Heavy as frost, and deep almost as life!" This recognition is not an affirmation but a gesture of resignation or regret—or, if that is too strong (given the last stanza's note of solace), a moment in Wordsworth's characteristic oscillation away from and towards the world, an oscillation so conspicuous also in Stevens. Yet this oscillation is really an attenuation of the movement of the dynamical sublime towards a self transcending the natural order, a movement whose imaginary completion would result in that condition Kant called rational raving. Transcendent subjectivity is thus, for romanticism, an imaginative ideal rather than a condition of actual existence. But this does not mean that its actual impulse is towards a merging with or incorporation into the world, for the price of this incorporation would be a condition of extinction—as in "A Slumber Did My Spirit Seal," where the incorporation of the "thing that could not feel / The touch of earthly years" into nature reduces it to something with no motion or force, which "neither hears not sees, / Rolled around in earth's diurnal course / With rocks and stones and trees."

I believe that Harold Bloom is right to insist that readings (like Cavell's) that associate Wordsworth, and romanticism generally, with pantheism and a quest for unity with nature are distortions, that the actual relation posited by romanticism between subjectivity and nature is an antagonistic one, and that "Romantic nature poetry, despite a long history of misrepresentation, was an antinature poetry."[9] Wordsworth's achievement, according to Bloom, was to empty poetry of any real content or subject other than pure subjectivity, by making it a field for an internalized quest whose hero is the poet himself, "in a reductive universe of death."[10] And the goal of this internalized quest is not, appearances to the contrary notwithstanding, the recovery of some sort of former union with nature, or the installation of the self in the world, but of a "former selfless self"[11]—which, I take it, is a condition of pure subjectivity, conceptually prior to its objectification in the form of the human person.

Such a condition is of course as unattainable as is the completion of the movement of the dynamical sublime. Yet its status as an unattainable ideal points to the opposition between what Paul de Man calls "the ontological status of the object"[12] and the demands of consciousness. Though romantic poetry manifests, in its language, a *temptation* for "the nostalgia for the object," this temptation actually seeks to thwart the impulse of romanticism; and to see the latter as aspiring to an "unmediated vision" that fuses matter and consciousness in a "happy relation" is to "fail to realize that the very fact that the relationship has to be established within the medium of language indicates that it does not exist in actuality."[13] Invoking Wordsworth's characterization of nature as a "blank abyss," de Man locates the trajectory of the romantic imagination in an attempt to tear itself away from a terrestrial nature and a movement towards an "other nature … associated with the diaphanous, limpid and immaterial quality of a light that dwells nearer to the skies."[14] This is not the conventional imagination of flower imagery but the idea of a savage and self-contained mode of consciousness, capable of existing "entirely by and for itself, independently of all relationship with the outside would, without being moved by an intent aimed at a part of this world."[15] And it is the fascination with some such possibility, unrealizable though it may be, that I take to be the animating force behind the internalized romantic quest.

De Man does acknowledge romanticism's temptation for a movement towards the world that runs counter to this underlying animus. And it is of course undeniable that the tendencies towards merging the self and the world that Cavell mistakenly identifies as romanticism's root impulse are present in its poetry. But I think such tendencies should be seen as a reaction, or countermovement, to the fundamental drive towards the affirmation of subjectivity. That drive tends towards the estrangement of subjectivity from the world, towards the isolation of the subject. But desire is an essential component of subjectivity (at least once it has fallen from that imaginary condition of the "selfless self" to which Bloom thinks it aspires); and a consequence of this withdrawal from the world is that desire remains unfulfilled. Thus the characteristic romantic longing, the impulse of unfulfilled desire, emerges as an inevitable countermovement towards the world—a world of the objects of desire—and the actual trajectory of the romantic imagination isn't de Man's smooth ascension from terrestrial nature but, rather, an oscillatory one, as the basic impulse towards an isolated condition of pure subjectivity is countered by the force of unsatisfied longing it trails in its wake.

The question I posed at the outset was of the relation between theses or positions that are properly philosophical, on the one hand, and, on the other, attitudes or outlooks that aren't really subject to philosophical argument or assessment but which typically inform the operations of the imagination. Specifically, the question was of the possible affinity between the root impulse of romantic poetry and either philosophical realism or antirealism. My thought was that the existence of such an affinity might both clarify the nature of that impulse and suggest a temperamental or affective dimension to those philosophical positions—and that this might, in turn, help explain what strikes me as the fact that individual philosophers' attractions or aversions to them often seem disproportionate to the strength of the actual arguments for or against them.

If one accepts the idea that what lies at the heart of romanticism is an affirmation of subjectivity, one's first thought would probably be that any affinity it might have with either realism or antirealism would likely be with the latter. Realism emphasizes the independence of the world from our thoughts or conceptions of it, while its denial typically construes the world as in some sense constructed out of subjective experience, or constituted by the beliefs and concepts we form in the course of the human activity of inquiry in the service of the satisfaction of our needs and interests. Antirealism thus seems to magnify or extend the range of the subjective or the human, or to locate the world within the domain of the human—and in doing this it might be thought to affirm the domination of the mind over a setting that would otherwise present an image of its annihilation. But in light of the foregoing account of romanticism, I think that one can see why this appearance of an affinity with antirealism is deceptive. By blurring the distinction between the self and the world, we in effect strip the self of that radical singularity that lies at the heart of the romantic imagination. Blurring the distinction between subjectivity and its objective setting doesn't so much establish its dominion over the latter as allow it to be swallowed up by it. This attempt at a recovery of the word, which Cavell celebrates as an overcoming of skepticism, is part of what I just suggested arises as a countermovement to the impulse of romanticism and threatens a correlative loss of the self as it becomes diminished or extinguished in the fulfillment of its desire for that recovery.

In treating the world as, in some sense, a projection of ourselves and our practices, antirealism challenges our ability to form a conception of a world possessing a character and nature that are independent both of our thoughts or representations of it and of our investigative practices directed towards it—indeed, it is the denial of our ability to form a complete conception of such an independent reality that is characteristic of antirealism in virtually all its forms, including Berkeley's idealism, Richard Rorty's version of pragmatism. Nelson Goodman's irrealism and Michael Dummett's critique of realism. And for reasons I shall try to bring out momentarily, a central element in the romantic affirmation of subjectivity is the attribution to it of the ability to form a conception of a world radically other than itself.

It may seem paradoxical to associate romanticism's valorization of consciousness with realism's view of the world as essentially inert and discontinuous with the mind, but this is where the affinity lies. The discontinuity may at first seem to diminish or marginalize subjectivity by removing it from the natural order, but I think that this impression is too hasty. The estrangement, in imagination, of consciousness from the world in effect purifies and isolates it, constituting the first step in the severing of its relation to the outside world that gestures towards that "selfless self" and freedom from "terrestrial nature" that Bloom and de Man identify as the basic impulse of romanticism. For in framing a conception of a natural order whose character and nature are independent of our representation of it in thought, one implicitly posits a vantage point or perspective on it that is not a part of that order but transcends it.

Remember the sequence of movements of the dynamical sublime: the apprehension of a physical enormity radically other than the self, by which the self seems diminished; next, the realization that one is able to comprehend that enormity, or contain it in thought; and finally (if carried to its conclusion), the positing of and identification with a transcendental subject of consciousness exempt from the natural world of causality to which the enormity belongs. The world portrayed by realism, it seems to me, amounts to an abstract version of that initially overpowering physical presence. And the mind's ability to form a conception of such a world strikes me as the analogue of the concluding movements of the experience of the sublime that gesture towards a transcendent subjectivity. Sometimes I think that the emblem of both realism and romanticism is that representation of tiny figures in a vast landscape characteristic of Chinese and Dutch landscape painting, in which the human person, externalized and reduced to objective terms, is swallowed up and dwarfed into insignificance—for the very experience of such a representation contains the idea of a subjective position outside that landscape, from which it can be apprehended.

Linking realism to a notion of transcendent subjectivity may seem odd, because realism is usually thought to incorporate, or at least allow for, a materialist position on the mind/body problem that would explain consciousness in natural terms and locate it within the natural realm. I am skeptical about the prospects for such a materialist explanation of consciousness. But whether or not this skepticism is justified is really irrelevant to the issue of romanticism's affinity with realism, for the *idea* of the self as not really part of the world seems to me to be latent in our subjective experience of ourselves; and any materialist account of consciousness and subjectivity would have to accommodate those aspects of our experience that give rise to such an idea. What romanticism requires is the positing by the imagination of an idea of a transcendent subjectivity and a movement or gesturing towards it. But as I've suggested, this movement inevitably gives rise to a countermovement back towards the world. And to insist on the actualization of that idea is to succumb to self-delusion, or to lapse into Kant's condition of rational raving.

One might also object that the conception of the world posited by realism is an unattainable one and that realism itself is an untenable philosophical view. This is in fact one of the main criticisms of realism (though it isn't one I find persuasive). But again, what is at issue here is neither the truth or viability of philosophical realism or the notion of a transcendent subjectivity posited by romanticism but their association. Michael Dummett, one of the most persistent critics of realism, recounts that he once considered an argument for God's existence to the effect that antirealism is incoherent but that realism is only tenable on a theistic basis.[16] Whether realism, theism, or such an argument are ultimately viable is really beside the point. What *is* important is the affinity between a certain philosophical doctrine and a certain way of conceiving of the self's relation to the world that the very idea of such an argument suggests.

This affinity can be seen in the work of many poets of consciousness. Elizabeth Bishop isn't often thought of in this way, but it seems to me that the sense of the subjective viewpoint is as strong in her work as it is in those poets in whom it is rendered more explicitly. Bishop was misconstrued early in her career by critics like M. L. Rosenthal as a passionless and genteel poet whose main strength was the depiction of surfaces but whose work was devoid of the furious sense of self informing the work of contemporaries of hers like Robert Lowell. It *is* true that Bishop's depictive abilities are remarkable; but what is so striking about her work is how she renders objects in a way that isn't merely accurate in a conventional sense but with a clarity that borders on the hallucinatory: a fish's eyes are "packed / with tarnished tinfoil / seen through the lenses / of old scratched isinglass" ("The Fish");[17] "The branches of the date-palms look like files" ("Over 2,000

Illustrations and a Complete Concordance").[18] Consider the stuffed loon in "First Death in Nova Scotia":[19]

> He kept his own counsel
> on his white, frozen lake,
> the marble-topped table.
> His breast was deep and white,
> cold and caressable;
> his eyes were red glass,
> much to be desired.

What this hallucinatory clarity evokes, as much as if not more than the depicted scene itself, is the sense of a subjective vantage point from which that scene is observed and which (as Wittgenstein remarks of the relation of the eye to the visual field) is absent from it. David Kalstone, in his discussion of Bishop's "Quai d'Orleans," notes that what gives her work its power is her "heightened receptiveness ... to a scene which, in the event, so excludes" the observer.[20] And it is through this almost palpable sense of exclusion permeating her work that subjective consciousness is rendered as an implied presence.

By contrast, in few poets is interiority rendered more explicitly than in Stevens, and in few is its external setting presented more obliquely. The late poems in *The Rock* are suffused, as Helen Vendler has remarked, with the ache of unsatisfied sexual longing.[21] Yet even there Stevens remains stoic in his isolation, gesturing towards the world only to reaffirm his withdrawal from it. "Long and Sluggish Lines" furnishes glimpses of the self's external setting, glimpses that reinforce the self's detachment from it:

> It makes so little difference, at so much more
> Than seventy, where one looks, one has been there before.
>
> Woodsmoke rises through trees, is caught in an upper flow
> Of air and whirled away. But it has often been so.

The world exists as a frame in which the ephemeral seat of the poet's consciousness finds its tenuous location:

> Wanderer, this is the pre-history of February.
> The life of the poem in the mind has not yet begun.
>
> You were not born yet when the trees were crystal
> Nor are you now, in this wakefulness inside a sleep.

"Not Ideas about the Thing but the Thing Itself" flirts with an embrace of reality prompted by unfulfilled desire, but this nostalgia for the object is deflected and transformed. The significance of the external is seen first as its representation in consciousness:

> At the earliest ending of winter,
> In March, a scrawny cry from outside
> Seemed like a sound in his mind.

The poem envisions a "new knowledge of reality"—supplanting "sleep's faded paper mache"—of the sun "coming from outside." But the sun remains "Still far away," and the experience, which is "*like* / A new knowledge of reality" (emph. added), seems not one of the recovery of the physical world but a second dawn of subjectivity as the poet's life approaches its close.

Nowhere is this sort of reversal, in which an emblem of externality is transformed into an affirmation of interiority, more striking than in "The Rock" itself, which opens with an acknowledgment of the ephemerality, indeed the unreality, of subjectivity:

> It is an illusion that we were ever alive,
> Lived in the houses of mothers, arranged ourselves
> By our own motions in a freedom of air.

But if the self is an illusion, "an impermanence / In its permanent cold," it is "an illusion so desired / That the green leaves came and covered the high rock" of its impersonal, extinguishing context. Ultimately, through the plenitude of the imagination,

>   the poem makes meanings of the rock,
> Of such mixed motion and such imagery
> That its barrenness becomes a thousand things
>
> And so exists no more.

As the mind, through the imagination, establishes its dominance over the rock, the latter becomes emblematic of the mind's life (unlike the rocks of "A Slumber Did My Spirit Seal," which become emblems of its extinction). Yet Stevens declines to carry this movement of the sublime towards transcendence to completion, and, as he returns to an acknowledgment of the self's ephemerality, the rock becomes both "The starting point of the human and the end":

> The rock is the gray particular of man's life,
> The stone from which he rises up—and—ho,
> The step to the bleaker depths of his descents.

The rock, transformed into an objectification of man's life, finally takes its true place in "Night's hymn of the rock, as in a vivid sleep."

One reason the issue of realism is cloudy is that neither the purest form of realism nor the purest form of antirealism is a tenable position. An extreme realism divorces the world so entirely from thought that the latter would not even have a role in forming the conceptual categories with which to accurately characterize the world—which makes it difficult to see how we might be able to think about the world at all. An extreme antirealism so merges the world and thought that it becomes hard to explain the obvious fact that through inquiry we seem to discover truths about the world that are not of our own making. Where one situates oneself between these extremes seems to me to some extent to be a question of philosophical temperament and not entirely a matter of argument and rational consideration.

Romanticism, as I have tried to understand it, is similarly torn between a vision of subjectivity as completely *other* than the world and a vision of the world as invested with and constituted by subjectivity. What I have tried to suggest is that romanticism's root affinity is with the first vision and that the second should be seen as a reaction to its austerity and isolation.

We can see this ambivalence in the work of the major romantic poets. Shelly and Wordsworth are both driven, by the apprehension of nature in its enormity and otherness, to a heightened awareness of consciousness. Both of them flirt with the temptation to then invest nature with the qualities of spirit, to project that consciousness upon it. Both are finally skeptical of this investment. And both gesture towards a transcendent vision of the self yet decline to embrace that vision fully and are, in this sense, poets of the attenuated sublime. Shelly's "Mont Blanc" opens as "The everlasting universe of things / Flows through the mind" and proceeds to a recognition of the mind's estrangement from it:

> Dizzy Ravine! And when I gaze on thee
> I seem as in a trance sublime and strange
> To muse on my own separate fantasy,
> My own, my human mind.

Mont Blanc is a site from which the human is absent—

> the snows descend
> Upon that Mountain; none beholds them there

—yet the poet still ascribes to it a "secret Strength of things / Which governs thought" and renders the mountain knowable. But the final image of the poem, which takes the form of a question, is of a nature that is inconceivable in its estrangement from consciousness:

> And what were thou, and earth, and stars, and sea,
> If to the human mind's imaginings
> Silence and solitude were vacancy?

Wordsworth's recollection—or perception—of the world is one of such tenderness that at times it can almost seem—and seem to him—to have been created by his imagination or apprehension of it, as at the conclusion of book 12 of *The Prelude*:

> I remember well
> That in life's everyday appearances
> I seemed about this period to have sight
> Of a new world, a world, too, that was fit
> To be transmitted and made visible
> To other eyes, having for its base
> That whence our dignity originates,
> That which both gives it being and maintains
> A balance, an ennobling interchange
> Of action from within and from without:
> The excellence, pure spirit, and best power
> Both of the object seen, and the eye that sees.

But the concluding vision of *The Prelude* exhibits the affinity that I've argued exists between the romantic affirmation of subjective consciousness and the conception of a world from which that consciousness is estranged—a magisterial vision of

> how the mind of man becomes
> A thousand times more beautiful than the earth
> On which he dwells, above this Frame of things.

Here the human figure is installed in the natural order. Yet the perspective that the human mind is able to take on that order *seems* to allow it to transcend it, to bestow on the mind an existence "above this Frame of things"—a frame of *things* (whatever their natures may be) that are independent of us, indifferent to us, and which lie at the heart of realism's conception of the world. And this, it seems to me, is romanticism's fundamental way of imagining the relation of the self to the world.

5

Poetry at One Remove (1998)

The installation of poets in the academy is now so complete that it is easy to forget that the relation of poetry and contemporary literature—let alone poets and contemporary writers—to departments of literature was once considered problematic. It was not really until the establishment of the New Criticism that contemporary poetry became an acceptable object of academic literary studies, and even then the methods of reading it applied, and the readings of the works of high modernism those methods yielded, tended to ignore issues of authorial presence and of the ways in which works of literature were actually produced. True, most of the major poets of the generation succeeding the high modernists—Delmore Schwartz, Robert Lowell, John Berryman, Randall Jarrell, Elizabeth Bishop—spent at least parts of their careers in English departments. But more often than not this was as teachers and scholars of literature, as with Berryman and Schwartz, or, as with Lowell and Bishop, as individual teachers of writing, whose roles were sui generis and left them only distantly connected to the departments to which they were formally attached. It is only recently, with the explosion in the number of creative writing programs, that the idea of poetry as the basis of an entire academic career has emerged, a career in which one receives formal instruction in the writing of poetry both as an undergraduate and as a graduate student and, having thus acquired the requisite credentials, joins the professoriate in a capacity structurally no different from that of a professor of German, philosophy, or economics.

My own situation as a poet has always placed me at one remove from formal literary studies and the teaching of writing. In high school I was deeply fascinated by literature, particularly modernist fiction, and did a certain amount of writing myself. But these were secondary to my primary interests in mathematics and physics, which I intended to pursue as a career. In college my interest shifted to philosophy, and I began writing poetry seriously. At that time there were at Princeton a number of undergraduate poets, most of them (even those who were English majors) united in their disdain for the English department and the contemporary poets of whom its faculty approved. R. P. Blackmur did serve as a source of encouragement and inspiration, though of course he was himself an autodidact whose relationship to academia was a somewhat uneasy one. Several little magazines were edited on the campus, some with ties to poets of the New York School, and discussions of poetry were usually intense exercises in what nowadays would be called theory. As a graduate student in philosophy at Harvard, I found the relation of students who were poets to the university to be different, with a much greater sense of allegiance to the institution and to the writers associated with it. I found this atmosphere uncongenial and came to think of my role in the university almost entirely in terms of my philosophical studies while associating myself as a writer with the poets and artists I knew in New York, in the completely uninstitutional setting of the small part of the literary world they constituted there. And I have continued to think of my role as a philosopher as a professional and academic one and of the writing of poetry as at some level an essentially gratuitous act. And, while it may be making a virtue of necessity, I have a vague feeling that this sense of estrangement from the idea of writing as an academic profession is not entirely disadvantageous and that it has had a distinctive effect on the way in which I think of poetry and on the actual poetry I write. At least that is what I want to try to explore here.

There are certainly incidental effects of coming to poetry from outside the arena of literary studies and of coming to it from the practice of philosophy in particular. There is a kind of orthodoxy in contemporary poetry that favors the concrete, the vivid, the evocative, and the particular and avoids the discursive and the abstract. I think that it is possible to endow the sort of theoretical reflection associated, at least in the popular mind, with philosophy with considerable emotional resonance—indeed, this is one of my primary poetic aims. The discursive and the abstract are philosophy's stock in trade, and a background in the discipline tends to make one at ease with these rhetorical modes. Eliot was one of the few poets trained in philosophy, and this manifests itself in the assurance with which he ventures into the realm of abstraction and the way in which his use of the conceptional idiom always seems casual and matter-of-fact, even at its most rarified. Stevens, by contrast, though often thought of as a philosophical poet, had no formal training in the discipline. And I think that this may be part of the reason why the language of his ruminations, usually so magnificent in its suppleness and profusion, occasionally seems a bit forced, as though he were trying to inhabit a rhetorical mode in which he was not entirely at home. This is not to say that a background in philosophy enables one to bring the conceptual methods of the discipline to bear on poetry. Meditation and speculation in philosophy are subject to severe constraints—this is, in a way, its point—whereas the movement of the mind in poetry is essentially unconstrained. And I think that an important consequence of having an identity as a poet that is not institutionally validated is that this freedom from conceptual constraint, which lies at the heart of the conception of poetry I hold, is reinforced and enhanced.

No doubt there are also incidental effects, some of them detrimental, on poetry written in the role of a literary scholar or a teacher of writing. The latter role is especially liable to have an adverse effect on one's work, since the fact that the poetry written in that role bears essentially the same relation to one's career and livelihood as does the writing of anyone in academia certainly has the potential to render it, over the course of time, formulaic and tired, issuing not from an impulse internal to the poetic act but from pressures external to it. Yet of course many poets who teach writing for a living manage to avoid these kinds of dangers, which in any case do not strike me as terribly interesting, being only externally related to poetic practice. What does interest me is the question of whether having an identity as a poet that does not coincide with an institutionally constituted role might have conceptual consequences internal to the poetic impulse itself, affecting the character of the relation between the authorial self or subject and the poetry that issues from that site.

The conception of poetry that animates my work is based on what I take to be the fundamental impulse underlying romanticism: the enactment and affirmation of subjectivity and the contestation of its inert, objective setting in a world that is emblematic of its annihilation. As I have described it in several essays in this book, the idea of subjectivity informing this conception is of a self not part of the real and objective world at all, a pure and impersonal subject of interiority prior to its objectification in the form of an actual person. It is in this sense a transcendental notion, though putting it this way verges on the delusional inflation of the self Kant called "fanaticism" and "rational raving."[1] It is better, I think, to think of it as a necessary illusion or fiction, a fiction to be enacted and affirmed in spite of the knowledge that it *is* a fiction. And one form this enactment takes is the representation of an attenuated version of the experience Kant, in the *Critique of Judgement*, called the dynamical sublime, in which the self, at first threatened by its perception of a world that reduces it to insignificance, attempts to attain a vantage point from which that world can be encompassed in thought.[2]

The situation of the romantic authorial self is in some ways a paradoxical one. On the one hand, it is bound to poetic practice by a sense of obligation or duty, an obligation to realize in language the abstract idea or form of the poem it is attempting to inscribe. On the other hand, that poem is something that does not yet exist to impose its demands on the poet, and the act of bringing it into existence is felt to be an exercise of unconstrained creation, an expression of subjectivity's freedom from externally imposed constraints that lies at the heart of the romantic imagination. Thus the notion of an obligation that is freely self-imposed is central to the conception of the genuine poetic act, and this odd combination of freedom and duty is again reminiscent of Kant, this time of his moral philosophy. Kant thought that the duties making up what he called the moral law flowed from the single formal principle that one must freely constrain one's conduct to accord with principles applicable to all rational beings. He may have been too optimistic in this: most interpreters of Kant doubt that substantive moral obligations can be derived solely from the formal principle he called the categorical imperative. In her important recent book *The Sources of Normativity*[3] Christine Korsgaard argues that in order to arrive at substantive duties incumbent on a person the categorical imperative has to be supplemented with assumptions about that person's *practical identity*, by which she means the self-conception he has adopted to define the kind of person he takes himself to be. *Practical* here is a theoretical term. A person's practical identity as, say, a mother sets limits on her actions, for since certain actions are at odds with this identity *she* cannot freely choose to do them, for if she were to act in these ways she would not be the kind of person she is. There are a variety of practical identities a person might adopt: as a mother, as a member of an ethnic or religious group, as a member of a certain profession, and so on. *Moral* obligations are those flowing from one's practical identity as merely a human being, as a member of "the party of humanity,"[4] an identity that it is in a way futile to resist acknowledging, since that is what, in the last analysis, one essentially is.

It strikes me that Korsgaard's version of Kantianism, with its notion of a chosen practical identity, helps make sense of the idea of freely self-imposed poetic obligation I take to be so central to the genuine poetic process. In adopting a practical identity as a poet, one obligates one's self to a poetic practice consonant with that identity. Yet as long as that identity is freely—even gratuitously—chosen, the obligations flowing from it are self-imposed and conformity to them a manifestation, rather than a limitation, of the freedom underlying the poetic act. Just as a range of practical identities are open to one, so there are a variety of poetic identities one might adopt, in particular those underlying what might be thought of as the poetics of a limited identity, in which one's work attempts to embody the perspective of some group, class, gender, or sexual identity, or, as in confessional poetry, of some actual individual. But if one conceives of poetry as I do, as an enactment of pure subjectivity, these kinds of poetic identities are liable to seem evasions of one's fundamental poetic identity as a locus of self-reflective consciousness—just as the adoption of a practical identity as a member of an ethnic group can be an evasion of one's basic practical identity as a member of the party of humanity. Indeed, since self-reflective consciousness is what is distinctive of human beings, it might seem that a poetic identity as a locus of pure subjectivity and a practical identity as a human being are one and the same, and it seems to me that an intriguing way of thinking about high Wordsworthian romanticism is to see it as trying to equate a poetic identity with an identity as a member of the party of humanity and so merging the aesthetic and the moral. But just as the full version of the experience of Kant's dynamical sublime is not really open to us, the only form of romanticism tenable now is a truncated and belated one, which enacts the claims of a transcendent subjectivity while at the same time acknowledging it to be illusory and which defines the poetic self by opposing it to the objective world to which we, as actual human beings, belong.

Central to my conception of poetry, then, is the notion of a freely assumed poetic identity as a subject of self-reflective consciousness, an authorial self that attempts to enact and portray that subjectivity in one's work. But if one's identity as a poet is institutionally constituted and sanctioned, one's relation to that work becomes problematic. It is essential that the relation between the poet and his work be an internal one between a freely adopted authorial self and a poetry that enacts that self's subjective consciousness—for only in that way can conformity to the obligations that relation engenders manifest the sense of freedom that lies at the heart of the romantic imagination of the self. But if one's poetic identity is in part a matter of an institutional role one occupies, there is always a danger that one will come to see it as externally imposed—in which case the relation between the authorial self and the work that flows from it will be altered. The work will no longer seem to be created in conformity to a self-imposed obligation but in conformity to a duty imposed from the outside. And this is liable to affect the character of the poetic act itself. Let me adapt and alter slightly an example of Bernard Williams's concerning moral deliberation to illustrate the point. A man's wife is drowning, and he acts, with some risk to himself, to save her, which is what morality requires of him. Were his deliberation to include the thought that he must save her *because she is his wife*, he surely would have, as Williams puts it, "one thought too many."[5] What would be objectionable here is the fact that his moral impulse would be mediated by the thought of a duty he has by virtue of the socially constituted relation he bears to her. He does, or course, *have* this externally imposed duty. But the idea of the thought of it intruding into his process of moral reflection seems repugnant. Similarly, the thought that one assumes a poetic identity *because it is part of one's job* seems foreign to the relation that should hold between the poet and his work. Of course assuming such an identity may indeed be required by one's institutionally defined role, and one may nevertheless assume it freely, unaffected by the thought that one is required to do so. But if such an externally imposed duty is in fact incumbent upon one, it is liable in practice to be difficult to resist having an awareness of it enter into the poetic process, thereby altering the character of that process.

But if one writes outside of the context of an institutional role that defines one as a poet, then the assumption of a poetic identity as an articulator of self-reflective subjectivity can only be freely assumed, since one is under no externally imposed obligation to assume it. There is an existential overtone here (as there is, I think, to Korsgaard's version of Kantianism): what makes the poetic process authentic is the fact that it proceeds from a freely chosen identity, rather, that from an identity one finds one's self to have. In fact, the whole conception of poetry I hold has an existential cast to it, for it insists on the affirmation of a subjectivity that is acknowledged not to be part of the objective natural order and in that sense not factual or real. And it is only on this conception of poetry that the occupation of an institutionally defined role as a poet threatens the integrity of the poetic process. If one conceives of poetry in other terms—formally, culturally, confessionally, or linguistically—one need not take one's poetic identity to be a locus of unconstrained subjective consciousness. Indeed, some conceptions of poetry do not presuppose a particular conception of poetic identity at all. And most academic disciplines presuppose no particular idea of the self. There is no tension between say, doing philosophy and being a professional academic philosopher, because philosophy is standardly conceived in terms of certain institutionally sanctioned texts, issues, problems, and methods, rather than as an activity to which the self bears an internal relation. If one thinks of philosophy differently, though, then professionalism *can* seem a threat to its practice. Wittgenstein thought of philosophy not in terms of texts and problems but as the continuing struggle of the mind "against the bewitchment of our intelligence by means of language"[6] and of "the real discovery" as "The one that gives philosophy peace, so that it is not longer tormented by questions which bring *itself* in question."[7] And he also famously loathed the company of academic philosophers and attempted to convince his best students not to pursue the discipline as a professional career, because of the threat this would pose to their intellectual and spiritual integrity.

Yet, there is something problematic about insisting on a distinction between the authorial self as a locus of pure subjectivity and the practical identity one has by virtue of a role one happens to occupy—a difficulty that is an instance of the more general problem of the relation between the authorial self and the actual person one happens to be and which emerges at the level of poetry's content. Subjectivity, even in a purely impersonal form, is intrinsically perspectival, since it can be grasped only from the first-person perspective each of us occupies. A poetry that attempts to enact and embody it, then, will almost inevitably be a poetry of the first person. Yet since one is of course a particular person, with a particular personality, a particular history, character, and temperament, and with particular relationships to other people, why, if one writes a poetry of the first person that is not simply devoid of content, will not the self of that poetry collapse into that actual personality? And if it does, rather than an enactment of subjectivity *simpliciter* will it not collapse into a confessional poetry of the concrete individual voice, with all the (to my mind retrograde) literary, theoretical, and political connotations this kind of poetry is usually taken to have?

The problem is that there is really no such thing as a self that is simply a locus of pure subjectivity *simpliciter*; yet there is a poetry that is animated the idea of this kind of self. One might try to evade the difficulty by renouncing the poetry of the first person altogether. But given subjectivity's essentially perspectival character, this would yield at best a truncated view of the interior. Or one might simply omit any reference to the personal or try to invest it with an ironic character that keeps it at arm's length. These strategies are not very satisfactory either—the first tends to yield to a poetry that seems either evasive or preciously thin and the second a poetry that seems smug and condescending. What I have tried to do in my own work—I cannot say with how much success—is to reimagine the first person by simply acquiescing in its poetry and incorporating the materials of personal life when the movement of the poem tends in that direction but enveloping them in a language that is dry, abstract, and matter-of-fact, yet with an insistent lyric undertone. The self of the poem is thus rendered in a way that seems factually adequate but which presents it as a partially fictitious entity, slightly off-center and out of focus, leaving the reader with a sense of a difference between the person of the poem and the authorial site from which the poem emanates, a sense of which I hope the reader is not entirely conscious.

The problem with the poetry of the concrete individual voice is that its demand for fidelity to the experience of the actual self is the internal analogue of the constraint resulting from an externally imposed practical poetic identity: both represent limitations on the freedom of the self of transcendent subjectivity and hinder the enactment of a poetry that embodies that conception of the self. One can escape the constraint of an externally imposed or institutionally sanctioned poetic identity simply by failing to have one; but the demand of fidelity to one's actual experience cannot be avoided so easily, since one cannot fail to be an actual person. I think the solution is not to either ignore or confront the conventional poetry of the first person but, rather, to acquiesce in its outward form while at the same time fleshing out that form through a process that is self-reflexively aware of its distance from the experience being described, so that in the end one stands to the seemingly confessional poem that results in something like the relation Borges's Pierre Menard stands to *Don Quixote*: the novel he writes is indistinguishable from Cervantes's, yet it is a different work, and a work of a different character from Cervantes's, because of the peculiarly self-conscious character of the process that produced it. When Eliot says in "East Coker" that "The poetry does not matter," one thing he means is that a poem is significant not so much as a verbal artifact but as a manifestation of the process—"the intolerable wrestle / With words and meanings"—by which it comes into existence.[8] And the poetic process underlying the conception of poetry I hold is one that insists on its freedom from the constraints of an externally imposed practical identity and from the internal demands of one's actual experience.

It might be felt that the notion of a transcendent subject of experience, of a self that is the locus of pure, unconstrained subjectivity, is an untenable one and that this vitiates any conception of poetry that incorporates that notion. This seems to me backwards. One does not decide on theoretical grounds whether to be engaged by a particular kind of poetry—to do so would be comparable to adopting a religious outlook because one had been persuaded, say, that the modal version of the ontological argument was valid. Rather, one simply finds oneself compelled by poetry of a particular sort and then acquiesces in the conception of the self that informs that poetry, even in the full knowledge that that conception of the self is illusory. A comparison might be with the status I take philosophical dualism to have. In its current form the mind–body problem basically amounts to the attempt to provide a materialist account of consciousness. Though I cannot give a conclusive argument for it, I have a strong intuition that because of the perspectival character of consciousness it is not possible to provide such an account. Instead, something about the character of our own reflective self-experience makes us unable to avoid thinking of ourselves as immaterial Cartesian egos, even though we may also be convinced that this conception of the self is untenable or even incoherent. Dualism thus has the status of a kind of necessary illusion, an unsatisfactory view to which we are unable to find any satisfactory alternative. Unlike dualism, the conception of the poetic self I have been describing is not a universal illusion, since, while everyone has the kind of reflective self-experience that gives rise to dualism, not everyone is engaged by poetry, let alone by the particular kind of poetry that engages me. But if one is engaged by poetry of this kind, then one will almost inevitably have a conception of the authorial self as a locus of transcendent, unconstrained subjectivity. That one acknowledges this conception to be illusory only makes one's willing acquiescence in it an even stronger enactment of it. As Stevens, our greatest poet of pure subjectivity, characteristically put it, "The final belief is to believe in a fiction, which you know to be a fiction, there being nothing else. The exquisite truth is to know that it is a fiction and you believe in it willingly."[9]

There is a temptation to read statements like this as expressions of the aestheticism for which Stevens is sometimes faulted. But I see them as an insistence on the autonomy of the authorial self, an autonomy which involves a freedom even from the demand of fidelity to the factual. It is worth remembering that a similar insistence on the self's autonomy lies at the heart of Kant's ethics, and far from taking Stevens to be espousing a kind of precious aestheticism, I see him, both in his work and in his reflections on the poetic process, as representing a poetic integrity possessing an almost moral weight.

The parallel with Kant's ethics may also help clarify what I have been trying to suggest about the relationship between the poet and the professional academy. Kant is sometimes taken to hold that, since to act morally is to act from the motive of duty, a person cannot act morally if he derives any pleasure or benefit from his action. But of course it is possible for one's motivation to be moral even if one happens to take pleasure in an action one performs from that motive. Similarly, nothing I have said is meant to suggest that occupying a professional role as a writer is somehow incompatible with writing from a genuine poetic impulse or that writing from outside such a role somehow endows the work one produces with a special distinction. I have been arguing for an internal or conceptual connection between a certain neoromantic conception of poetry and the idea of a freely assumed poetic identity, an identity that is a necessary though not a sufficient condition for the successful enactment of poetry of that kind. Whether one is able to combine such a freely chosen identity with an externally sanctioned professional identity, or whether the latter is liable to displace the former, depends, I believe, on a poet's contingent psychological makeup and temperament. There are certainly accomplished poets who are able to combine the two roles—perhaps because they are able to so compartmentalize them that they really have little to do with each other or perhaps because their roles as teachers of writing are simply extensions of their identities as poets and only incidentally professional. I can only say that in my own case I have found the sense of a disjunction between my identity as a poet and my academic role as a philosopher to be a strangely liberating one, engendering in me a conviction that, at least for those of a certain temperament and cast of mind, poetry may sometimes be engaged most intimately when it is engaged at one remove.

6

Thought and Poetry* (2000)

Though I write both poetry and philosophy, and teach the latter, I don't have settled views about the relations or affinities between the two activities, which I engage in at different times of the year and involve habits of thought which in my experience are quite distinct. But in a number of occasional essays written over the past twenty-five years or so, I have made some tentative suggestions about possible relations between these two forms of reflection.[1] First, they both seem to me to be speculative activities engaging some of the same subjects (for instance, the relation of the self to the world), in that both involve the entertaining of abstract and general thoughts and propositions in the absence of empirical, or for that matter any clear-cut, ways of establishing them. Moreover, philosophy's abstract and discursive rhetoric can and should be used to serve poetry's ends (this despite the fairly prevalent orthodoxy which tries to limit poetry to narrative sequence, plainness of language, and concreteness of imagery). But the difference is that speculation in philosophy is subject to rather severe constraints of clarity, consistency, argumentation, self-interrogation, and so on, while speculation in poetry is unconstrained, and a poet is free to entertain or enter into ideas without the obligation to support them, to which philosophers are subject.

A second relation between poetry and philosophy involves what lies at the heart of the kind of broadly romantic poetry that engages me, namely, the enactment of subjectivity, and the affirmation of it against the claims of an objective natural setting which threatens to annihilate it. Poetry is particularly suited to enacting the movement of thought which Kant called the experience of the dynamical sublime, in which the mind is at first overwhelmed, almost to the point of extinction, by some external natural enormity, but then by its realization of its ability to conceive of an even greater magnitude, and to contain the natural one in thought, experiences itself as transcending the latter.

And third (and largely because of poetry's ability to enact this characteristic romantic movement of thought), I've suggested that poetry can embody or have affinities with various philosophical conceptions and outlooks. For instance, I have suggested that the conception of the self that informs John Ashbery's poetry resembles the conception of the transcendental subject (something I shall have more to say about here) found in Kant, Schopenhauer, and the early Wittgenstein, while the notion of the self found in other poets' work is closer to, say, Descartes's or Hume's.[2] And I have also argued for an affinity between romanticism and the kind of philosophical realism which emphasizes the objective reality of the world and its independence from our thoughts, experiences, and conceptual schemes.[3]

All this strikes me as plausible as far as it goes, yet it still seems to me to fall short, in that the role it assigns to poetry in relation to philosophical themes is a merely illustrative one: poems can enact patterns of thought that may be of philosophical significance, and they can embody or have affinities with particular philosophical conceptions and theories, but none of this amounts to allowing poetry a positive role in establishing or supporting views that might properly be called philosophical. And I have the sense that poetry can indeed play such a role, though it is not at all easy to say just how. I hasten to say that what I have in mind is not the incorporation of philosophical theorizing or argumentation into poems, which would only result in poetry and philosophy which were both third-rate. What I have in mind is something more indirect: that the imaginative strategies and movements of thought characteristic of certain poems might be seen as lending support to certain philosophical views. At any rate, that is what I want to explore here.

The particular philosophical conception I want to consider is the conception of the self I mentioned earlier: the notion of the transcendental subject found in Kant, Schopenhauer, and the early Wittgenstein. According to this conception, the self is something existent, yet it isn't part of the natural, factual, material world, and can't be identified with anything belonging to the natural order. This might be thought of as a form of dualism, since the self it posits is something additional to the objects constituting the material world; yet it differs from Cartesian dualism in that Descartes held that the world itself contains two kinds of substances, material substance and the mental substance constituting the self or mind. The transcendental subject isn't something in the world constituted of some substance different from matter; rather, it isn't part of the natural world at all. Moreover, while Descartes held that we have a "clear and distinct" conception of a nonmaterial self,[4] the transcendental subject, according to Kant, is "nothing more than a feeling of existence without the least concept,"[5] a subject of which we "cannot have … any knowledge whatsoever."[6]

My own view—or intuition, really—is that dualism in a broad sense, and this form of dualism in particular, is deeply rooted in the character of our own self-experience, so deeply that even if we profess to know, on principled grounds, that some form of materialism must be true, we still cannot help conceiving of ourselves on the model of the transcendental self (whether or not we are willing to acknowledge this). It may be an illusion, but it is an illusion to which we are necessarily subject, and traditional arguments for dualism such as Descartes's are best seen as attempts to articulate what it is about our self-experience that makes this conception of the self so compelling. Yet these arguments, or attempted articulations, are, for reasons I shall turn to next, inconclusive. They require a certain exercise of the imagination, and it is problematic whether that exercise can be completed successfully. This is where I want to suggest a role for poetry in validating this conception of the self.

Let me rehearse the dialectic of the arguments and counter-arguments concerning the conception of a self distinct from the world. Two things have to be established. The first is that there *is* such a thing as the self in the first place. This may seem to go without saying, and Descartes of course maintained, in the cogito, that the existence of the self is the first of all certainties, and immune from any possible doubt. But what is at issue is not, say, the existence of a human being, but of a self conceived of as the locus or subject of consciousness. Hume famously reported that "when I enter most intimately into what I call *myself*, I always stumble on some particular perception or other, [but] … I can never catch *myself*, without a perception, and can never observe anything but the perception."[7] Kant, in a passage I quoted earlier, admitted that we have no conception or knowledge of the self (though he did maintain its existence). Daniel Dennett, in *Consciousness Explained*, denies not only the existence of a locus or seat of consciousness, but even, apparently, consciousness itself.[8] (I think he does so because he realizes that once you posit the existence of a locus of consciousness, it becomes very difficult to render it in physical terms.) And some of the later Wittgenstein's remarks on the first-person pronoun suggest a kind of "no self" view as well. My own view is that the ground for insisting on the existence of the self is the inherently qualitative and perspectival character of conscious mental states. As Thomas Nagel has repeatedly emphasized, there is something *that it is like* to consciously experience, say, pain or redness.[9] And if there is something that it is like to *be* in a conscious mental state, then there must be someone *for* whom it is like something to be in that state.

The second thing that has to be established is the *distinctness* of this self from any object in the world, including the human body. Here I shall just assert, without going into detail, that because of the logical relations between the concepts of identity, necessity, and possibility, what this requires is the establishment of the *possibility* of the self existing in the absence of whatever object with which we might be tempted to identify it. And since imaginability is usually taken to be a criterion of possibility, this in turn requires that a state of affairs involving, say, a disembodied existence be imaginable or conceivable. And this may seem relatively easy. After all, I can easily imagine the following sequence of events: as I look in the mirror one morning I am puzzled to see empty space where my eyes should be; curious, I investigate further by removing the top of my skull with a surgical saw, only to find it empty; and as I continue to watch in fascination, the rest of my body slowly fades away, leaving *me* gazing into an empty mirror. Isn't this an example of imagining disembodied existence?[10]

The trouble is that imagining a state of affairs establishes its possibility in the relevant sense only if we can *genuinely* imagine it. And it is quite easy to be mistaken about what one has imagined. For instance, since lightning *is* a discharge of electricity, it isn't possible, and hence not imaginable, for lightning to occur in the absence of an electrical discharge. And while this may seem quite easy to imagine, on reflection it turns out that what is easy to imagine is the occurrence of something that *looks like* (but isn't) lightning in the absence of electricity. In the case at hand, it might be said that I haven't really imagined a disembodied self at all, but rather a sequence of movie-like images representing, say, the experiences of a fully embodied person suffering an odd hallucination (and moreover, some sort of "no self" view might be invoked to deny that these are even the experiences of an existing self at all). This points to the trouble with the exercise of the imagination involved in typical philosophical thought experiments: it is usually rather shallow, involving a sequence of tableaux or images, together with a claim about what state of affairs those images represent. But these imagined images can't by themselves distinguish between the purported state of affairs and various other ones to which it is phenomenologically similar. What is called for, and what the use of the imagination involved in typical philosophical reflection seems incapable of providing, is an exercise of the imagination which possesses a conviction and depth that does not allow it to be called into question in the way just indicated.

I want to suggest that such exercises of the imagination can be found in the work of many poets of consciousness. I noted earlier that John Ashbery's poetry seems to me to embody a transcendental conception of the self, though this sense of self so pervades his work that it is difficult to localize it in particular poems or passages. Wordsworth, especially in *The Prelude*, offers a similar view of the self, though his cultural and spiritual distance from us may make it difficult to enter into his imagination as fully as required. Certain poems of Emily Dickenson's—for instance, "I Heard a Fly Buzz When I Died"—might be cited, but let me take instead as my example Elizabeth Bishop's "In the Waiting Room."

Bishop was once thought of, and sometimes is still thought of, as a vivid depicter of scenes and settings. But what strikes me as most distinctive about her poetry is the powerful sense of consciousness it conveys, a consciousness which, as David Kalstone noted, involves a "heightened receptiveness … to a scene which, in the event, so excludes" it.[11] This sense of a conscious self excluded from the world is powerfully rendered in "In the Waiting Room,"[12] a poem which begins with the speaker's recollection of accompanying, as a young child, her aunt to a dentist's appointment. In the dentist's waiting room she peruses an issue of *National Geographic* which contains exotic scenes from around the world and pictures of human beings strange to her:

> Babies with pointed heads
> wound round and round with string;
> black, naked women with necks
> wound round and round with wire
> like the necks of light bulbs.

The onset of an experience of detachment from her body and the world is a cry of pain she initially takes to be her aunt's. But then she is stunned to realize "that it was me;/my voice, in my mouth." She experiences

> the sensation of falling off
> the round, turning world
> into cold, blue-black space.

She tries to arrest the sensation by telling herself that she will be seven years old in three days, and that

> you are an *I*,
> you are an *Elizabeth*,
> you are one of them.

Here the *I* that she tries to assure herself she is is not the *subject* of the disorienting experience being described, but "an *Elizabeth*," "one of *them*," a member of a human race which includes the figures in the issue of *National Geographic*. The attempt to reinstall herself in the familiar world is unsuccessful, for the thought of being a part of humanity makes no sense to her:

> *Why* should you be one too?
> I scarcely dared to look
> to see what it was I was.

Implicit in this fear is the thought that whatever she might see would *not* be what she was. She can't understand what similarities "held us all together/or made us all just one," or how she came to seem a part of the setting of the waiting room in the first place:

> How—I didn't know any
> word for it—how "unlikely" …
> How had I come to be here,
> like them …?

Finally the world of the waiting room is obliterated:

>   it was sliding
> beneath a big black wave,
> another, and another.

Then as abruptly as the experience began, it ends, and the world is restored:

> Then I was back in it.
> The War was on. Outside,
> in Worcester, Massachusetts
> were night and slush and cold,
> and it was still the fifth
> of February, 1918.

"In the Waiting Room" imagines the self in a way that incorporates the two elements needed to validate the conception of the transcendental subject. There is a powerful sense of the self's presence: the poem emanates from a locus of consciousness whose reality is undeniable. And it also imagines the self in a way that makes clear its distinctness from its setting, including its human setting. The possibility that the speaker is merely "an *Elizabeth*," one human animal among others, "one of *them*," is not affirmed but confronted, and what emerges from that confrontation is a strong sense of the self's uniqueness and isolation. Because of its emotionally freighted confrontation with that possibility, and because the poem so engages the reader and can be entered into so immediately, the imagination of the self it enacts has a power to convince simply not possessed by the exercise of the imagination at work in philosophical thought experiments.

Earlier I suggested that the problem with philosophical thought experiments is that they can be taken to be mere sequences of mental imagery whose representational content is indeterminate. Given the complexity of its internal dialectic, I don't think the same can be said of the exercise of the imagination in Bishop's poem. But a broader sort of objection might be made, one implicit in writings of some deconstructionists and some of the theorizing associated with language poetry. It involves what might be called the *materialization* of language generally, and of poetic language in particular. The claim is made that both amount to nothing more than the manipulation of signs according to contingent, historically conditioned conventions; and the conclusion is drawn that representational content generally, and the kinds of imaginative experiences enacted by poems like Bishop's, is simply illusory. Where the objection to philosophical thought experiments reduced them to sequences of inert images, this line of thought reduces the contents of the poetic imagination to sequences of inert signs.

This isn't the place to explore this view in detail, but I want to make two brief points about it. The first is that the move from "contingent and conventional" to "therefore, illusory" is a non sequitur. The second, more important point is that this mode of criticism is simply not successful in practice, since it is powerless to dispel the "illusion"—if that is what it is—certain poems have to compel and convince. It's important here to recall what I said at the outset about the conception of the transcendental subject: not that it is a *correct* view of the self, but that, correct or not, it is a conception grounded in our own self-experience which we are unable to avoid, an illusion—if that is what it is—to which we are necessarily subject. I've tried to link this conception of the self to a certain kind of imaginative experience which poetry seems able to enact, and if that experience is illusory too, it doesn't really matter, as long as the illusion remains compelling and inescapable, as I think it does.

An easy view is that thought, and philosophy as a kind of distillation of thought, is essentially propositional. On this view poetry enters the domain of thought and philosophy only by incorporating discursive reasoning into its subject matter, by aspiring to the status of a "meter-making argument." I don't find this a useful conception of either thought or poetry. As I said at the outset, I think that poetry ought to incorporate and exploit the discursive and abstract rhetoric and cadences associated with philosophy; but the fact remains that reflection in poetry is not, and shouldn't be, subject to the kinds of constraints essential to philosophy. What I've tried to suggest instead is that the conceptual role of poetry is not so much a propositional as a performative one. There are certain topics and themes—here, the nature of the self and the conception of the transcendental subject—which are properly philosophical, but whose consideration requires resources not readily available to philosophy, resources involving movements of thought and exercises of the imagination that lie at the very heart of poetry, at least as I conceive it.

7

Styles of Temptation and Refusal in Wittgenstein and Stevens* (2003)

I would guess that Ludwig Wittgenstein and Wallace Stevens never heard of, let alone read, each other. It is hard to imagine two more different personalities or temperaments: contrast Wittgenstein's abstemiousness with Stevens's indulgence in sausages and cheeses on his forays into New York, or Wittgenstein's haughty disdain for Karl Popper in their now legendary encounter in Cambridge with Stevens's getting knocked down by Hemingway in their fistfight in Key West; or think of Wittgenstein holed up in Ross's Hotel in Dublin while Stevens was enjoying the comforts of the Hartford Canoe Club. And though it might be said that they had philosophy in common, for Stevens philosophers were something like unworldly figures of authority, while for Wittgenstein they were seducers whose entrapments were to be spurned.

Yet I think a similar style or movement of thought, an oscillatory one, is to be found in both. Wittgenstein's anti-philosophical tendencies are associated with the interlocutory style of *Philosophical Investigations* and other late compilations, in which a voice making a claim or raising a question that invites constructive philosophical theorizing is countered by another voice that tries to deflate it by rejecting its presuppositions. And a similar movement seems to me to occur in Stevens's poetry, where the temptation of romanticism's imaginative transformation of reality is deflected by an acknowledgment of the futility of that idea. Stevens often goes on to affirm the imaginative gesture in full awareness of its futility, and this may seem an important difference between Stevens and Wittgenstein in the dialectic of temptation and refusal, since Wittgenstein typically ends with the refusal. But I think that Wittgenstein believed that avoiding the temptations of philosophy is far more difficult than he is usually taken to, and that, as with Stevens, its pictures hold us captive despite our knowledge that they are illusory.

There is a common view of Wittgenstein's anti-philosophical tendencies that strikes me as simplistic in several respects. On it, the deflation of philosophy constitutes the entire thrust of his work, which is seen as containing no constructive views or arguments (concerning, say, the social constitution of linguistic meaning). Associated with this is the idea that philosophical perplexity is the result of mere linguistic confusion, to be dissolved by paying attention to the details of ordinary usage, along the lines of J. L. Austin's dismissal of skepticism and sense-data theory on the grounds that they involve a departure from the ordinary usage of words like "know" and "real." (It is probably this view of Wittgenstein's attitude towards language and philosophy that so enraged Popper, at least on to David Edmonds and John Eidinow's account of their meeting in *Wittgenstein's Poker*, a view of the later Wittgenstein perhaps shared by Bertrand Russell.) A kindred view (though one which does not take philosophical confusions to be shallow) is the so-called resolute reading of the *Tractatus* proposed by Cora Diamond and others, on which *Tractatus* 6.54's characterization of the book's sentences as nonsensical is taken to indicate that it does not actually embody substantive views about the relation between language and the world, but rather that Wittgenstein was from the outset, including in the *Tractatus*, engaged in a deconstruction of philosophy in the traditional sense.

But Wittgenstein speaks of the temptations of philosophy with what seems a passion borne of experience: "A *picture* held us *captive*. And we could not get outside it, for it lay in our language and language seemed to repeat it to us *inexorably*" (*Investigations* 116, last two emphases added); "The real discovery is the one that makes me capable of stopping doing philosophy when I want to—The one that gives philosophy peace, so that it is no longer tormented by questions which bring *itself* into question" (*Investigations* 133). And in 1929's "A Lecture on Ethics" he says that "my whole tendency" in trying to talk about ethics or religion "was to run against the boundaries of language," which, while he describes it as "perfectly, absolutely hopeless," he acknowledges to be "a tendency in the human mind which I personally cannot help respecting deeply and [which] I would not for my life ridicule."

What exactly are the philosophical temptations Wittgenstein insists on declining? It is not easy to say just what "philosophy," in this pejorative sense, is supposed to be, though philosophers have a long history of accusing one another of committing it (think of Berkeley's attempt to pass off idealism as a piece of philosophically uncontaminated common sense). I think the specific target of Wittgenstein's refusals is what might be called the temptation to *posit*.

The theory of elementary propositions embodied in the *Tractatus*, which (the resolute reading notwithstanding) he came to regard as a paradigmatic example of a captivating philosophical picture, posited an elaborate semantic and metaphysical theory in which states of affairs composed of "simple" objects shared a "logical form" with propositions composed of "names," a theory imposed a priori on language and the world with no regard for their actual nature or structure. And the typical object of refusal in the later work is the positing of "superlative fact[s]" (*Investigations* 192), states and processes of meaning, understanding, remembering of inner, private experiences. *Investigations* 308 describes the "decisive movement in the conjuring trick … the very one we thought quite innocent" as a willingness to "talk of states and processes and leave their nature undecided. Sometime perhaps we shall know more about them—we think. But that is just what commits us to a particular way of looking at the matter." This comes just after his having said in *Investigations* 305 that what he wants to reject is "the picture of the 'inner process'" which "stands in the way of our seeing the use of the word ["remember"] as it is."

It is one thing though to decline to posit the baroque semantic and metaphysical machinery of the *Tractatus*, since the temptation to do so derives from the acceptance of certain theoretical principles, such as the doctrine of the determinacy of sense, which are simply assumed without argument and which are specific targets of criticism in the later work. But it is much harder to refuse the offer of facts, states, and processes of meaning, understanding, or remembering of which we seem to have something like a direct experience or awareness. Wittgenstein's rejection of "the picture of the 'inner process'" in *Investigations* 305 follows his imagining the interlocutor insisting, "Still, an inner process does take place here," and going on to say, "After all, you *see* it." He claims, in *Investigations* 308, that he only wants to "deny the yet uncomprehended process in the yet unexplored medium," but does not want to deny mental processes. But it is hard to see how to do the former without doing the latter.

What makes Wittgenstein's refusal of philosophical temptation problematic is, I think (and in this I share the late Rogers Albritton's reading of Wittgenstein) that he really does mean to deny the reality of something of which we *seem* to have a direct experience or awareness. In *Zettel* 487, following the interlocutor's outburst of "But 'joy' surely designates an inward thing," he says in his own voice, "No. 'Joy' designates nothing at all. Neither any inward nor any outward thing."

It seems paradoxical to deny the reality of something we think we know from experience to exist. The feeling of paradox may be mitigated somewhat by the fact, I would argue, that Wittgenstein in his later work continues to retain something like the showing/saying distinction of the *Tractatus*, and holds that mental and semantic properties, while not factually real, are *shown* or *manifested* by what we say and do. But talk of "showing" has an air of mystification about it (though I think there are ways of making at least some sense of it), which is why, I believe, the "real discovery ... that gives philosophy peace" remains deferred, and the struggle against the bewitchment of intelligence by language remains just that, a struggle. Let me suggest an analogy with the status of mind–body dualism. There is something about the character of our self-experience which makes it difficult, if not impossible, for us to really conceive of ourselves as part of the natural, physical order, even if we are convinced that that is exactly what we are. Deep down we are almost all dualists, even if we know better. Dualism thus has the status of a kind of inescapable illusion, "a tendency in the human mind" it is difficult if not impossible to resist. I think that something like this is true of the temptations of philosophy Wittgenstein refuses, which *should* be refused, but which maintain their force even in the face of that refusal, leading to an oscillatory movement of thought in which we continue to be drawn to something we repeatedly push away.

A similar movement towards and away informs Stevens's poetry, though the characters of both the temptation and the refusal differ from Wittgenstein's. In Wittgenstein the temptation of philosophy is something he is passively drawn to and actively rejects, whereas the object of temptation for Stevens is something actively wished for or insisted on, while his refusal takes the form not so much of an active rejection of it, but of an acknowledgment of its futility. This object is always some kind of imaginative transformation of the world, yet the form it takes varies from poem to poem (indeed, it often changes within the same poem) and with the stages of Stevens's career, ranging between immanence and transcendence, but always playing the role of something that might relieve the pervasive sense of dissatisfaction that animates his work. And his refusal of it, his acknowledgment of its futility, would represent the triumph of that dissatisfaction or disappointment were it not for the fact that Stevens usually persists in affirming it, or at least asserting it, in the face of that acknowledgment.

In his early poems the imaginative transformation sometimes takes the form of a sense of the immanence or fullness of the world, conveyed through a verbal lushness. At the opening of "The Comedian as the Letter C" we find Crispin,

> The lutanist of fleas, the knave, the thane,
> The ribboned stick, the bellowing breeches, cloak
> Of China, cap of Spain, imperative haw
> Of hum, inquisitorial botanist,
> And general lexicographer of mute
> And maidenly greenhorns,

who is then "washed away by magnitude"

> > until nothing of himself
> Remained, except some starker, barer self
> In a starker, barer world, in which the sun
> Was not the sun because it never shone.

In the second canto he once again "felt the Andean breath" and becomes "free/And more than free, elate, intent, profound," as "the thunder, lapsing in its clap,/Let down gigantic quavers of its voice,/For Crispin to vociferate again." The movement from being "washed away by magnitude" to becoming "more than free" enacts the experience of the sublime, about which more in a moment. But what I want to note now is that the third canto enacts its denial: the hope that

> > the Artic moonlight really gave
> The liaison, the blissful liaison,
> Between himself and his environment

becomes a "voyaging ... / ... up and down between two elements,/A fluctuating between sun and moon," until finally "The moonlight fiction disappeared," and with its disappearance he comes to see

> > how much
> Of what he saw he never saw at all.
> He gripped more closely the essential prose
> As being, in a world so falsified,
> The one integrity for him, the one
> Discovery still possible to make,
> To which all poems were incident, unless
> That prose should wear a poem's guise at last.

Sometimes Stevens's acknowledgment of futility is not registered explicitly, but is implied by a willful and heightened insistence and the use of interrogatives. He begins "Notes toward a Supreme Fiction"—and of course the title itself is already a kind of acknowledgment—by registering his location at the center of the poetic imagination:

> In the uncertain light of a single, certain truth,
> Equal in living changingness to the light
> In which I meet you, in which we sit at rest,
> For a moment of the central of our being

He proceeds to define the dimensions of that imagination through a series of injunctions—*It Must Be Abstract, It Must Change, It Must Give Pleasure*—each of which, in its insistence, plants seeds of its undoing. The impulse is to conceive of the world as pure form—"The inconceivable idea of the sun"—prior to its disappointing actualization in the familiar:

> You must become an ignorant man again
> And see the sun again with an ignorant eye
> And see it clearly in the idea of it.

Stevens has it that the apprehension of the first idea of the world results not from an act of will, but from a passive receptivity:

> ...
> But to impose is not
> To discover. To discover an order as of
> A season, to discover summer and know it,
>
> To discover winter and know it well, to find,
> Not to impose, not to have reasoned at all,
> Out of nothing to have come on major weather,

Yet this evocation of the longed-for apprehension of reality through acquiescence is immediately followed by a remarkable outburst of desperate insistence that betrays his own disbelief:

> It is possible, possible, possible. It must
> Be possible. It must be that in time
> The real will from its crude compoundings come,
>
> Seeming, at first, a beast disgorged, unlike,
> Warmed by a desperate milk. To find the real,
> To be stripped of every fiction but one,
>
> The fiction of an absolute.

"What am I to believe?" the poet asks. But rather than abandon the vision in the face of the recognition of its unattainability, the poem moves towards its conclusion in a melancholy affirmation of "the more than rational distortion/ The fiction that results from feeling":

> They will get it straight one day at the Sorbonne.
> We shall return at twilight from the lecture
> Pleased that the irrational is rational,
>
> Until flicked by feeling, in a gildered street,
> I call you by name, my green, my fluent mundo.
> You will have stopped revolving except in crystal.

"The Auroras of Autumn" is the great American poem of the sublime, that movement of thought described by Kant and central to romanticism in which the self's fear of being overwhelmed by some physical enormity is replaced by its realization that by comprehending and surpassing that enormity in thought it can transcend the natural order. But where Wordsworth moves swiftly towards and affirms that transcendence, in Stevens this trajectory of thought is attenuated, as each successive realization is followed by a renunciation. "The scholar of one candle's" fear of being overwhelmed by the aurora—

> An Arctic effulgence flaring on the frame
> Of everything he is. And he feels afraid.

—is followed, as it is in Kant, by an intimation, however tentative, of transcendence:

> Is there an imagination that sits enthroned
> As grim as it is benevolent, the just
> And the unjust, which in the midst of summer stops....
>
> To imagine winter?"

But the temptation of the sublime is refused in favor of a desperate ("But it exists,/It exists, it is visible, it is, it is") embrace of innocence:

> So, then, these lights are not a spell of light,
> A saying out of cloud, but innocence.
> An innocence of the earth and no false sign

And this embrace of innocence, "As if the innocent mother sang in the dark," is in turn replaced by images of isolation, first of the innocent mother

> when she came alone,
> By her coming became a freedom of the two,
> An isolation which only the two could share,

and finally of death:

> Shall we be found hanging in the trees next spring?
> Of what disaster is this the imminence:
> Bare limbs, bare trees and a wind as sharp as salt? ...
>
> It may come tomorrow in the simplest word,
> Almost as part of innocence, almost,
> Almost as the tenderest and truest part.

The strong late poems Stevens wrote after the impulse behind his long poems was spent are poems of pure desire and of the frustrations of desire, in which the longing for a kind of completion is palpable. "The World as Meditation" conjures Penelope, in the guise of a self "She has composed, so long, a self with which to welcome him," poised for the imminent arrival of Ulysses:

> She wanted nothing he could not bring her by coming alone.
> She wanted no fetchings. His arms would be her necklace
> And her belt, the final fortune of their desire.

But then comes the characteristic refusal or acknowledgment ("But was it Ulysses? ... // ... It was only day.//It was Ulysses and it was not."), leaving her suspended between an obsessive brooding on the object of her desire and the realization of its permanent deferral:

> She would talk a little to herself as she combed her hair,
> Repeating his name with its patient syllables,
> Never forgetting him that kept coming constantly so near.

And in "As You Leave the Room" the poet insistently—too insistently—denies that he has "lived a skeleton's life,/As a disbeliever in reality." He has been "Part of a major reality, part of/An appreciation of a reality//And thus an elevation" that leaves him "With something I could touch, touch every way." But his final gesture is to concede the unreality of this consoling transformation of the world:

> And yet nothing has been changed except what is
> Unreal, as if nothing had been changed at all.

Wittgenstein and Stevens share a movement of thought in which the thinker is drawn to something from which he tries to distance himself. Within this movement there are asymmetries: Wittgenstein insistently rejects something whose reality can seem to us completely obvious, while Stevens's refusals are reluctant, as he insists on inhabiting illusions whose unreality he recognizes. As masters of the art of disillusionment both are quintessentially modern figures, and in his persistent assertions in the full awareness of their futility, Stevens might even be thought of as an existential poet (an odd way of thinking of a poet once commonly regarded as an aesthete and a dandy). I think that both are exemplars of modernism in another way as well, for I would suggest that something that distinguishes modernism from whatever we want to call its successors is the way in which it acknowledges the strength of the vessels it breaks, the temptations it refuses.

8

On John Ashbery's
"Definition of Blue"* (2007)

I first encountered "Definition of Blue" in the *Times Literary Supplement* (as it was then called) in 1967 or 1968, and was immediately enthralled by it. I'd discovered John's poetry about two years earlier, in *The Tennis Court Oath*, followed quickly (for me anyway) by *Rivers and Mountains*; and I thought that this poem took his habit of incorporating "unpoetic" language and material—demotic or prosaic or nonfigurative language—to new heights (or depths, if your prefer). It's a familiar strain in his work, from the incorporation of bits of the pulp novel *Beryl of the Biplane* into "Europe," the faux-philosophical idiom of "Clepsydra" (another of my great favorites), the quotation from the Declaration of Independence that opens "Decoy" (also in *The Double Dream of Spring*), the undigested chunks of art history in "Self-Portrait in a Convex Mirror," and right down to today, as in "Wolf Ridge" in *Where Shall I Wander*, which begins "Attention, shoppers." "Definition of Blue" opens with academic boilerplate that could be straight out of a history of ideas textbook: "The rise of capitalism parallels the advance of romanticism/And the individual is dominant until the close of the nineteenth century." Some critics see this impulse in John's poetry as a deconstructive one, a dismantling and debunking of some sort of traditional idea of poetry; but I tend to agree with Allen Grossman's observation that "Ashbery is a conservator of traditional resources," and prefer to see him as exploring how far one can go in creating what, in their spiritual and affective aspects, are undeniably and powerfully poems, while at the same time eschewing the traditional materials and resources of poetry.

The invocation of "home" at the end of the fifth line has, as it has so often in his poetry, a galvanizing effect (think of the poem I believe Jorie Graham is going to talk about, "As One Put Drunk into the Packet Boat"). The poem becomes insistent, proceeding "in one steady, intense line" to a point "where the action became most difficult" and acknowledging the futility of the heroic aspirations of modernism: "there is no point in looking to imaginative new methods/Since all of them are in constant use." The act of self-portrayal (not to mention self-creation) becomes a passive one, in which "erosion" supplies "a medium/In which it is possible to recognize oneself," a medium which yields "A portrait, smooth as glass" of no public significance and bearing "no relation to the space and time in which it was lived."

The climax of the poem is a diffident enactment of the experience of the sublime, in which the speaker finds himself adrift in an overwhelming urban landscape, the glassy canyons of the metropolis, "In which the blue surroundings drift slowly up and past you." It's a marvelous moment, and one is apt to have one's own private associations with it. I think of the inhuman and overwhelming cityscape of *Blade Runner*, or if that seems too anachronistic, of the vast subterranean computer banks of the Krell in the 1950s science-fiction masterpiece *Forbidden Planet*. But unlike the traditional experience of the sublime of high romanticism, the outcome here isn't an expansion and celebration of the self, but rather its diminution and literalization, as it remains intact and safe in a way, yet limited to its local surroundings, to its precise dimensions, as you "Waken each morning to the exact value of what you did and said, which remains."

I think there's an affinity between "Definition of Blue" and another favorite poem of mine from *The Double Dream of Spring*, "The Chateau Hardware," a perfect miniature. It opens with another invocation of home—though not described as such, what else could it be but the Ashbery homestead in Sodus, New York: "It was always November there," where "The little birds/Used to collect along the fence." The speaker goes about the business of his private, quotidian life, "As I pursued my bodily functions," oblivious in a way of his surroundings, bereft of higher aspirations, "wanting/Neither fire nor water." And yet everything turns out alright in the end, but on a small and literal scale, with home consigned to an irrecoverable past and the speaker safe in a diminished present, "turning out the way I am, turning out to greet you."

9

Wittgenstein and Lyric Subjectivity* (2007)

Wittgenstein is almost unique among philosophers in the so-called analytic tradition in being of interest to people outside the discipline of academic philosophy, a writer of influence to people engaged in a wide variety of intellectual and creative studies and pursuits. Modernist and postmodernist artists and writers in particular have found him to be a figure of fascination. In the visual arts one thinks of Jasper Johns, Bruce Nauman, and the younger Peter Wegner, not to mention the exemplary work of modernist architecture, the Kundmanngasee house, Wittgenstein himself designed for his sister Gretl. And Marjorie Perloff, in her seminal book *Wittgenstein's Ladder*, has brought out affinities between his work and that of a host of canonical modernist writers, including Gertrude Stein, Samuel Beckett, Thomas Bernhard, Ingborg Bachmann, Robert Creeley, and the poets and writers of the *Oulipo* and Language Poetry movements.

What are some of the aspects of Wittgenstein's thought that account for its affinities with literary modernism? One is certainly his dismantling of the Cartesian conception of the self and mentality, on which the mind is a kind of private arena accessible only to the person whose mind it is, and whose thoughts and sensations have the status of private objects apprehensible only through introspection, and only by the person to whom they belong. This conception is deeply rooted in our self-experience, and represents the idea of the subjective self that informs romanticism, a locus of subjectivity that identifies itself in opposition to its objective setting in the world. It is, however, a precarious conception, always on the brink of sliding into skepticism about other minds and solipsism. Against it Wittgenstein offers a conception of mentality as essentially public, not (or not only) in the sense that our application of mentalistic concepts to others is guided by observable behavioral criteria, but in the stronger and more puzzling sense that thoughts, sensations, and other mental phenomena can be said to be manifested or *seen*, and that we can speak literally of *pictures* of mental states and even of the mind ("The human body is the best picture of the human soul"). I believe that this theme of the "displayability" of the mental is a vestige of the showing/saying distinction of the *Tractatus*, and would note that its pervasiveness in Wittgenstein's later thought has been explored most fully by Bernie Rhie.

(I'm not going to try to bring out connections between Wittgenstein and particular writers here—Perloff has already done a thorough job of that—but I do want to add an autobiographical aside. I first encountered Wittgenstein's work and John Ashbery's poetry at about the same time, and when I came across lines like these from Ashbery's poem "Clepsydra" I thought that surely he must have been reading Wittgenstein:

> The sum total of all the private aspects that can ever
> Become legible in what is outside …
> What is meant is that this distant
> Image of you, the way you really are, is the test
> Of how you see yourself, and regardless of whether or not
> You hesitate, it may be assumed that you have won, that this
> Wooden and external representation
> Returns the full echo of what you meant
> With nothing left over …

—which of course he hadn't.)

A second obvious point of contact with literary modernism is the manner of Wittgenstein's writing. Even in the *Tractatus* it is aphoristic, disjunctive, and nonlinear (despite a contrived numbering system, which tries to impose a somewhat artificial organization on it); and the later work, with its characteristic interlocutory style, adds to this a cacophony of multiple voices and shifting perspectives. There is a conspicuous absence of sustained argumentation and "the costly stuff of explanation," in Ashbery's phrase; and while it is possible to supply argumentative contexts for much of what Wittgenstein says (as in Robert Fogelin's account of the *Tractatus* and Saul Kripke's controversial reading of the *Investigations*), his work is clearly intended to achieve its purpose without this supplementation, and it remains a matter of contention whether Wittgenstein actually adduces any of the arguments that have been attributed to him, or whether his work embodies any substantive theses at all. Also largely absent are the references to other philosophers and the usual scholarly paraphernalia which would enable the reader to situate his writings in some familiar intellectual landscape, allowing them to be seen (if one wants to see them) as freestanding verbal constructions.

The third affinity I want to mention is Wittgenstein's deflationist attitude towards the theoretical and his insistence on the priority of the ordinary, something also emphasized by Perloff. He rejects the pretensions of traditional philosophy to offer unifying, systematic explanations of meaning and representation, regarding these as symptomatic of a kind of intellectual delusion brought on by a "craving for generality" and involving the positing of "superlative fact[s]"and "*super*-concepts" which are simply not there; and this deflationism can be extended without too much license to totalizing narratives generally, and to attempts to penetrate or transcend everyday reality, as in the Kantian experience of the sublime that constitutes the core of romanticism. Against these pretensions he insists ("Nothing is hidden") that the only legitimate uses of language are the "humble" ones attaching to ordinary words like "table," "lamp," and "door," uses they have in largely autonomous patterns of linguistic activity or "language-games," which aren't bound together by any underlying unity or essence (as he had supposed in the *Tractatus*).

All this is familiar enough, but it bears repeating because I want to suggest that something puzzling emerges when we turn from received Wittgensteinian doctrine—and by "doctrine" I don't necessarily mean substantive philosophical claims, but simply the received sense of what Wittgenstein is about that I've been rehearsing—to examine the sensibility and temperament embodied in the writings themselves. For there seems to be a tension between what they represent at the level of doctrine and what they enact at the level of performance. Consider the famous interlocutory style of the later works. True, it works in the service of Wittgenstein's deflationary aims, as a philosophical suggestion floated by one voice is brushed aside by another in turn. But it is also steeped in interiority, presenting an intense example of the characteristic mode of the romantic poetic meditation: *talking to yourself.* The reason Harold Bloom, for whom poetry basically *is* romantic poetry, titled a book *Shakespeare: The Invention of the Human* is that he took the Shakespearian soliloquy—an *internal* soliloquy—to be emblematic of the self-reflexive subjectivity that makes us what we are, that constitutes the human mental condition. On this model (one to which I subscribe, for what it's worth), the poetic meditation isn't addressed to a reader or audience, which would be a kind of death— though a reader or audience is invited to *overhear* it, which is more or less what Wittgenstein's students did with the relentless philosophical self-examinations he conducted in his rooms at Cambridge. But of course the real performance takes place in that inner theater or arena which, at the level of doctrine, his work is supposed to dismantle.

Wittgenstein's inner soliloquy is punctuated at intervals by passages that, quite apart from their doctrinal significance, are of a marked lyric intensity, like this expression of romantic futility from *Investigations* 115:

> A *picture* held us captive. And we could not get outside it, for it lay in our language, and language seemed to repeat it to us inexorably.

Or consider this image of self-estrangement from *Investigations* 398:

> Think of a picture of a landscape, an imaginary landscape with a house in it.—Someone asks "Whose house is that?"—The answer, by the way, might be "It belongs to the farmer who is sitting on the bench in front of it." But then he cannot for example enter his house.

Again, consider this melancholy note of quiet intimacy on which "On Certainty" ends:

> Someone who, dreaming, says "I am dreaming," even if he speaks audibly in doing so, is no more right than if he said in his dream "it is raining," while it was in fact raining. Even if his dream were actually connected with the noise of the rain.

These episodes of romantic lyricism shouldn't be surprising if we remember Wittgenstein's obscure discussion of "the mystical" towards the end of the *Tractatus* (as well as his autobiographical remark that the positivists considered what he called his "mystical streak" to be his "yellow streak"). I've alluded to the centrality of the Kantian experience of the sublime to high romanticism, an experience in which one overcomes the sense of diminution occasioned by an encounter with the overwhelming magnitude of the physical world by the realization that it can be contained in thought, a realization that leads to a sense of transcending the world. This is quite close to what I take Wittgenstein's characterization of the mystical to amount to:

> To view the world sub specie aeterni is to view it as a whole—a limited whole.
>
> Feeling the world as a limited whole—it is this that is mystical.

Of course, whereas Kant (and Wordsworth, in whose poetry it figures prominently) affirms this experience, Wittgenstein considers its apparent content as literally nonsensical, since thinking of the world as a totality or whole is prohibited by the theory of representation contained in the *Tractatus*. Yet, despite his deflationary approach to theoretical conceits like this, his attitude towards them is far from dismissive, but rather one of deference and respect, as shown by the conclusion of "A Lecture on Ethics," where after describing "This running against the walls of our cage" (which amounts to basically the same thing as what he earlier called "the mystical") as "perfectly, absolutely hopeless," he ends by saying that "it is a document of a tendency in the human mind which I personally cannot help respecting deeply and I would not for my life ridicule it."

The disparity between doctrine and sensibility persists when we turn from his writings to Wittgenstein himself. Underlying his privileging of the ordinary over the theoretical is the picture of a community of individuals of an almost Tolstoyan simplicity and naturalness, unselfconsciously engaged in shared patterns of activity or "forms of life"—a picture that takes on the status of a sentimental ideal when contrasted with Wittgenstein's own sense of a mental isolation verging on the solipsism his work is intended to render incoherent, and his estrangement from the everyday life of his fellow human beings. There is more than a bit of the aura of the romantic hero about Wittgenstein. The title of Ray Monk's biography *Ludwig Wittgenstein: The Duty of Genius* alludes to the obligation Wittgenstein felt, because of what he regarded as his unique intellectual endowments (encapsulated in the romantic notion of genius), to a life of relentless self-examination and moral seriousness. His charisma, the devotion of his disciples, and the allegiance he demanded from them are all legendary. In some comments published a few years ago in *The Paris Review* Bloom cited Wittgenstein's remarks on Shakespeare in *Culture and Value* as symptomatic of the anxiety he felt at the threat Shakespeare represented to the authority of philosophy. The anxiety poetry occasions for philosophy is of course an old one, going back at least to Plato. But when I suggested in correspondence that it seemed an unlikely reading of those particular remarks, in light of the fact that Wittgenstein didn't think that philosophy *had* any authority, Bloom's response was simply to reiterate that the remarks are fraught with anxiety, as they well may be. But to the extent that they are, I'd suggest it would be on account of the threat Wittgenstein perceived Shakespeare represented to *his* authority.

What, if anything, should we make of this disparity? On the one hand, it may be seen as of merely psychological interest, symptomatic of Wittgenstein's odd psychopathology and of no relevance to our understanding of the philosophical significance of his work. At the other extreme, it might be taken to indicate a paradox internal to his work, in something like the way a recent influential (though to my mind misguided) reading of the *Tractatus* takes its concluding remark to the effect that the sentences making up the book are nonsensical to indicate that it doesn't really present the kind of systematic philosophical views it appears to (e.g., the so-called picture theory of propositions), but is rather intended to bring out the futility of any sort of philosophical theorizing. I think that neither of these responses is correct. Wittgenstein's conflicted personality did of course affect the manner of his writings, but I think that this disparity between doctrine and sensibility has implications for how we should assess his work's significance. But I don't think it should be taken to mean that his work doesn't really aim at the deflation of the Cartesian conception of mentality, or of the coherence of the experience of the mystical or of the sublime that is usually attributed to it. Rather, I think it helps us understand how radical and difficult that aim is, as well as something about the affinity between Wittgenstein's philosophy and poetry.

The model of the mind as an inner arena in which various "private" objects are on display is one of the "pictures" said to captivate us, and from which it is Wittgenstein's avowed aim to free us or, in the famous metaphor, "To shew the fly the way out of the fly-bottle." So is the account of representation presented in the *Tractatus*, which was his own early attempt to answer the question "How do we manage to represent the world in language and thought?" and which is the target of the first hundred or so sections of the *Investigations*. In the latter case the job of demolition is relatively easy, since that picture rested on a few unargued assumptions which were simply accepted a priori; and it falls of its own weight once these assumptions are abandoned (though it's worth noting that Wittgenstein's new answer to that question, if he has one, isn't easy to make out, once we reject the simplistic response attributed to him by philosophers like Richard Rorty, viz., "We don't"). Similarly, the attentive reader of the later work is supposed to come to see through the Cartesian model of the mind and walk away from it, as Wittgenstein himself was supposedly able to do.

This, it seems to me, is entirely too facile. Wittgenstein says of the "picture[s] that held us captive" that "we *could not* get outside" them because language seems to repeat them to us "inexorably" (emphasis added). It is one thing to realize that a certain picture or way of looking at things is untenable (and I think that Wittgenstein does establish the untenability of the Cartesian model in the various considerations lumped together under the rubric "private language argument"). It's quite another to stop looking at them in this way, or to arrive at an alternative way of conceptualizing them. The case of dualism, which the Cartesian model pushes us towards so strongly, is illustrative. There's something about our self-experience, which encourages the idea that the mind is both real and incapable of being understood in physical terms. We may think we know (as indeed I think we do know) on independent grounds that nothing like dualism in its traditional form can possibly be true; and yet deep down inside we all remain dualists, or are at least powerfully drawn to dualism: even though we know better, it has the status of an inescapable illusion, or at least one we find it extremely difficult to avoid; Wittgenstein perhaps encourages the idea that it's easy to rid ourselves of illusions like this by blaming them on "language," or on a misconstrual of the "grammar" of our ways of describing, say, our sensations (e.g., on the model of "object and designation"), as though we could dispel them by simply adopting a different way of talking. This is misleading: when he says they "lay in our language" what he means, I take it, is that we feel compelled to conceptualize our experience in certain ways, and that we find it difficult, if not impossible, to arrive at alternative ways of conceptualizing it.

The radical nature of Wittgenstein's views on mentality, and the difficulty of breaking with our customary ways of thinking of it, is brought out in a circulated but unpublished paper by the late Rogers Albritton, "A Difficulty in Understanding Wittgenstein." Albritton is trying to make sense of the remark in *Investigations* 305 that a sensation "is not a *something*, but not a *nothing* either," and a related remark in *Zettel* 487 to the effect that the term "joy" "designates nothing at all. Neither any inward nor any outward thing." He argues that the latter isn't meant to be peculiar to joy or emotions, but represents Wittgenstein's view of mentalistic discourse generally, and he argues against attempts to render this view more palatable by, for example, treating psychological terms as family resemblance terms, or construing talk of sensations and so on adverbially rather than referentially. Wittgenstein allows that we do indeed talk about and refer to introspectibilia, according to Albritton, and yet they are, as he puts it, "metaphysically thin," in the sense that there simply *isn't* anything they are. But how can this be? "After all," as one of Wittgenstein's voices says of the "inner process" under discussion, "you *see* it." He appears to be asking us to break with a picture of mentality and inner processes that seems to be forced on us by the very nature of our own experience. And how are we supposed to go about doing *that*?

The picture of interiority whose hold on us he aims to loosen is thus one to which he himself is powerfully drawn, as witnessed by the interlocutory voice's commitment to it. Wittgenstein's interlocutor is sometimes regarded as a kind of philosophical patsy along the lines of Berkeley's Hylas, giving voice to confused views merely in order to be straightened out by the voice representing the author himself. This seems wrong to me: the interlocutor's commitments are temptations Wittgenstein himself recognizes and shares, just as he shares and respects the temptations of the mystical and the sublime; and the intensity of the lyric subjectivity that pervades his writings is a measure of the strength of their attraction for him.

Philosophy and poetry can certainly share themes, like the relation of the self to the world, or of emotion and experience to memory and the passage of time. The difference, it seems to me, is that philosophy is basically doctrinal (in a broad sense of "doctrine" that encompasses Wittgenstein's antitheoretical aims): there is a commitment to some sort of view (again in a broad sense), and an obligation to explain, motivate, or justify it. Poetry isn't so much concerned to establish the validity of the ideas it engages as to *inhabit* them, to enter into an imaginative possibility to see what it feels like and where it leads—or, if you like, to allow one's self to be gripped by a picture Elizabeth Bishop's "In the Waiting Room" makes palpable, the idea of a disembodied existence detached from the physical world that is the crucial step in traditional arguments for dualism, though she isn't trying to argue for or establish anything at all. Wittgenstein's work combines doctrinal commitments with the imaginative exploration of ideas (including the very ideas he wants to exorcize), which is perhaps why he is so often described as doing philosophy in poetry. It might be said that the former links him with modernism and the latter with romanticism, though this strikes me as a bit too neat—I think that modernism is really a continuation of, or a successor to, romanticism, though this isn't the place to pursue their connection. In any case, Wittgenstein's doctrinal and affective aspects bear a symbiotic relation to each other, something like the relation Eliot suggests in his remark on poetry, emotion, and personality, when he says that poetry, far from being a release or expression of emotion and personality, is an escape from them; but then adds, "of course, only those who have personality and emotion know what it means to want to escape from these things."

Wittgenstein's interiority and lyric subjectivity seem to me to be manifestations not only of the strength of the attraction of the ideas of the mind and the self from which they spring, but also of the strength of his desire to be free of them, an aim he pursued throughout his life in quest of the discovery "that gives philosophy peace." But I don't think he was able to realize that aim completely, and I don't think we can either.

10

Comments on Susan Wolf's *Meaning in Life* and *Why It Matters* (2007)

I find Susan Wolf's account of what makes a life meaningful persuasive on the whole, and do not intend to criticize it.[1] What I want to address are some consequences of a particular application of it. Some may find these consequences troubling, though I myself do not.

On Wolf's account a life is made meaningful by a subjective commitment to, or a love for, a project or activity of objective worth. The subjective component precludes the possibility of someone's life being meaningful for reasons of which she is not cognizant (e.g., because it happens to have beneficial effects), which seems implausible. And the requirement that the project be objectively valuable precludes a life's being meaningful by virtue of a blind passion for something ridiculous, such as assembling the world's largest ball of string. There's an ambiguity as to whether calling a project or activity objectively valuable means that it's of a *kind* we value (artistic activity, for instance), or whether it means that the project or activity is successfully completed or pursued (say, by actually producing works of artistic value). I'm inclined to think that Wolf means the latter, for she speaks of a scorned artist sustained by the thought that her work is good, and elsewhere she offers the example of a scientist's quest for an important discovery whose significance is compromised when someone beats him to it.

Having a meaningful life is something we value. One would think then that it ought to be a source of comfort and satisfaction, and that it ought to contribute to one's sense of well-being. Wolf distinguishes between happiness and meaningfulness, between a happy life and a meaningful one. The pursuit of a project of objective value may involve sacrifices and disappointments at odds with living a life that is happy in any conventional sense. But in that case the thought that one's life is a meaningful one, devoted to the pursuit of something objectively worthwhile, would at least seem to offer comfort and consolation.

I imagine that I have been asked to comment on Wolf's lectures both as a poet and as a philosopher, and so I want to consider in particular some possible consequences of her idea of a meaningful life that might apply when the projects involved are certain kinds of aesthetic ones. In an essay on the avant-garde written in the 1960s, the poet John Ashbery remarks that religions are beautiful because of the strong possibility that they're founded on nothing, which he thinks is also true of the kind of art he's discussing. The comparison is apt, though I find the possibility less exhilarating than he does. After modernism, acting on aesthetic impulses of a certain kind involves a "recklessness," as Ashbery puts it, which makes the possibility of failure inherent in or internal to the enterprise itself. I'm not entirely sure how to characterize the kinds of aesthetic impulses and commitments I have in mind, except to say that they are ambitious ones. Of course, like the scientist who's beaten to the discovery to which he's devoted his life, one can always fail in acting on commitments to projects of any sort. But in such a case, it is at least clear what would *count* as success in trying to fulfill the commitment, which is precisely what is *unclear* in the case of the kinds of aesthetic commitments I am talking about.

Let me try to clarify the point by considering a series of examples, starting with Bernard Williams's discussion of Gauguin in his essay on moral luck. Gauguin abandoned his family in Denmark to pursue painting in Paris, an act we may reluctantly excuse on the grounds that (as Wolf might put it) his aesthetic commitments gave him reasons to do what he did additional to his moral reasons to support his family. But as Williams suggests, our verdict would be different if he had turned out to be an untalented hack gripped by a delusion that he was engaged in work of artistic significance, something not precluded by the intensity of his passion for art. The example shows that the meaningfulness of a life depends not just on one's commitments but also on one's success in acting on them. But this, too, is potentially misleading: Gauguin's achievement is so nearly universally recognized that we might suppose success in pursuing aesthetic aims to be typically so clear-cut. Let's consider then three other examples, in which the status of the artistic accomplishment is increasingly problematic.

In *The Banquet Years*, Roger Shattuck describes a dinner held in Picasso's studio in 1908 in honor of the painter Henri Rousseau, attended by, among others, Apollinaire, Gertrude and Leo Stein, Marie Laurencin, and Alice Toklas. Rousseau is now regarded as one of modernism's canonical figures, though an anomalous one, but at the time his work was dismissed by art journalists as fraudulent, and the banquet has been interpreted "as a lampooning of Rousseau, as a magnificent farce organized for everyone's enjoyment at [his] expense."

Moreover, Rousseau's own assessment of his own and others' work, as when he described himself and Picasso as "the two great painters of this era, you in Egyptian style, I in modern style," seems close enough to delusional to make history's subsequent verdict on his work appear, from the vantage point of 1908, far from inevitable.

Or consider the French poet, novelist, and dramatist Raymond Roussel, whose works describe imaginary tableaux in minute and stupefying detail. His first publication was dismissed as "more or less unintelligible" and "very boring," and while he remains largely unknown, he's had a distinguished list of champions, including the surrealists, André Gide, Jean Cocteau, Marcel Duchamp, Michel Foucault, Alain Robbe-Grillet, and Ashbery. Yet the achievement to which this list testifies falls short of his own assessment of it, for he claimed to his psychiatrist Pierre Janet that he was the equal of Dante and Shakespeare, and that he had to close the curtains of his room when he wrote, lest the intense light emanating from his pen endanger the world outside.

Consider finally the "outsider" artist Henry Darger, a reclusive Chicago janitor who gained prominence when an epic narrative of over fifteen thousand pages, *The Story of the Vivian Girls, in What Is Known as the Realms of the Unreal*, profusely illustrated with hundreds of watercolors and drawings, was discovered after his death in 1973. His work, the paintings and drawings in particular, has had considerable cultural effect, inspiring, for example, a book-length poem, *Girls on the Run*, by (who else?) Ashbery. And while Darger's work is undeniably powerful, simultaneously innocent and sinister, with vibrant coloration and complex compositional qualities, it is also unsettling in ways that have little to do with aesthetics: it can be extremely violent, and the girls are often depicted with male genitalia, quite possibly because Darger didn't know any better; and it is unclear whether what one sees in looking at it is the fulfillment of an aesthetic commitment or the manifestation of a disturbing psychological compulsion. Probably the right thing to say is that it is simply indeterminate, which it is.

These are extreme examples, and the three artists described seem oblivious to the possibility that they might be affected by delusions. But they are meant to suggest something that is true of more typical cases as well: namely, that it is difficult to distinguish, from the vantage point of the artist, between the successful achievement of serious aesthetic aims and the delusion that one has them and that they've been achieved; and this difficulty complicates the question of whether one's life is meaningful or wasted. One has to work, as it were, in the shadow of an awareness of the latter possibility. One can of course always be mistaken in thinking that one has fulfilled commitments one has undertaken, whatever their nature. What's distinctive about the kinds of aesthetic aims I'm talking about is that the possibility of delusion is internal to them, and that by their very nature, clear criteria for success in fulfilling them are lacking. Stanley Cavell makes a similar point in "Music Discomposed," when he suggests "that the possibility of fraudulence, and the experience of fraudulence, is endemic in the experience of contemporary music," a possibility he takes to be inherent in the very nature of the kinds of musical compositions he's discussing. I think Cavell is responding to the popular suspicion of the 1940s and 1950s as to whether avant-garde music, painting, and so on were really art at all ("Why, my kid could do that if she'd just stop drawing Thanksgiving turkeys and stoop to it!"), which in retrospect seems quaint. *Of course* they're art. But the question remains whether in any given case the art is of significance or importance.

None of this is meant to suggest that aesthetic value isn't objective, or at least as objective as Wolf takes it to be. The judgments others make of my work or I make of others' work can be objectively correct, and they need not be subject to the inherent possibility of self-deception or delusion I'm talking about. The possibility I have in mind seems viewpoint-dependent (as Cavell's worry about fraudulence doesn't), one that appears from my first-person perspective as an artist, and that neither the phenomenological character of my subjective commitments nor the assurances of others suffice to dispel—since the former could be the same whether or not the work succeeds, and (quite apart from *banquet Rousseau*-like worries) a too ready acceptance of my work by others could well be a sign that it has failed. Something comparable occurs in arguments for philosophical skepticism, where a crucial premise is my inability to rule out some outlandish hypothesis like, for instance, that I'm a brain in a vat. *You* know perfectly well that I'm not, but the problem is how *I* could know this. Ordinarily, if you know something and inform me of it, I can thereby come to know it too. But this doesn't work in the case of skepticism, and it doesn't work in the artistic case either. I don't want to press this comparison too far though, or treat the possibility of aesthetic delusion as merely a special instance of a general skeptical worry, for while it is perfectly alright for me to ignore the skeptical possibilities as ridiculous (even if I cannot rule them out in a principled manner), it is part of the nature of artistic endeavor that I cannot dismiss the possibility of delusion or self-deception out of hand.

How disturbing is this? Even if it jeopardizes my ability to derive satisfaction and comfort from a life based on aesthetic commitments, and of appealing to the nonmoral reasons that flow from them, I do not myself think that it is cause for much concern—it is simply a predicament I have to live with. ("For us, there is only the trying. The rest is not our business."—T. S. Eliot, "Burnt Norton") But if the reader finds it unsettling, there are several possible ways to handle the problem within Wolf's framework. One is to take the criterion of success in fulfilling aesthetic ambitions to be a readily recognized competence. A second is to take it to be acceptance by a suitably constituted community. And a third is to take it to be helping maintain the artistic enterprise you are engaged in, whatever the ultimate importance of your own work. ("One who marched along with, 'made common cause,' yet neither the gumption nor the desire to trick the thing into happening."—Ashbery, "Sortes Vergilianae") I don't find the first two strategies appealing, and the third is hard to spell out, but for reasons of time I will not explore them here. I will close instead with an illustrative anecdote. In 1968, I was driving across the country and stopped in Iowa City to see Ted Berrigan, who had just begun a year of teaching at the Iowa Writers' Workshop. In those days there really *was* a distinction, as I don't think there is anymore, between academic and nonacademic poetry, and it seemed odd to think of Berrigan, the presiding figure of the quintessentially nonacademic second generation of New York School poets, teaching at what many considered, perhaps unfairly, a main training ground for academic poetry. Naturally I wanted to know what he thought of his students, and he said they were fine, except that they all wanted to be minor poets, which he took to betray a crippling lack of ambition. It is ironic then that that's what Berrigan, who died in 1983, is—a minor poet, something I mean as high praise. Major poets are such because of the range and depth of their accomplishment and influence, but to be an enduring minor poet— as opposed to just a representative figure of a certain period and milieu—is a tremendous achievement. All the same, I'm not sure how much satisfaction Berrigan would have taken in it.

11

Poetry and Truth* (2009)

Last fall I participated in a conference on poetry and philosophy at the University of Warwick, where I heard a paper on poetry and abstract thought by the philosopher Peter Lamarque which interested me for two reasons.[1] One was that he discussed a long poem of mine, "The Secret Amplitude," something that's always gratifying; and the other was that what he said struck me as eminently sensible, and suggested to me some additional ideas about the relationship between poetry and truth. I should say at the outset though that in preparing today's lecture I came to suspect that what I'd thought were further ideas were actually contained in Lamarque's paper to begin with, and so I make no claims to originality. Still, I thought it might be of interest to hear the subject addressed by someone who is both a poet and a philosopher.

When I talk about poetry and truth, the truth I'm talking about is the truth of the kind of abstract thoughts that get expressed in the course of many poems—and not just in poems, but literature generally. Lamarque observed quite correctly that abstract thought is unavoidable in poetry, and thus that it makes no sense to claim that poetry is somehow better off without it. Now I know that there is a kind of tradition in modern and contemporary poetry that holds that you ought to avoid the abstract and discursive and stick entirely to the concrete and particular—"No ideas but in things." I even recall listening to a panel once in which two well-known poets seemed to be vying with each other to see who could come out most strongly against ideas and in favor of stupidity in poetry. But the simple fact is that part of our experience—and I take it to be the role of poetry to respond somehow to experience—is the experience of thinking abstractly. And if we proscribe it, I think we're working with a very attenuated conception of experience. I've discussed this elsewhere and am not going to argue for it today.[2] But that's my view.

Let me give you some examples of what I mean by abstract thought expressed in poetry. In "Sunday Morning," Wallace Stevens writes at one point:

> Death is the mother of beauty; hence from her,
> Alone, shall come fulfillment to our dreams
> And our desires.

And a little later on:

> Death is the mother of beauty, mystical,
> Within whose burning bosom we devise
> Our earthly mothers waiting, sleeplessly.

And in "Little Gidding," T. S. Eliot says:

> There are three conditions which often look alike
> Yet differ completely, flourish in the same hedgerow:
> Attachment to self and to things and to persons, detachment
> From self and from things and from persons; and, growing
>   between them, indifference
> Which resembles the others as death resembles life,
> Being between two lives

I'm not going to try to unpack these particular thoughts, but I think you recognize their kind when you read them. The question I want to address is whether, given that thoughts like these do get expressed in poems (whether one likes it or not), is it important to the success of a poem, or to what's going on in a poem, that they be true? Do poems aim at truth in anything like the way that writings in philosophy or science or history aim at truth?

I think that the answer to this question, subject to considerable qualification, is no, though I'll need to explain in what sense it's no, and what the relation is between poetry and the truth of the thoughts that get expressed in it. But first a few disclaimers. I'm not going to talk about whether thoughts of this kind can be true in some full-bodied sense of the word. I think it could reasonably be questioned whether, for example, the sorts of psychological generalization and metaphorical claims one finds in poems really can be true in the way more "factual" and objective-sounding statements can be, but I'm going to put this question to one side and simply assume that they can be. In a similar vein, I should note that my claim that truth isn't the point of poetry doesn't stem from any skepticism about the whole notion of objective truth, as is the case in some discussion of truth and literature. Philosophically I'm a diehard realist, at least about a broad range of statements, for whom objective truth is the coin of the realm.

There are a couple of other issues about truth and poetry I want to note in order to set aside. It is certainly the case that some poems include concrete descriptions of mundane facts and historical or personal day-to-day occurrences and things. In recent years I've regularly written "memory" poems in which I'll recount some perfectly banal sequences of events that have come back to me in an episode of Proustian recollection. I intend them to be accurate, though sometimes I'll discover later that I've gotten some of the facts wrong. And Frank O'Hara is often associated with what he called his "I do this, I do that" poems, often consisting of accounts of what he saw or did during his lunch hour. How important is it that the details of such poems be true? If O'Hara didn't actually buy Mike Goldbert the bottle of Strega he says he did in "The Day Lady Died," but bought him a bottle of Pernod instead, would it make any real difference? Probably not, but in cases like these I think the thing to say is that if the poet were simply indifferent to the truth of details like these such poems would lose much of their point, that it would be difficult to write them, and that they wouldn't have the freshness or force or conviction they do have. But certainly no one cares whether it was Strega or Pernod.

The other issue concerning poetry and truth that I'm not really concerned with here (though it does slide into an issue I am concerned with) has to do with poems of relentless, passionate self-examination. Sometimes this is associated with so-called "confessional" poetry, though I don't think it's confined to such poetry. One thinks though of Robert Lowell's well-known line "Why not just write what happened?" Here I think that what may appear to be a direct concern with truth is sometimes more a matter of the poet adopting a certain guise, the guise of the "truth-teller," and of guarding against self-deception, the easy consolations poetry sometimes traffics in, or facile ways of thinking of one's self and others. In Part II of *Philosophical Investigations* Wittgenstein, in a discussion of dreams, suggests a distinction between truth and truthfulness, where the latter is in some way independent of the former. I think that truthfulness in this sense (whatever it is exactly) rather than truth is what's relevant to poems of self-examination, and that it's not crucial that the details and explanations they offer actually be true. But the issue is complicated by the fact that what a poet says in an effort to reveal and understand himself is often underwritten by the kinds of abstract and often psychological generalizations that I do want to talk about now.

My interest in the issue of the truth of such statements began in college when I was plowing through *Remembrance of Things Past*. Somewhere in either *The Captive* or *The Sweet Cheat Gone* (I've never been able to find the passage again)

I came across a sentence that read, if memory serves, "What is love but the heart grown conscious of separation in time and space?" a rhetorical question obviously intended as a claim about the nature of love. I had that familiar feeling of assenting to a striking insight we often experience in reading great literature ("How true!"), but then it occurred to me that the same feeling of asset could also be prompted by the near negation of that sentence, "What is love but the heart grown unconscious of separation in time and space?" While the latter is more banal than, and not strictly the negation of, the former, clearly the two observations are in tension with one another. No doubt there's a certain ambiguity to the meaning of "conscious" in the two sentences, but it seemed clear enough that this couldn't be the whole explanation of why one could put one's self into a frame of mind in which the first observation could strike one as true, and another frame of mind in which the second could strike one the same way. This suspicion that there's something problematic about the relation between truth and imaginative literature was bolstered when I read some years later that Robert Lowell, when he was obsessively revising the sonnet-like poems that make up *History* and some other late volumes of his (he never seemed to be able to let well enough alone), would often go through them and insert the word "not" into sentences at appropriate places, apparently finding the negations of those sentences at least as compelling as the originals.

Earlier I offered some passages from Eliot and Stevens as examples of the kind of abstract generalizations I have in mind. Both are commonly thought of as "philosophical" poets (Eliot was actually trained as a philosopher, and wrote a dissertation on F. H. Bradley at Harvard), which to my mind is something of an oxymoron. Let us assume (somewhat tendentiously perhaps) that generalizations of this kind can occur in both poetry and philosophy. The practices of each are still very different, in that philosophy is subject to certain constraints to which poetry is not. In philosophy the theses at issue have to be fairly precisely framed, with an effort made to clarify them if there is a chance of their being misunderstood. Considerations have to be adduced in their favor, and objections to both the claims and the arguments have to be anticipated and defused, all this subject to norms of coherence and consistency. Poetry is largely free of these constraints, which lends it a certain freedom I've always found exhilarating. The kinds of objections one might make to a philosophical paper would usually be inept as criticisms of poems. Harold Bloom subtitled his big book on Shakespeare *The Invention of the Human* because he thinks that the internal soliloquy so characteristic of Shakespeare is emblematic of the human form of consciousness; and I share his view that poetry is basically an elevated form of talking to yourself. You can talk to yourself about just about anything, and while the subjects of philosophical concern are also wide and various, in philosophy you're essentially addressing an audience and your aim is to persuade, which it usually isn't in poetry. (This, by the way, is why I'm somewhat dubious about political poetry in the sense of poetry intended to have political effects, for to do this it also would have to be directed towards an audience.)

With this background, let me turn to some reasons for thinking as I do that truth figures rather differently in poetry than it does in philosophy, as well as in history, science, and other forms of writing which do aim at truth. Here again I want to draw on Lamarque's paper, in which he writes, "Where philosophical reflection does occur in poems, its role is quite different from that in philosophical prose." I think this is right. For example, I mentioned that it's usually inept to object to statements as they occur in poems in ways that you could object to them in other forms of writing. At the conclusion of Elizabeth Bishop's great poem "At the Fishhouses," she in effect makes the assertion that knowledge is historical:

> It is like what we imagine knowledge to be:
> dark, salt, moving, utterly free,
> drawn from the cold hard mouth
> of the world, derived from the rocky breasts
> forever, flowing and drawn, and since
> our knowledge is historical, flowing, and flown.

It's a powerful ending to the poem, and it would be bizarre to respond to it by objecting that knowledge is really timeless, on the grounds that even though we know things at some times and not at others, since you can always express knowledge claims by means of time-indexed eternal sentences, it's not historical in any interesting sense. To do so would be to miss the point of what such statements are doing in poems like Bishop's.

Another observation Lamarque makes has to do with paraphrase. It's a commonplace, and I think an overworked commonplace, that poetry can't really be paraphrased, that something is lost when you deviate significantly from the words in which a thought is expressed in a poem (think of the chapter titled "The Heresy of Paraphrase" in Cleanth Brooks's book *The Well-Wrought Urn*). I think this claim is somewhat overblown, in that there's rarely a *unique* effective formulation of a thought in a poem. Be that as it may, what we're inclined to forget, as Lamarque points out, is that if paraphrase is difficult or impossible in poetry, paraphrasability is obligatory in philosophy and various other disciplines. A genuine philosophical claim or statement can't be limited to one specific formulation: if a point is actually being made, a thought expressed, or a proposition being asserted as true, then it ought to be possible to reformulate it, or to put it in other terms; and to the extent that this isn't so in poetry, it suggests that the role of truth in poetry is very different than it is in philosophy and other allied disciplines.

A final point I'd like to mention draws on some interests of mine in epistemology and philosophy of language concerning what are called norms of assertion. Assertion is an activity, and activities are usually governed by rules, explicit or implicit. So we can ask what the rules or norms are that govern the making of assertions in ordinary contexts. When are we entitled or in a position to make an assertion that something is the case? The view I subscribe to is a variant of what's called the knowledge account of these norms, which says that when you make an assertion, you have to know that what you're saying is true, or at least be able to respond to a challenge to explain how you know that what you're saying really is the case.[3] Yet that sort of challenge to something said in a poem is usually inept (unless it's a very wrongheaded or excessively didactic poem), as it would be to respond to the ending of "At the Fishhouses" by asking how Bishop knows that knowledge is historical. So the fact that the use of declarative sentences in poems doesn't seem to be governed by the same sort of norms or rules that govern them in other contexts seems to me to be a third reason for thinking that the role of truth in poetry is different from what it is in those contexts.

This last point, about the relation between poetry and knowledge, is connected with Plato's worries in the *Republic* about poetry that led him to banish it from the ideal society he described there. These worries were twofold. First, he regarded poetry as the main rival to the authority of philosophy in the governance of society. And second, he thought that poets don't know what they're talking about. The first worry is apt to seem quaint now—it's hard to imagine people looking to the poetry of, say, Sylvia Plath or Anne Sexton for guidance on how society ought to be run. But to feel the force of Plato's complaint, we should, as the philosopher Alexander Nehamas has suggested, replace poetry as we understand it now with the mass media, including television and movies, since that's what plays the role in the popular imagination today that Plato saw poetry playing in his day.[4] I think Plato's second point remains valid though, since I don't believe that poetry *is* based on knowledge (though since it's no longer even a candidate for the social role Plato envisioned for it, it's none the worse for that).

How then does truth figure in poetry? Lamarque makes another point that's helpful here: that thought in poetry is inherently *perspectival,* in the sense that it's always attached to the point of view of the poet or the speaker of the poem. Earlier I remarked that I basically accept Harold Bloom's idea of poetry as a kind of internal soliloquy, a form of talking to yourself that is emblematic of the distinctively human form of experience, self-consciousness. Poetry as I conceive it attempts to communicate what this sense of life is like, to involve the reader in the experience of an individual consciousness, something which is at the same time the most extraordinary and the most ordinary thing in the world. Since abstract thinking of the sort I'm considering here is an integral part of this experience, successful poems have to involve the reader in the experience of entertaining such thoughts, and this means endowing them with enough initial plausibility that the reader can see how the speaker of the poem can, from his point of view, entertain them and find them compelling enough to acquiesce in them and, if the poem succeeds in involving the reader in that point of view, acquiescing in them himself. This need not—indeed should not—involve the kind of critical scrutiny of those thoughts that would be appropriate if what the poem were trying to establish were their truth, rather than trying to recreate and communicate the experience of entertaining and accepting them. What the poem tries to do is not to persuade the reader of the truth of those thoughts, but to get him, so to speak, to enter into them.

Here I find useful some ideas the philosopher Cora Diamond uses to support her reading of Wittgenstein's difficult book, *Tractatus Logico-Philosophicus,* which concludes with a remark to the effect that anyone who understands Wittgenstein will realize that the sentences making up the whole book are nonsense.[5] Most interpreters of Wittgenstein, myself included, take this to mean that while the sentences are nonsense in a technical sense developed in the *Tractatus,* a reader who works through them in the right way nevertheless comes to grasp something important and illuminating. Diamond and some other interpreters reject this and take Wittgenstein to mean that the sentences in the book are literal nonsense on a par with "Socrates is frabble," and convey or illuminate nothing. The problem of course is not only that many readers do claim to find illumination in the book, but that the sentences deemed literally nonsensical include not only those of the *Tractatus,* but also those we utter when we attempt to make ethical declarations, pronouncing certain things right or wrong, good or bad. Diamond's response to this is to say that her "resolute" reading of the book involves a distinctive exercise of the imagination, entering into the mind or viewpoint of someone who puts forward and entertains these literally nonsensical sentences as though they were expressive of thoughts.

Now I think this reading of Wittgenstein is quite wrongheaded: there's no evidence that he intended his book to be read this way, and much to suggest the opposite; and moreover, the fact that we can enter into the mind or adopt the perspective of someone who entertains its sentences and finds them illuminating is enough to show that they *aren't* literally nonsensical. But the present point isn't about this reading of the *Tractatus*, but rather that the kind of imaginative exercise Diamond thinks it involves, in which one tries to enter into the mind of someone who entertains and accepts certain thoughts, is, I think, what poems expressive of such thoughts enable us to accomplish.

What I've been saying may leave the impression that this imaginative entering into an idea is basically something the reader does; and so I want to emphasize that it applies equally to what the poet does. Let me use an example I've used before to illustrate what I mean, that of philosophical dualism, the idea that the mind of self or soul—call it what you will—isn't a part of the physical world.[6] Almost no one in philosophy would defend dualism, and yet there's something about the character of our experience that draws us towards it almost inexorably, so that deep down we're almost all dualists, even if we know better. Dualism has deep connections to romanticism, and one thing I sometimes find myself doing in poetry is trying to enter into that idea, to inhabit that conceptual possibility, knowing full well that it's illusory (the poem of mine that Lamarque discusses, "The Secret Amplitude," is an example of this). And I find this sort of imaginative exercise taking place in the work of other poets too. In the paper I just alluded to, I discussed Elizabeth Bishop's poem "In the Waiting Room," in which she recounts an episode as a child in which she experienced a radical sense of detachment both from her social identity and from her physical, biological self. Of course Bishop almost certainly didn't have philosophical dualism in mind, but I think her poem can be seen as implementing one of the key steps in a classical Cartesian argument for dualism, in which one attempts to vividly imagine the distinctness of the mind and body in an effort to establish the conceptual possibility of their separation (from which one then tries to infer the metaphysical possibility of their separation). And so one thing poems of the sort I have in mind can do is convey what it's like to take an idea like dualism seriously, to entertain it and acquiesce in it, even if one believes on other grounds that it's untenable. Why is this something that's important to do? I think it's because being drawn to thoughts like these, whether or not they're true, and whether or not they can survive strict philosophical scrutiny, is a central part of human experience; and attempting to capture and convey even these elusive aspects of human experience is a central aim of poetry, at least as I conceive it.

There's a worry that occurs to me about this view of the relation between poetry and truth. What I've been suggesting seems to imply a certain indifference to truth on the part of poets and readers. Some of you might be familiar with a book by the philosopher Harry Frankfurt called *On Bullshit*, which was originally a short essay in the journal *Raritan* before becoming a surprise best seller when it was reprinted as a small—a *very* small—book.[7] Frankfurt offers a wonderful analysis of what it means to say that something is bullshit, or that one is engaging in bullshit, and his conclusion is that it involves not lying or deliberately trying to mislead, but rather a certain *indifference* to truth. And the worry that occurs to me is this: why isn't poetry, on the view of it I've been suggesting, really a form of bullshit, since it does involve a kind of indifference to truth? I think that this is a fair question, but that the reason most poetry isn't bullshit is because of a qualification implicit in Frankfurt's analysis: bullshit involves an indifference to truth in contexts in which you're supposed to be aiming at, or are reasonably taken by others to be aiming at, truth. (I'll remark in passing that this may disqualify a paradigmatic example of the art, the college dorm room bull session, as an instance of bullshit, if we regard it as what it often is, a spirited verbal free-for-all rather than an irresponsibly conducted exercise in inquiry.)

And this brings me to a final point about poetry and truth. Earlier I referred in passing to excessively didactic poetry. What I had in mind is a certain strain in modern poetry often associated with the Stein–Williams–Zukofsky version of modernism (as opposed to the Eliot–Stevens version, e.g.), continuing through poets like Charles Olson, and represented more recently by certain Language poets. Poems in this tradition are often underwritten by quasiphilosophical views about language, thought, and the self, and their concern is often with the nature of representation and perception, with the poems either addressing such issues explicitly or being offered as proof texts for theses about them. The problem I have with poetry like this is that it *does* take itself to be aiming at truth in the way that philosophy aims at truth, and yet it doesn't subject itself to the constraints I described earlier that philosophy is subject to. Its avoidance of such constraints represents, it seems to me, an indifference to truth in a context in which one is aiming at truth, and so does qualify it as a kind of bullshit in Frankfurt's sense.

In my previous lecture on romanticism and modernism I argued that the latter is really a continuation of the former, though I noted that this wouldn't hold for the modernist strain I've just characterized as excessively didactic. The central modernist strain I talked about in that lecture is a continuation of romanticism, not in the sense of something celebratory or pastoral, but in its focus on the individual consciousness, even in fragmentary and disjointed forms. If what I've said today about the relation between poetry and truth is at least vaguely on the right track, that would seem to bolster the view I share with Bloom and many others that takes romanticism, including the strain of modernism that represents a continuation of romanticism, to be central to poetry as we (or is it just I?) have come to understand it.

12

Poetry, Philosophy, and the Syntax of Reflection (2012)

Western philosophy and poetry have enjoyed a neighborly but vexed relation at least since Aristophanes ridiculed Socrates in *The Clouds* and Plato, one of the West's great literary stylists, returned the compliment by banishing poets from his *Republic*. Both can be motivated by any number of common concerns, including the nature, knowledge, and persistence of the self; the character of experience and its relation to time and memory; the phenomenology of perception; skepticism and the extent of our knowledge of the world and of our own minds; and the relations of individuals to each other and to society. Of course there are areas of philosophy which may seem to have little connection to poetry, but even philosophy of mathematics is concerned with the recognizably poetic fascination with the idea of a realm of reality graspable through intellectual or imaginative apprehension, and philosophy of science and philosophy of physics are concerned with the notion of a fundamental order underlying or transcending the world of appearance. And I haven't even mentioned moral philosophy or philosophy of religion.

Yet though philosophy and poetry can often be found in close proximity to each other, I think there's something about them that makes "philosophical poetry," as I'm going to use the phrase, almost an oxymoron. By philosophical poetry I don't simply mean poetry that alludes to or even takes as its subject matter properly philosophical themes. I think poetry can be about almost anything, and there are many powerful examples of philosophical poetry in this sense to be found—to take just a few examples from the modern period, in the works of Eliot, Stevens, Richard Wilbur, Howard Nemerov, Charles North, and Troy Jollimore. But doing philosophy and writing poetry are activities people can engage in, and sometimes even the same person can engage in. Philosophical poetry, as I want to understand it, would be poetry which itself engages in the activity of philosophy. This kind of poetry, it seems to me, is extremely rare, and what interests me is why this should be so. The broad answer I want to suggest is that philosophy and poetry are, as the saying goes, separated at birth, in the sense that while both can be motivated by certain protophilosophical experiences, the two activities proceed from or develop these originating impulses in very different ways, subject to and characterized by different constitutive constraints, conventions, and strategies. I'll try to flesh out this answer in a number of different ways, but let me begin with some examples of the kinds of experiences I think can give rise to both philosophy and poetry.

The first two examples are ones I've discussed elsewhere, and concern the ontological status of the self.[1] Few philosophers would be willing to defend Cartesian dualism or its religious counterparts, and yet it seems to me that deep down we're all dualists, even if we know better, and that dualism is a kind of necessary illusion which we find difficult or impossible to avoid. The reason is that there's something in the nature of our self-experience that pushes us very strongly towards dualism, and I take it that traditional philosophical arguments for it, like the four considerations Descartes adduces in the Sixth Meditation, are really attempts to articulate just what it is about our experience of the self that does this. The most conspicuous aspect of it is the immediacy of subjective experience, and our inability either to call it into question or to make sense of it within the framework of the physical order—an inability that seems to support at least the imaginative possibility of the existence of a subjective self independent of the physical body. And it is this same immediacy of subjective self-experience that lies at the heart of high romanticism (of which I take modernism to be a continuation). I've argued elsewhere that what's central to romanticism is the affirmation of individual subjectivity in opposition to its setting in an objective material world, a world that can seem to threaten it with annihilation.[2] And as an example of how intense introspection can lead to a vivid sense of the distinctness of the self's existence from the body's, I've previously cited Elizabeth Bishop's great poem "In the Waiting Room," in which the speaker has a sudden experience of detachment from the world of tangible human beings:

> I said to myself: three days
> And you'll be seven years old.
> I was saying it to stop
> the sensation of falling off
> the round, turning world
> into cold, blue-black space.
> Why should I be my aunt,
> or me, or anyone?

My second example is the experience of what Kant calls the sublime. As he describes it, it begins with the self's sense of its insignificance or diminution in the face of some physical enormity, like towering mountains or a vast, open sea. But this sense of diminution is countered by the realization that this enormity, great as it is, can nevertheless be contained in thought, which leads in turn to a sense of the mind's transcendence of the natural order. It forms the basis for arguments for another form of dualism, which unlike Cartesian dualism doesn't simply expand our conception of the natural order to include mental as well as material substances, but rather removes the transcendental ego from the natural order altogether. One needn't subscribe to all the details of Kant's conceptualization of the experience of the sublime—indeed, I think it can be generalized to start with a sense of the insignificance of what Thomas Nagel calls the subjective viewpoint when thought of objectively, *sub specie aeternitatis*, and continuing with oscillations between his subjective and objective viewpoints.[3] What's important here is that it's a genuine experience, as I and no doubt many of you can attest, an experience central to the poetry of high romanticism and its descendants, as in the concluding vision of Wordsworth's *Prelude*, a vision of

> how the mind of man becomes
> A thousand times more beautiful than the earth
> On which he dwells, above this Frame of things.

My final example of a protophilosophical experience common to both philosophical and poetic reflection comes from Hume's analysis of causation or necessary connection. We have a conviction that our concept of causation involves more than a repeated succession of cause and effect, but includes as well a tie between them which makes the former necessitate the latter; but when we try to find the source of this binding element in our experience of nature we come up short, and discover instead only constant repetitions of events. As good empiricists then we have to either reject our received concept of causation as empty, or at best (on a somewhat controversial reading of Hume) trace it to a confused projection of our own habitual associations of ideas onto nature. Now this may seem like a rather arid metaphysical dispute with little poetic resonance, but in fact the sudden apprehension or realization of the apparent contingency or unconnectedness of the stream of experience, an apprehension which can be both exhilarating and terrifying, underlies a great deal of poetry, particularly modern poetry with its characteristic obsession with disjunction and discontinuity. One might think here of Frank O'Hara's "I do this / I do that" poems, or poems written in accordance with Charles Olson's injunction in his poetic manifesto "Projective Verse" (which he attributes to Edward Dahlberg), "ONE PERCEPTION MUST IMMEDIATELY AND DIRECTLY LEAD TO A FURTHER PERCEPTION."[4] But to me, the most powerful expression of the felt lack of connection between events we've taken to form a cohesive whole is to be found in another poem of Elizabeth Bishop's, "Over 2000 Illustrations and a Complete Concordance," where after an increasingly anxiety-ridden catalog of the speaker's travels the poem is interrupted by a sudden realization: "Everything only connected by 'and' and 'and' "; and then concludes with an enigmatic vision of a thoroughly demystified world:

> Why couldn't we have seen
> this old Nativity while we were at it?
> —the dark ajar, the rocks breaking with light,
> An undisturbed, unbreathing flame,
> colorless, sparkless, freely fed on straw,
> and, lulled within, a family with pets,
> —and looked and looked our infant sight away.

There are other examples of experiences or felt concerns that can motivate both philosophy and poetry: the mind independence (or dependence) of the world; the way time feels in passing; the apprehension of others' mentality. But rather than multiply examples, let me return to the question that interests me here: why is it, despite so many shared underlying impulses, that poetry which is genuinely philosophical, in the sense of engaging in philosophy or advancing recognizably philosophical aims, is so uncommon? One way to approach this question is to ask how poetry might be enlisted to function in the service of philosophy by poets with broadly philosophical interests.

One answer can be found in the works of poets with interests in philosophy of language, like many so-called Language Poets, who seek to highlight the materiality and socially constructed nature of language, and to undermine what they take to be a received idea of language as a transparent, naturally given medium for the representation of reality. Certain poems might be taken as proof texts for various views of language which one wants to support or condemn. For instance, the idea of words as transparent natural symbols might be thought to stem in part from our habituation to the familiar sense of the coherence and inevitability of both everyday linguistic expression and heightened poetic utterance. A way to deflate this idea would be to demonstrate that this kind of coherence can be generated by the adoption of arbitrary compositional techniques like those of the early-twentieth-century French writer Raymond Roussel or the late-twentieth-century French Oulipo group, or the appropriational tactics of recent Flarf poets, thereby bringing out the role of arbitrary conventions and constructions in the generation of sense. And poets employing this strategy typically go on to argue that the putative subject matter of poems generated in this way has a similarly conventional or constructed status.

The trouble with this way of enlisting poetry in the service of philosophy is that it's often superficial and directed at straw men. While it's sometimes helpful to be reminded that meaning, or the illusion of meaning, can be produced by virtually random techniques, what serious philosopher of language would have thought otherwise, given the obvious role of arbitrary conventions in the establishment and use of language, or what Hilary Putnam called "trivial semantic conventionalism"? It's one thing to emphasize the conventionality of language and linguistic (including poetic) practices. It's quite another to project that conventionality, as is often done, onto what we use language to talk and write about, whether it's the mundane paraphernalia of ordinary life or the intense transports of high romanticism.

Something else that makes the idea of a genuinely philosophical poetry problematic is the fact that philosophy—or at least what I've heard described as "nine-to-five philosophy"—and poetry are, as I've suggested elsewhere, subject to different constitutive constraints.[5] Philosophical reflection typically begins with an identifiable question or problem, often one that has been formulated and addressed by other philosophers. It has to be clarified, its ambiguities removed, and then, if one's aim is constructive, an approach or answer to it proposed, which has to be clarified and disambiguated in turn (or if the aim is critical, objections to previous answers or approaches have to be proposed and clarified). Misunderstandings of or objections to this proposal have to be anticipated and deflected, and a case in favor of it has to be adduced, subject to the further constraints of consistency, coherence, and plausibility. Possible objections to these arguments need to be addressed, and remaining difficulties and issues to be resolved have to be noted. These constraints flow out of the traditional aim of philosophy, which is to arrive at the truth (however infrequently this aim may be achieved), an aim it shares with science, and even though its arguments are largely a priori rather than empirical, the basic structure of philosophical inquiry is similar to that of scientific investigation.

Poetry, by contrast, typically doesn't aim directly at truth.[6] Though assertions of the same abstraction and generality as those encountered in philosophy may occur in a poem, it would be inept to criticize the poem with the sorts of objections and counterexamples that would be appropriate to a philosophy paper (even when the poem seems to be asking for them, as with Keats's "Beauty is truth, truth beauty"). Rather, as I've argued elsewhere, poems may traffic in philosophical generalizations or present the kinds of protophilosophical experiences I discussed earlier, but the aim is not to *establish*, say, the truth of Cartesian or Kantian dualism, but rather to *inhabit* positions like these, or to allow the reader to enter into the viewpoint of someone who inhabits and accepts these imaginative possibilities; and the poem is successful if it achieves this aim. This doesn't mean that poetry is devoid of philosophical interest. For example, a crucial step in the traditional argument from possibility for dualism is the claimed imaginability of a disembodied mind, but this imaginability is always open to challenge. I might imagine looking at myself in the mirror, noticing that my eye sockets are empty, sawing off the top of my skull and finding it empty too, and then watching my entire reflection fade, leaving me staring at an empty mirror.[7] Am I really imagining myself existing in the absence of my body, or just a weird hallucination? The vividness with which an experience of the distinctness of the self from the body can be presented, as in the Bishop poem "In the Waiting Room," may help bolster the sense of its genuine imaginability. (Someone remarked during the discussion when I suggested this on an earlier occasion, "So you're just saying that poems can provide better thought experiments"—a not entirely inaccurate, if not very sympathetic, way of putting the point.) But what's missing from even the most vividly imagined Cartesian scenario, and which is essential to the philosophical case for dualism, is the crucial step from imaginability to real possibility, a step it's hard to see a poem taking.

Much of the foregoing is, as I've indicated, by way of rehearsing and amplifying what I've said previously about the difficulty of a genuinely philosophical poetry. I still think it's right as far as it goes, but it invites an obvious rejoinder. If the problem is that poetry isn't subject to the constraints constitutive of philosophy, why not contemplate the possibility of a poetry that *is* written subject to something like these constraints? I'm not an essentialist about poetry, and I'd be the last person to maintain that a "poetry" that aims at truth in the way philosophy does wouldn't really *be* poetry at all. The kinds of constraints I described a moment ago may indeed be constitutive of philosophy—or at least nine-to-five philosophy—but it seems narrow-minded to maintain that a *failure* to be subject to them is somehow constitutive of poetry. I'm not sure what such a poetry would be like, and I'm certainly not advocating it—perhaps it would be tedious, or fail to draw the reader into an imaginative viewpoint in the way we expect poems to do, or lack the rhythmical and musical qualities needed to sustain a poem (though I don't see why these things should necessarily be so). But at least it seems possible.

It strikes me though that there's another difficulty with the idea of a poetry that would be philosophical in this sense, a difficulty that's in a way less deep but more immediate than the one I've talked about so far; and I want to spend the rest of my time discussing it. I'm enough of a Fregean to think that the sentence is the unit of thought. I recently heard a reading by a much (and justly) celebrated younger poet, a poet whose poems were lively and energetic, jumping around in something like the way Frank O'Hara's do, and often moving and involving. But I began to feel a certain sameness to them, and it suddenly struck me that almost all the sentences in the poems were straightforwardly declarative ones. And then it occurred to me that because of this there were kinds of thoughts that this poet was simply incapable of expressing. What kinds of thoughts? Well, among them would be those typical of philosophical reflection as I tried to characterize it earlier, an activity that involves such subordinate activities as clarification, qualification, the drawing of distinctions, digression, revision, the adducing of reasons and arguments, and the making of inferences. And a language in which such activities can be carried out is almost bound to have a syntax rich in conditional and subjunctive constructions, subordinate clauses, qualifiers like "and yet," "nevertheless," and "but not," quantifiers, and logical and inferential connectives. And this is not the syntax of the language of most poetry, especially lyric poetry.

Before saying more about the link between philosophical reflection and syntactic complexity, let me give some examples of the contrasting styles I have in mind. Consider first James Wright's "Lying in a Hammock at William Duffy's Farm in Pine Island, Minnesota":

Over my head I see the bronze butterfly
Asleep in the black trunk,
Blowing like a leaf in green shadow.
Down the ravine behind the empty house,
The cowbells follow one another
Into the distance of the afternoon.
To my right,
In a field of sunlight between two pines,
The droppings of last year's horses
Blaze up into golden stones.
I lean back, as the evening darkens and comes on.
A chicken hawk floats over, looking for home.
I have wasted my life.

The poem presents nothing like a consecutively unfolding train of thought, but rather a passively observed and plainly described setting in which the speaker experiences a sudden devastating epiphany. The poem is an example of what Mary Kinzie has called "the rhapsodic fallacy," in which a plain style is deployed towards the end of an outburst of pure subjectivity, which can take the form of a sudden insight or realization, or a Zen-like extinction of thought in a swoon of sensation, a tendency both exemplified and given a sophisticated articulation by Robert Hass in "Meditation at Lagunitas."

By way of (extreme) contrast, consider this excerpt from John Ashbery's long, unbroken poem "Clepsydra" (the title means "water clock"):

> Thereafter any signs of feeling were cut short by
> The comfort and security, a certain elegance even,
> Like the fittings of a ship, that are after all
> The most normal things in the world. Yes, perhaps, but the words
> "After all" are important for understanding the almost
> Exaggerated strictness of the condition, and why, in spite of this,
> It seemed the validity of the former continuing was
> Not likely to be reinstated for a long time.
> "After all," that too might be possible, as indeed
> All kinds of things are possible in the widening angle of
> The day, as it comes to blush with pleasure and increase,
> So that light sinks into itself, becomes dark and heavy
> Like a surface stained with ink: there was something
> Not quite good or correct about the way
> Things were looking recently: hadn't the point
> Of all this new construction been to provide
> A protected medium for the exchanges each felt of such vital
> Concern, and wasn't it now giving itself the airs of a palace?
> And yet her hair had never been so long.

Almost all the syntactic devices I just described are on display here: qualifications, digressions, inferential transitions, second thoughts, and so on (the excerpt also illustrates a strategy Ashbery often uses to maintain dramatic tension in his long mediative poems, by casting them in the form of conceptual narratives). I hasten to say that I'm *not* offering "Clepsydra" as an example of genuinely philosophical poetry: readers of Ashbery will recognize that to a great (though I think not complete) extent what he's trying to capture is the experience or sensation of abstract mediative thought, in the absence of any clearly defined subject matter (the poem opens with a question in search of a subject, "Hasn't the sky?"). The same can be said of his *Three Poems*, and to a lesser extent of other examples of a syntactically complex mediative style, like Stevens's ruminations in "Notes toward a Supreme Fiction" or Auden's channeling of Henry James in Caliban's address to the audience in "The Sea and the Mirror." And in the case of the rare imaginative writer like Proust in whose work something like sustained philosophical reflection does occur, it seems inextricably linked to those endlessly uncoiling sentences that can sometimes stretch over several pages.

The current climate in contemporary poetry is, to say the least, inhospitable to styles of such syntactic complexity, let alone ones that traffic heavily in abstractions. But highly disjunctive poems, while quite common, seem best suited to serve as proof texts for philosophical ideas, rather than as exercises in philosophy itself, for they lack the conceptual continuity characteristic of philosophical reflection. And variants of the plain style illustrated by the Wright poem seem ill-suited to the enactment of philosophical thought as well, for such thought seldom moves in a straight line. Consider, for example, how one might proceed from the protophilosophical experience of disconnectedness to a Humean conclusion about a lack of necessary connection in nature (indulge me in the fantasy that this is something a poet might want to do). One would first have to conceptualize the experience (Eliot: "We had the experience but missed the meaning"), and then defend the empiricism that insists that if there were such connections they would have to be disclosed in experience. Along the way, one would have to rule out other, a priori sources for the idea of necessary connection (something Kant didn't think Hume succeeded in doing). The point is that none of this is straightforward, and involves exploring a lot of blind alleys, returning, and starting over. I've suggested that this requires considerable syntactic complexity, but the broader point is that it requires indirection, digression, and casting about, however linguistically framed—something in tension with the directness of apprehension we typically expect of poems. Indirection in philosophy is not only a matter of syntactical complexity, but can also be accommodated by other stylistic devices even more foreign to poetry. Kenneth Winkler has an interesting paper in which he builds a case against so-called causal realist readings of Hume by looking at changes to the footnotes in successive editions of the *Enquiry*, arguing that "in an effort to make his presentation less abstruse, Hume, I think, made a decision to force three kinds of material to the bottom of the page: contextualization and controversy; elaborate clarification; and technical detail."[8] Winkler also cites a fascinating book by Anthony Grafton that examines the use of footnotes in historians' writings, in which the proposed historical narrative is presented in the main text and the case for it, primarily in the form of textual citations, is presented in the footnotes (which differs from their use in philosophical writings, where, as in Hume's case, they are often used primarily for corral digressions and clarifications).[9]

It might be objected that attributing the rarity of philosophical poetry to the styles and linguistic resources available to the poet is, so to speak, putting the cart before the horse. Surely, the objection goes, if poets were really interested in engaging in philosophical reflection, they'd simply adopt a style appropriate to the exercise; and thus the rarity of genuinely philosophical poetry must have a different explanation. And indeed I agree that the explanation isn't entirely stylistic, as shown by my earlier discussion of the constraints to which philosophy and poetry are subject. But the objection fails to appreciate just how language-driven poets and the poems they produce actually are. One seldom starts a poem with a fully thought-out conception of its subject matter (broadly construed), and then proceeds to discover a linguistic medium adequate to its expression. One more often starts with certain words, phrases, lines, scraps of language, images, rhythms, and prosodic forms, and then tries to fashion a poem out of them. In my own practice I often begin with a sense of what I like to call the poem's "architecture," a kind of abstract image or idea of the poem that includes its rough length, how it's going to look on the page, the sorts of sentences it's going to employ, its cadences, its density of expression, its affective tone—in short, almost everything about it except its content—and then work to fill in that architectural template. In fact, I once wrote a long, dense, unbroken poem ("The Constructor") in which I started with the last line and then worked backwards to arrive at the beginning of the poem over two hundred lines earlier.

Against all this, it might be suggested that the works of a number of philosophers serve as counterexamples to the idea that there's something inherently problematic about writing that embodies both philosophical and poetic qualities. Wittgenstein in particular is both one of the most important philosophers of the twentieth century and one whose writings are of interest to a wide range of imaginative writers, visual and conceptual artists and composers with little interest in technical philosophy. Marjorie Perloff, for instance, an important critic of contemporary poetry, has written a book, *Wittgenstein's Ladder*, that attempts to bring out affinities between his work and that of a number of modern and postmodern figures, including Gertrude Stein, Samuel Beckett, Thomas Bernhard, Robert Creeley, and Language Poets like Charles Bernstein.[10]

Now I share the assessment of Wittgenstein both as a great philosopher and as a writer whose works often exhibit a striking poetic resonance (one of my own touchstones is *Investigations* 115: "A *picture* held us captive. And we could not get outside it, for it lay in our language and language seemed to repeat it to us inexorably"). And I've written previously about the romantic lyricism that I think informs much of his philosophical work.[11] But it also seems to me that reflection on his example reinforces, rather than undermines, the idea of a tension between philosophical and poetic ways of writing. Wittgenstein is sui generis and it would be dangerous to generalize from his example, but anyone familiar with Wittgenstein studies knows that the most conspicuous fact about them is the extreme degree of disagreement among his interpreters over what his views are, or even whether he has any. True, there are interpretive disagreements about many philosophers (I've alluded to some concerning Hume), but one usually has the sense that they're in principle resolvable, a sense I find lacking in many of the disputes concerning Wittgenstein. And the source of the uncertainty in his case is to a great extent stylistic, as his presentations are often terse, epigrammatic, and devoid of explicit argumentation. And beyond these obvious impediments to understanding him, there's the characteristic interlocutory style of his later works, which involves two different voices, both written in fairly plain styles—one offering philosophical temptations and the other declining the gambits. I'll close with an example of this style and of the interpretative difficulties it poses, *Investigations* 308:

> "Are you not really a behaviorist in disguise? Aren't you at bottom really saying that everything except human behavior is a fiction?"—If I do speak of a fiction, then it is of a *grammatical* fiction.

What exactly does Wittgenstein mean by a grammatical fiction? Rogers Albritton, one of Wittgenstein's most clear-minded and relentless interpreters, spent many years trying to figure out what he might be getting at in this (and the surrounding) passage(s), an effort that resulted in what I think is an extremely important paper (characteristically unpublished at his death), "A Difficulty in Understanding Wittgenstein," in which he considers and rejects a number of ways of glossing it until he feels he's arrived at a tentative sense of what Wittgenstein is suggesting:

> But I don't honestly quite see how the suggestion should be put, or understood. I do (I think) obscurely see that the notion of the pain in my neck (and in yours, no doubt, by this time) is what I called <u>thin</u>, a minute ago, but I can't honestly see the absurdity, the emptiness, of the inference that <u>pain</u> is "thin," so to speak. A metaphysical inference. Pain a something after all, just metaphysically <u>thin</u>. Maybe as thin as a <u>number</u>, though <u>particular</u>.[12]

Two things leap out at once about this assessment: first, its extreme tentativeness; and second, its metaphorical character ("metaphysically thin"). I think, though I can't argue it here, that these two things are going to be true of honest interpretations of much of Wittgenstein's work; and I also think they're due, to a great extent, to the manner in which he chose (if that's the right word) to present it.

One last thought to forestall a possible misunderstanding: I've been arguing that there's something problematic about the idea of a poetry that embodies philosophical reflection, and some might think I see this as a shortcoming on poetry's part. I don't. The problem I've considered has to do with poetry's trying to aim at truth in the way philosophy is supposed to, but whether this is a desirable aim for poetry is something I haven't even discussed, though I'm inclined to think it isn't. (In a discussion of poetry's positive qualities, I would emphasize its self-legislating character, which allows it to serve as a vehicle for the manifestation of imaginative, and hence human, freedom.) Philosophy and poetry can both be reflective endeavors capable of transforming the way we see ourselves and the world, but they go about this in very different ways; and it may well be that in many areas of human concern, poetry is more effective than philosophy at bringing about this kind of imaginative transformation. At least that was part of what Plato was worried about.

13

On John Ashbery's "Clepsydra" (2013)

John Ashbery's "Clepsydra," which I regard as one of his (many) masterpieces, is a poem of about two hundred and sixty lines, first published in *Art and Literature*, a magazine he co-edited, and then included in his 1966 collection *Rivers and Mountains*. That book had been preceded by 1962's *The Tennis Court Oath*, one of the most radically disjunctive books in American poetry, and I suspect that most readers found the poems in *Rivers and Mountains* to mark a distinct shift in Ashbery's development, since the syntactic fragmentation so prominent in the earlier book was almost completely absent from the new one. But I had discovered *The Tennis Court Oath* only in early 1966, just before *Rivers and Mountains* appeared, and reading the two books in close proximity to each other I had a greater sense of a kinship between them than I probably would have if I'd read the latter four years after reading and musing on the former. "Europe," the longest poem in *The Tennis Court Oath*, is both conceptually and syntactically fragmented, though, like many of the poems in the book, with a sense of a narrative or story invisibly unfolding beneath the fragmented surface. "Clepsydra," the central (though not the longest) poem in *Rivers and Mountains*, renounces that syntactic fragmentation, unfolding in labyrinthine but nevertheless complete sentences; yet it retains the conceptual disjunctiveness and the sense of an invisibly unfolding narrative. Like the earlier poem, it remains a verbal artifact: its hundreds of lines are dense, relentless, and without stanza breaks, and Ashbery has said that his governing image of the poem was of a tall, narrow marble slab down which a single drop of water slowly trickles (the title "Clepsydra" means "water clock").

The poem opens with a question in search of a subject ("Hasn't the sky?"), and to the extent that it *has* a subject, it is, as James Longenbach has observed, the feeling of the passage of time—indeed the poem begins in the morning ("The reason it happened only since you woke up") and concludes at the end of the day, when "the body is changed by the faces of evening." But if the passage of time is its only real subject, I want to suggest that the poem is also (like many of Ashbery's long poems) a kind of quest-narrative. In this regard, it is usefully compared to Marianne Moore's "An Octopus," which seems to me one of the precursor poems of "Clepsydra." Moore's poem, which Ashbery has suggested may be her greatest, is comparable in length to his, if a bit shorter, and is also a verbal slab, in this case with one stanza break. It is (as many of her poems are) a linguistic collage, and though more static and impersonal than "Clepsydra," it traces, by stringing together a variety of quotations from disparate sources, an ascent of Washington's Mt. Rainier, from the fir trees at its base to the "snow falling on the peak," a movement in which "you have been deceived into thinking you have progressed." Ashbery's poem even contains what may be an allusion to "An Octopus" in a passage about travelers ascending a mountain:

>   the way
> A telescope protects its view of distant mountains
> And all they include, the coming and going,
> Moving correctly up to other levels, preparing to spend the night
> There where the tiny figures halt as darkness comes on,
> Beside some loud torrent

The object of the quest-narrative of "Clepsydra" is more abstract and indeterminate than Moore's summit and emerges only gradually. The poem moves forward in a meandering, lackadaisical fashion that seems like the external representation of some drama occurring in a private, inner realm it both manifests and guards, until a little over halfway through it reaches its first moment of crisis, with the realization that this poetic enactment has taken on a life of its own, a realization the speaker finds both disturbing and liberating:

>   there was something
> Not quite good or correct about the way
> Things were looking recently: hadn't the point
> Of all this new construction been to provide
> A protected medium for the exchanges each felt of such vital
> Concern, and wasn't it now giving itself the airs of a palace?
> And yet her hair had never been so long.

From this point on it becomes increasingly clear that the goal of the quest is the possibility of poetry itself, the possibility of poetry that is recognized and acknowledged (a goal that animates much of Ashbery's subsequent work—e.g.,

"Soonest Mended" and "Grand Galop"), which the speaker more and more despairs of attaining:

> It seemed he had been repeating the same stupid phrase
> Over and over throughout his life; meanwhile
> Infant destinies had suavely matured; there was
> To be a meeting or collection of them that very evening.
> He was out of it of course for having lain happily awake
> On the tepid fringes of that field

(Though Ashbery wrote "Clepsydra" in his mid-thirties, well before he had gained the wide recognition he now enjoys, he was already a kind of senior figure to a small group of younger poets, something about which he seemed ambivalent.) The fear that poetic validation requires the communication of something incommunicable, something on the tip of one's tongue that eludes formulation, leads to a second, terrifying crisis:

> That we shall never see in that sphere of pure wisdom and
> Entertainment much more than groping shadows of an incomplete
> Former existence so close it burns like the mouth that
> Closes down over all your effort like the moment
> Of death, but stays, raging and burning the design of
> Its intentions into the house of your brain, until
> You wake up, the certainty that it
> Wasn't a dream your only clue to why the walls
> Are turning on you and why the windows no longer speak
> Of time but are themselves, transparent guardians you
> Invented for what there was to hide.

Yet this mood of despair is suddenly dissipated by the almost Wittgensteinian realization that the picture of a realm of introspected, incommunicable thoughts and meanings that poetry has to strive, vainly, to articulate is a kind of inescapable illusion:

>   It is not a question then
> Of having not lived in vain. What is meant is that this distant
> Image of you, the way you really are, is the test
> Of how you see yourself, and regardless of whether or not
> You hesitate, it may be assumed that you have won, that this
> Wooden and external representation
> Returns the full echo of what you meant

And with that realization the poem proceeds to its serenely beautiful conclusion, ending with two lines Ashbery had jotted down and saved before it was written:

> Moving in the shadow of
> Your single and twin existence, waking in intact
> Appreciation of it, while morning is still and before the body
> Is changed by the faces of evening.

"Clepsydra" is an astonishing performance, possibly the purest poem Ashbery has written and one of the great poems of the twentieth century.

14

Perplexity and Plausibility: On Philosophy, Lyrical and Discursive (2013)

Mainstream Anglo-American philosophy—or what I have heard described as "nine-to-five philosophy"—is a reflective activity conducted in accordance with certain broad constitutive constraints. It typically begins with an identifiable question or problem, often one that has been formulated and addressed by other philosophers. The problem has to be clarified, its ambiguities removed, and then, if one's aim is constructive, an approach or answer to it proposed, which has to be clarified and disambiguated in turn (or, if the aim is critical, objections to previous answers have to be proposed and clarified). Misunderstandings of or objections to this proposal have to be anticipated and addressed, and a case in favor of it has to be adduced, subject to the further constraints of consistency, coherence, and plausibility. Possible objections to these arguments need to be addressed, and remaining difficulties and issues to be resolved have to be noted. These constraints flow out of the traditional aim of philosophy, which is to arrive at the truth (however infrequently this aim may be achieved)—an aim that philosophy shares with science, and even though its arguments are largely a priori rather than empirical, the basic structure of philosophical inquiry is similar to that of scientific investigation.

There is a familiar complaint, coming from both outside mainstream philosophy and within it, that philosophical reflection conducted on this model is sterile and unsatisfying, incapable of arriving at the insight and understanding that philosophy is traditionally supposed to provide. Jan Zwicky shares this dissatisfaction over the standard model, a model to which she adds, somewhat tendentiously, several additional elements. According to Zwicky, philosophy as practiced by "analysts" (a word that should set off alarm bells, as references to "the Democrat Party" would) is characterized by the assumption that the meaning of a whole is a function of its component elements, combined according to syntactic rules (an idea also said to be associated with "the Newtonian concept of cause"), and by the assumption that all meaning is linguistic in form and does not exist prior to language. What makes these additions tendentious is that both are substantive philosophical positions that are the subject of debate within mainstream philosophy itself and so can hardly be among its presuppositions. The first is a version of what is often called the principle of compositionality, an explanatory hypothesis first articulated by Frege (though anticipated to some extent by Plato and Locke) and accepted by many, but far from all, philosophers of language; while the second would be denied by the many philosophers who subscribe to the language-of-thought hypothesis. (As for "the Newtonian concept of cause," Newtonian mechanics consists of laws relating various physical magnitudes to one another, and it makes no mention of causation.)

Against this model of philosophy, Zwicky offers the prospect of what she calls lyric philosophy. Her characterization of it is admittedly sketchy and contains few illustrations, but it includes a number of central elements. Lyric philosophy "presupposes that ... meaning exists prior to and independently of language" and that such "lyric meaning" is "gestural" and based on "human experience of the world, unconditioned by language." Lyric meaning is holistic rather than compositional, experiential rather than discursive—grasping it is likened to experiencing a gestalt shift—and Zwicky appeals to Wittgenstein's discussion in the *Investigations* of aspect-seeing (of which she takes metaphor to be an instance), in order to illuminate the idea. Lyric thinking "desires wordlessness," something she equates with phenomenological selflessness, and she contrasts it with "the technocratic worldview" with its "distrust ... of intense emotion, and ... [its] insistence on the generic superiority of the rational intellect to emotions, desires, and sensations." Surprisingly, she also contrasts it with romanticism, but since she identifies romanticism with "an absolute distinction" between art and science, rather than (as I would) a felt tension between subjectivity and its objective setting in the world, I am inclined to take this contrast between lyric philosophy and romanticism with a grain of salt. Finally, Zwicky's characterizations of lyric philosophy make scarcely any mention of truth.

It is difficult to know what to make of all this. My first, unsympathetic reaction was to be reminded of what the poet and poetic theorist Mary Kinzie calls the rhapsodic fallacy, a poetic mode in which a plain style is deployed in preparation for the end of a sudden outburst of subjectivity, a Zen-like extinction of thought in a swoon of sensation or a sudden epiphany. James Wright's well-known poem "Lying in a Hammock at William Duffy's Farm in Pine Island, Minnesota," in which a presentation of a minutely observed and plainly described natural setting is followed by the devastating realization, "I have wasted my life," is an example—and Zwicky herself supplies another, Rilke's "Archaic Torso of Apollo," in which a meticulous description of a statue of Apollo is followed by the abrupt injunction, "You must change your life." The poem, she says, is a description of what she calls "seeing-into," a kind of "ontological attention" which "is a response to particularity" and in which "we perceive [something] as a *this* [and] experience its meaning": "*This*ness is the experience of a distinct thing in such a way that the resonant structure of the world sounds through it."

Kinzie's choice of the phrase "rhapsodic fallacy" to describe this mode of poetic imagination betrays her skepticism of it, a skepticism I share. But the affinities between poetry and Zwicky's lyric philosophy suggest to me a more sympathetic way of thinking about it, one that involves the relations between philosophy, poetry, and experience. Both philosophy and poetry can be motivated by certain protophilosophical experiences, though they proceed from or develop these originating impulses in very different ways, subject to and characterized by different constitutive constraints, conventions, and strategies.

Let me give four examples of the kinds of experiences I think can give rise to both philosophy and poetry. The first two concern the ontological status of the self. While few philosophers would be willing to defend Cartesian dualism, it seems to me that deep down we are all dualists, for there is something in the nature of our self-experience that pushes us very strongly towards dualism, and I take it that traditional philosophical arguments for dualism are really attempts to articulate just what it is about our self-experience that does so. The most conspicuous aspect is the immediacy of subjective experience and our inability either to call it into question or to make sense of it within the framework of the physical order—an inability that seems to support at least the imaginative possibility of the existence of a subjective self independent of the physical body. And this same immediacy of self-experience lies at the heart of romanticism, to which my second example is also central: the experience of what Kant calls the sublime. As he describes it, this experience starts with the self's sense of its insignificance or diminution in the face of a physical enormity, like towering mountains or a vast, open sea—a feeling of diminution that is countered by the realization that this enormity, great as it is, can be contained in thought, which leads in turn to a sense of the mind's transcendence of the natural order. One need not subscribe to all the details of Kant's conceptualization of the experience of the sublime; what is important is that it is a genuine experience, one that forms the basis for another sort of argument for dualism and is also central to the poetry of high romanticism (it is particularly prominent in Wordsworth's *Prelude*).

My third example of a protophilosophical experience common to both philosophical and poetic reflection comes from Hume's analysis of causation or necessary connection. We have a conviction that our concept of causation involves not only repeated successions of cause and effect but also a tie between them that makes the former necessitate the latter; yet when we try to find the source of this binding element in our experience of nature, we come up empty and discover instead only constant repetitions of events. This may seem at first like a rather arid metaphysical problem with little poetic resonance, but the sudden apprehension or realization of the sheer contingency or unconnectedness of the stream of experience, an apprehension that can be both exhilarating and terrifying, underlies a great deal of poetry, particularly modern poetry with its characteristic obsession with disjunction and discontinuity. (One of its most powerful expressions is to be found in Elizabeth Bishop's poem "Over 2000 Illustrations and a Complete Concordance," where she writes, "Everything only connected by 'and' and 'and.'") My last example of an originating experience also concerns contingency: a deep feeling of astonishment or puzzlement that anything should exist at all, an experience of which Wittgenstein, in his "Lecture on Ethics," contends that "the best way of describing it is to say that when I have it I wonder at the existence of the world" and which in the *Tractatus* he identifies with "the mystical."

These are genuine and deeply important human experiences that, by themselves, remain inchoate: merely having them constitutes neither philosophical thought (at least as usually conceived) nor poetry. For them to lead to philosophy requires them to be conceptualized or articulated in ways that lead to formulable positions or theses (or, as in Wittgenstein's response to the wonder at the existence of the world, to the view that the questions the experience gives rise to are illegitimate), which then are developed and defended in accordance with something like the model of reasoning that I sketched at the outset and governed by the overall aim of truth. Alternatively, originating experiences like these can give rise to reflective poetry, where the aim is not to arrive at the truth about various competing hypotheses but rather, I would argue, to explore or inhabit the imaginative possibilities that philosophical hypotheses try to capture, or to render vivid what it would be like for those possibilities to be realized. Elizabeth Bishop, for example, makes palpable the feeling of the estrangement of the mind or self from the human person in "In the Waiting Room"; and Wordsworth, in *The Prelude*, portrays the freedom of the transcendental self from the natural order: "How the mind of man becomes

/ A thousand times more beautiful than the earth / On which he dwells, above this Frame of things."

Zwicky, as I am reading her, suggests a different perspective on protophilosophical experiences like these, one from which the having of them is itself a form of thought, "lyric thought," and from which the effort to attain them is itself a form of philosophy, "lyric philosophy." I have no objection to extending the terms *thought* and *philosophy* to cover activities centered on such experiences: they are certainly of tremendous human significance, and philosophy that is not ultimately rooted in them is bound to be shallow and sterile. But the danger of forsaking the discursive model of philosophy entirely and replacing it with a quest for grasping ineffable experiences is that one thereby not only forsakes any attempt to articulate just what it is one grasps or what its significance is but also is in danger of succumbing to an illusion of grasping something of significance (whatever it is), when in reality one has not grasped anything at all. Wittgenstein is one of Zwicky's presiding figures, and in mulling over her remarks on ontological attention, on experiencing something as a *this* and thereby coming to "experience its meaning," I was reminded of nothing so much as his attempt, in the so-called private language sections of the *Investigations*, to debunk the illusion that one can give oneself a private ostensive definition of a term by inwardly concentrating one's attention on a sensation-token and thereby grasp what kind of sensation it is ("but I can inwardly undertake to call THIS 'pain' in the future").

Something ought to be said about Wittgenstein's role in Zwicky's conception of philosophy. Although I think there is a tension between her views and his in this instance, I also think that she is right in important ways about how he thinks of meaning and significance. Wittgenstein's extended discussion of aspect-seeing, which figures so prominently in her remarks, was, as she notes, motivated by the light he thought it shed on what it is to experience the meaning of a word. Aspect-seeing actually first appears in the *Tractatus*, where it is used to illuminate what it is to grasp the sense of a proposition. The ocular metaphors of showing and seeing are of course central to that book's account of language, according to which aspects of language, including semantic properties and relations, that can be shown or seen are nonfactual and cannot be described. Zwicky is right to emphasize the persistence, in Wittgenstein's later account of how one sees or grasps an aspect, of the idea in the *Tractatus* that language's semantic properties are seen or grasped. She is right to note as well, in his later work, other notions central to the *Tractatus*, such as those of internal properties and relations. She is not offering an overall reading of Wittgenstein here, but where I suspect

I would differ with her is on the issue of the extent to which he is a systematic, constructive philosopher, an issue that has dominated Wittgenstein studies in recent decades. Despite the concluding pronouncement of the *Tractatus* that its sentences are nonsense, and despite Wittgenstein's repeated insistence that the *Investigations* merely reminds us of obvious facts and embodies no philosophical theses or arguments, I would maintain that the former is a deeply systematic and constructive work, and that the latter continues to embody the semantic (and psychological) nonfactualism of the earlier book, in support of a community-based conception of language. (I think, e.g., that the "private language argument" is not only a genuine argument but a sound one to boot.) Here, though, is not the place to pursue the issue.

Much of the attraction of the alternative mode of philosophical thought Zwicky offers comes from the contrast she draws between it and philosophical reflection conducted in accordance with the standard discursive model. But her sketches of the latter are cruel parodies, bearing little resemblance to the practice of most philosophers working in that mode. I have noted some of the tendentious assumptions, like compositionality, with which she saddles it. But the parodies encompass the whole manner and style of standard philosophy, which she appears to equate "with systematic logico-linguistic analysis," written in "the academically safe vocabulary of positivism" and in a "technocratically acceptable prose" devoid of all emotion or metaphor and confined to a straightjacket of deductive inference. I do not recognize the work of most of the important (and many less important) philosophers working in the discursive mode in characterizations like these. And I am not thinking only of philosophers whose work is essayistic, like Thomas Nagel, Bernard Williams, Harry Frankfurt, Susan Wolf, K. Anthony Appiah, Stanley Cavell, and many others. I am also thinking of philosophers whose work is often dry, detailed, and systematic, like John Rawls, Thomas Scanlon, Christine Korsgaard, or Derek Parfit, and of metaphysicians whose work is often quite formal, like David Lewis and Theodore Sider.

It is not hard to see why such philosophers do not fit the mold Zwicky suggests. Illuminating discursive philosophy is based neither on axiomatic deductive systems nor on mechanical counterexample mills but, rather, on perplexity and plausibility: on finding that protophilosophical experiences of the sort I described earlier give rise to philosophical puzzlement, and on finding that some ways of responding to such puzzlement are more compelling than others. And both of these modes of philosophical reflection involve precisely the same conceptual gestalt that Zwicky identifies with lyric philosophy: being struck by how certain combinations of experiences and ideas feel inherently problematic (think of Wittgenstein's remark about philosophers who suffer from "loss of problems"), and grasping how certain combinations of ideas that attempt to address these problems hang together while others do not (which I think is what really lies behind the overworked talk of "intuitions"). Moreover, the thought and language in which discursive philosophical reflection is conducted are frequently affective and metaphorical. I have often been struck by how philosophers approach perennial issues like realism and skepticism can be as much a matter of temperament as it is of argument; and the elaborate metaphysical and semantic system of the *Tractatus* (to take just one salient example) is couched in deeply metaphorical terms. What I find most troubling about Zwicky's model of lyric philosophy is not its direct appeal to the idea of unconceptualized experience, since I am inclined to agree that there are aspects of human experience that resist conceptualization (though I find this idea more troubling than she does). Rather, it is that the mode of making sense that is supposed to characterize lyric philosophy and distinguish it from its discursive counterpart is one that strikes me as central to the discursive model of philosophy itself.

15

On Helen Vendler's Wallace Stevens* (2014)

It's an honor and a pleasure to participate in this session on Helen Vendler's influence on how we read Wallace Stevens, and it's easy too, since all I have to do is reminisce. I never really "got" Stevens until I read *On Extended Wings* as a philosophy graduate student in the late 1960s, and while part of the reason involved my own poetic predilections and biases, it also involved how Stevens was read prior to Vendler's book. First, my own biases: I began writing poetry in 1964 inspired by a course on modern American literature in which I first read the poetry of high modernism (though oddly enough, not including Stevens). My first model was the Eliot of "Gerontion" and "The Waste Land," but when I moved on to more contemporary poets the ones I tried to emulate were those associated with the Black Mountain School and the Objectivists. I espoused an anti-symbolic, "no ideas but in things" aesthetic, though the poems I was writing—pretty bad ones—spent more time elaborating this aesthetic than enacting it. When I then read Stevens in a modern poetry course in 1965, I was put off by what struck me as his excessive verbosity, lack of concrete imagery, and the general aura of significance that tended to surround what images there were. (I'll remark parenthetically that I later came to realize that his images could be amazingly precise—"The necklace is a carving, not a kiss"—though rarely in the "red wheelbarrow / faces in the metro" style.) Moreover, he was presented as a somewhat dandyish poet engaged in systematic philosophizing about reality and the imagination couched in highly symbolic terms (all those seasons, heavenly bodies, elements, and so on). As a philosophy rather than an English major this immediately seemed to me suspect, since it didn't feel like real philosophy at all (I never had similar qualms about Eliot, but he was trained as a philosopher). This was how Stevens was often read at the time, and my aversion to it was hardly atypical—think, for example, of Randall Jarrell's antipathy to Stevens's later poems (and Auden's too) for what he took to be their excessive abstraction, argumentation, and aridity.

Vendler's rehabilitation of Stevens had, for me, two components, linguistic and conceptual. Unsympathetic readers tended to complain about the excessively dandyish language of many of the early poems (which still isn't to my taste) or, like Jarrell, about what they took to be the abstraction and desiccation of many of the late poems. Vendler made us see how language-driven his poems were (something she has done so well with other poets too), and moreover that the language driving them was of a Keatsian or Shakespearian lushness (though she had yet to write extensively on Keats or Shakespeare). Not only was this the last nail in the coffin of the linguistic austerity I'd been so enamored of when I first started writing; more importantly, by bringing out the linguistic underpinnings of what had seemed like content-driven utterances, she helped dismantle the view of Stevens as a systematic thinker and led us to focus instead on the movements of the poems themselves, which are the movements of consciousness. Stevens was never really a philosophical poet, but rather a meditative one, and meditation is an activity in which the feeling of the ebb and flow of thought is as important as its ostensible subject matter, for to capture that feeling is to represent what it's like to be human. In Stevens, the movements of thought are oscillatory, seduced by the temptations of romantic possibility and then refusing them, only to be drawn to them again in turn. The guiding impulse of his poetry is thus not an intellectual construction but rather a sense of dissatisfaction, of disappointment and, as Vendler has observed of the great final poems of *The Rock*, of sublimated desire (a point I believe she makes in *Part of Nature, Part of Us*, though I can't put my finger on the passage).

Let me end with a problem. The great meditative poets of the twentieth century are, it seems to me, Stevens, the late Eliot, and middle-period John Ashbery. Vendler has written admiringly about Stevens and Ashbery, and about the phantasmagoric Eliot of "The Waste Land," but is dismissive of *Four Quartets* (and of Eliot's plays, which, whatever their merits as drama, contain passages of powerful reflection). I suspect, though I'm not really sure, that the reason is twofold. Just as there was a linguistic and a conceptual aspect to her rehabilitation of Stevens, her disdain for the late Eliot may be due, to some extent, to his language, which, though exquisite (I think Eliot has the best ear of all the great modern poets), lacks the Keatsian lushness of Stevens's or the kineticism and dynamism of Ashbery's. It may also be due to the fact that Eliot, trained as he was in philosophy, is a more systematic thinker than either Stevens or Ashbery (though I'd still hesitate to call him a philosophical poet), and that Vendler isn't sympathetic to this quality of his work. Whatever the reason, the contrast between her attitudes towards Stevens and the late Eliot continues to puzzle me.

16

The Microcosm: Poetry and Humanism (2016)

I think of poetry as what Wallace Stevens called a soliloquy of the interior paramour, or less grandly, as a form of talking to yourself, rather than addressing an audience. But I have the sense that when people first hear this description of poetry, they take me to be offering a conception of poetry lying somewhere between the narcissistic and the solipsistic, and react accordingly. Yet in thinking of poetry in this way, I take myself simply to be agreeing with much of what Harold Bloom says about it—that it's emblematic of our most characteristically human trait, what distinguishes us from our fellow creatures: our capacity for self-consciousness. I now feel that my idea of poetry as a form of talking to yourself is a basically humanistic conception of poetry, and I want to try to say a bit about what that means.

Human beings are the ultimate source of value, and what makes human beings valuable—or what Kant called "ends in themselves"—is human consciousness, human self-consciousness, which is the most commonplace and, at the same time, most unique thing in the world. Even though there are and have been billions and billions of us, each of us is uniquely aware of ourselves in a way unimaginable by anyone else; and while we all inhabit the same natural world and the same historical time, each one of us also inhabits a world of our own. As Wittgenstein put it: *I am the world.* (*The microcosm.*) Kant and Wittgenstein both also recognized the transcendental character of this subjective consciousness and its sense of its distinctness from the natural order—Kant in what he called the experience of the sublime, in which the mind attempts to contain the natural world in thought, and Wittgenstein in what he called the experience of the mystical, in which it tries to see the world as a limited totality. And what I mean by a humanistic conception of poetry is one that takes its goal to be the creation of a sense of the unimaginable reality of the individual life. Thinking of poetry as a form of talking to yourself is simply in the service of that goal, for it's only by enacting the experience of the self-conscious self that one creates this sense—or so it seems to me.

While it's true that poetry as a form of talking to yourself works to create a representation of the individual life, and in that sense is self-centered, it isn't inherently self-absorbed or narcissistic, since you can talk to yourself about virtually anything. You can talk to yourself about isolation and the privacy of your own experience; but you can also talk to yourself about the quotidian, the dailiness of ordinary life, the immediacy of the natural and social worlds, love, sex, physics, and politics. The range of the great poets of consciousness is astonishing: One rarely has a sense of the external world in Stevens, or else it's so transformed by the imagination as to be unrecognizable. Yet in Eliot and Ashbery it's often vividly present but so fragmented that it moves in and out of focus, while in O'Hara and Schuyler it's carried forward by the momentum of attention. Merrill's microcosm is an inherently social one, while Bishop's natural world is observed with such hallucinatory clarity that it's suffused by the subjective consciousness which (as David Kalstone has remarked) it so painfully excludes. The work of all these poets is informed by a palpable sense of self, whether or not that self is explicitly referred to or addressed.

I've attempted to realize this idea of poetry in my own work. Some years ago I argued, in commenting on the philosopher Susan Wolf's views on meaning in life, that in the wake of modernism artists, including poets, are often not in a position to know just what their aims are and whether they've succeeded in realizing them; and that this is not just because of the human penchant for self-deception, but is somehow inherent in modernism itself. Moreover, the humanist conception of poetry I've been trying to describe is not something I decided one day would be a great idea and then set out to implement; rather, it's one I've come to think informs my work in retrospect. That said, when I first started writing in college in the mid-1960s, my models were Black Mountain poets like Olson and Duncan, in whose work language (along with perception) is the focus, and from which that aforementioned palpable sense of the self was usually (and deliberately) absent. As I began to find this model of poetry stultifying, I discovered the work of New York poets like Ashbery, O'Hara, and Schuyler, which was even more interesting linguistically, but in which a feeling of a self behind the poems was vividly present. For a long time afterward, the poems I wrote, while self-centered in the first sense I just talked about, were disjunctive and surreal, and then conceptual and abstract, culminating perhaps in a poem called "The Constructor" (1988), a long first-person meditation on poetic belatedness with no concrete setting at all. In the early 1990s, I worked for almost a year on an even longer poem, "Falling Water," one of the first poems I'd written that was explicitly autobiographical, though I also continued writing abstract meditations like "The Secret Amplitude" (1966). Later I started writing what I think of as "memory poems," based on a Proustian recollection of a past incident of no particular significance in itself, but the memory of which seemed to me to capture the feeling of the passage of time more directly than I'd been able to in conceptual terms (these, including the title poem, make up the last section of *Sally's Hair* [2006]). I've continued to write in that mode, including the title poems of *Ninety-Fifth Street* (2009) and *ROTC Kills* (2012), and to some extent in the title poem of my new book, *The Swimmer*. That book seems to me more various and open to the idea that you can talk to yourself about almost anything, while still conveying a sense of the individual self. Though it contains abstract meditations, like a long poem on the experience of individual time I alluded to above ("*La Duree*"), it also includes poems centered on physics, model trains, cats, jazz, ceramics, men's clothes, rock and roll, Ernest Hemingway, mathematics, and cosmology, as well as two long social meditations on the Civil War and recent American history. I'd like to think it's a fuller realization of the humanistic idea of poetry I've been trying to describe, one that conveys a more robust sense of what it's like to be alive. But as I said, I'm not really in a position to say.

17

On *Wordsworth's Fun* (2021)

When I told the poet Kevin Hart that I was reading Matthew Bevis's book *Wordsworth's Fun*, he replied, "Must be a short book." I suspect Bevis wouldn't be surprised by Hart's quip, for it reflects a prevalent view of Wordsworth that his book seeks to undermine. On this view, Wordsworth is a poet of solemn and settled pronouncements, carefully distilled from experience and characterized by their seriousness, earnestness, and generality. Much of what little humor there is in his work is due to the unintentional lapses that account for his prominence in *The Stuffed Owl*. He's an unabashed representative of the high romanticism who celebrates and affirms the self's transcendence of the natural order manifested in the emotional trajectory of the experience of the Kantian sublime. While he is the first modern poet in the sense that he's the first to make subjectivity itself the subject of his poetry, his work embodies the kind of confidence and complacency that is the target of twentieth-century modernism's fragmentation, ambivalence, and uncertainty, and is in this sense one of modernism's foils.

Bevis isn't suggesting that, contrary to this view, Wordsworth has been an unrecognized jolly poet all along. Rather, what he means by Wordsworth's "fun" is that, first, his poetry embodies much more confusion, tentativeness, ambivalence, and a sense of the ridiculous and ludicrous than is usually recognized; and second, that Wordsworth himself is aware of this and takes considerable pleasure in it, a delight in following a poem's meditative course cognizant of its futility, and in the unforeseen verbal byways through which it leads. Instead of the clear conception of the transcendent self that is the conclusion of the emotional trajectory of the sublime, he's nagged by a sense of the ridiculousness of that romantic gesture, and the conception of the self that actually informs his poetry is a confused and comic one. But rather than being a source of despondency and discouragement, the unsettled nature of Wordsworth's poetic reflections is a driving force of his work and something in which he finds enjoyment, and even fun.

Bevis develops his take on Wordsworth by accretion, calling attention to nuances of individual words and lines, concentrating on sustained readings of particular poems, and finally arguing along broadly thematic lines for a deflationary view of *The Prelude*. He's the closest reader of poetry that I know of, treating every word as an individual choice whose significance emerges from comparisons with alternative choices. For instance, in "I wandered lonely as a Cloud," he argues that the choice of the word "oft" in the lines "For oft when on my couch I lie / In vacant or in pensive mood, / They flash upon that inward eye / Which is the bliss of solitude," instead of "now" or simply no temporal qualification, implies that the consolation provided by the recollection of the daffodils isn't constant and continuous, but rather sporadic and transitory, and that loneliness, vacancy, and bliss are entangled together in what he calls "the integrity of incoherence." Or again, in "Strange fits of passion I have known," he seizes on the stunning, and often remarked, incongruity of the last two lines, coming abruptly after the dreamy, meandering reflections of the moonstruck lover approaching his beloved's cottage: "'O mercy!' to myself I cried, / 'If Lucy should be dead!'" But he cites an early version of the poem Wordsworth sent to Coleridge that contained a concluding stanza apparently meant to bring these lines into the poem's perspective and rationalize them ("I told her this; her laughter light / Is ringing in my ears;"), and argues that Wordsworth's decision to omit the stanza should be seen as his acknowledgment of their incongruity and of his comfort with their provocative character.

A more sustained example of a revisionist reading of one of Wordsworth's major poems is provided by Bevis's treatment of "Resolution and Independence." On a conventional reading, the Leech-gatherer, in his self-sufficiency, is an antidote to the despondency into which poetry has led the speaker, an emblem of the availability and consolation of the ordinary. But the closer you look at him, the less he seems like an emblem of anything, and more like a merely uncommunicative or at best reluctantly communicative figure oblivious to the barrage of inanities ("'This morning gives us promise of a glorious day,'" "'What kind of work is that which you pursue?'") the speaker hurls at him. Rather than a resonant fellow traveler, he's a bare factual presence emblematic of nothing, who lies before the speaker "As a huge Stone is sometimes seen to lie." In talking about Wordsworth, Bevis often brings in modern and contemporary poets (about whom I'll say more later), and in his discussion of "Resolution and Independence" he quotes a letter from Elizabeth Bishop to Robert Lowell in which she speaks of wanting to write poems that were "great clumsy structures like Wordsworth's Leechgatherer," whose greatness, Bevis observes, is inseparable from their clumsiness. And I couldn't help thinking of her great poem "The Moose" as comparable to Wordsworth's in the way both culminate in an encounter with a presence that simply exists in its clumsy, brute factuality in the midst of a welter of banalities.

But the core of Bevis's revision of Wordsworth, it seems to me, is his delineation of the poet's entanglements with the self. In no other poet is the sense of the self as strong as in Wordsworth, and yet it remains maddeningly indeterminate and elusive. Bevis quotes Mark Strand's contention that "for Wordsworth the self precedes experience ... It makes a silent claim for primacy and we almost feel that Nature is its invention," and then remarks, "When reading Wordsworth we *almost* feel that. The claim for primacy, the very strength of the need to make it, gestures toward a sense that the self is made rather in its resistance to experience, its refusal to be defined by—or to be beholden to—what has happened to it." What this suggests to me is that the self of Wordsworth's poetry is what Kant called the transcendental subject, which he characterized as "a feeling of existence without the least conception of it"; and that the sense of comic oscillation Bevis sees at the heart of Wordsworth's poetry, his repeated insistence on and attempts to affirm something he knows to be ludicrous, derives from his efforts and inevitable failures to articulate or conceptualize that self. Let me explain.

A hallmark of high romanticism is the experience of the sublime Kant describes in *The Critique of Judgment*, and the conception of the self it gives rise to. The experience begins with the apprehension of some overwhelming physical enormity—tours of the Alps were popular at the time—that induces in the self a sense of its own insignificance. But this feeling of diminution is followed by the realization that however great that magnitude is, it's still bounded, and can be contained in thought and grasped by a mind capable of forming the conception of an unbounded magnitude. And finally, this realization leads the self to a realization of itself as something that transcends the natural order it's able to comprehend and contain in this way. Because he's the greatest poet of high romanticism, I'd always taken Wordsworth's work to affirm this experience of the sublime and the attendant conception of a transcendent self—by contrast with modernism, which in its obsession with subjectivity and the self is a continuation of romanticism, but which in its belatedness and disillusionment acknowledges the temptations of the sublime but is incapable of acquiescing in them. And indeed there are plenty of passages in Wordsworth's poetry that appear to accept it at face value and celebrate it—for instance, this one from the concluding Book XIII of *The Prelude*:

> how the mind of man becomes
> A thousand time more beautiful than the earth
> On which he dwells, above this Frame of things.

But there's something fishy, not to say ludicrous, about the Kantian experience of the sublime and the realization it's supposed to lead to. Unlike, say, traditional Cartesian arguments for the immateriality of the mind or self, it isn't a logical inference from supposedly acceptable premises. Rather, it's an aspirational emotional gesture, an oscillation between feelings of diminution and wonder capable of instilling in someone experiencing it a conviction of the self's transcendence of the natural order, whatever that might mean. I'm very much in the minority among philosophers in thinking that, properly understood and qualified, some of the Cartesian arguments for dualism are sound. But considered as an argument, Kant's formulation of the experience of the sublime is simply a nonstarter. What does it mean to say that the physical enormity that engenders the original feeling of diminution and insignificance can be "contained in thought"? It's not literally *in* the mind, but rather something I'm capable of thinking about, which is hardly a basis for thinking I transcend it. Moreover, there's a kind of incoherence about this affirmation of the self, a kind of paradox of self-consciousness, for once I form a conception of my self's transcendence, don't I thereby "contain it in thought" or make it an object of thought, and so become distinct and estranged from it?

Bevis brings out Wordsworth's ambivalence about this whole romantic confabulation of the sublime and the self. The poet certainly recognizes it, is drawn to it, and often affirms it; but at the same time he's plagued by a suspicion of its underlying ridiculousness and a subsequent need to distance himself from it. Bevis offers "'Beloved Vale!' I said, 'when I shall con'" as "an exercise in the antisublime," or better, as "an encounter with the oddity of the sublime," in which the speaker, rather than being cowed by nature's immensity, is surprised "To see the trees, which I had thought so tall, / Mere dwarfs; the Brooks so narrow, Fields so small." And rather than inducing an expansion of the self, the shrinkage of the trees, brooks, and fields leaves the speaker lost in a tender wonder verging on amusement in which all sadness has vanished ("I looked, I stared, I smiled, I laughed, and all / The weight of sadness was in wonder lost"). And instead of the self's expansion into grandiosity as in the Kantian sublime, Wordsworth presents the self as an anomaly, an odd singularity each of us has in common with others, as in *The Prelude*:

> Points have we all of us within our souls,
> Where all stand single; this I feel, and make
> Breathings for incommunicable powers.

The self is thus for Wordsworth in his deflationary moments something simultaneously singular and ordinary; and Bevis quotes Auden's observation that humor arises from "the simultaneous conscious[ness] of … each [of us being] a unique person and of being in common subjection to unalterable laws" to suggest that this sense of the self as both unique and utterly commonplace is tantamount to "a kind of fun, a potential and a prowess at once egotistically sublime and ridiculous—a sublime self-unimportance, even."

This sense of "a sublime self-unimportance" lies at the heart of Bevis's conception of *The Prelude*. *The Prelude* is of course an autobiographical epic, and *Paradise Lost* is among its models. But what Bevis emphasizes is that it is, more exactly, a *mock*-epic of self-creation, rather than an earnest recounting of a life as a settled totality of experience. "In writing, Wordsworth makes himself up as he goes along," Bevis remarks (recall Strand's observation that "for Wordsworth the self precedes experience"); and while "*The Prelude* is never quite a progress narrative, it is nevertheless in search of a humored self that would mark a progress of sorts."

And rather than Milton, the models Bevis emphasizes are Ariosto, whose *Orlando Furioso* Wordsworth translated, and whose central figure Angelica continues her ceaseless running through the woods of his own mock-epic; and Cervantes, for him an "enduring preoccupation." (The cover illustration of *Wordsworth's Fun* is a Daumier drawing of Don Quixote and Sancho Panza.) Bevis sees Ariosto's "repeatedly staging foilings of consummation" as prefiguring Wordsworth's never to be completed quest for self-definition or self-creation; and Quixote's mock-heroic exercises as anticipations of the underlying ludicrousness of the elevation of anything as ordinary and commonplace as the self to the grand scale of the sublime. *The Prelude* also illustrates his contention that Wordsworth's uncertainty and ambivalence about his ongoing efforts at self-creation are for him a source of enjoyment and invention, and he quotes a forty-line passage towards the end of Book VII, in which the poet returns to Ann Tyson's bedroom, in its entirety in support of it—lines remarkable for their verbal exuberance, despite the fact that "commentators have often been unwilling to admit what demonic fun it must have been to write this passage."

What *is* the source of this semi-comic sense of the futility of self-creation Bevis sees as the sustaining impulse of *The Prelude* and of Wordsworth's poetry generally? It seems to be what he calls "the peculiar ridiculousness at the heart of Being," which strikes me as akin to what I earlier called a kind of paradox of self-consciousness. If the self of Wordsworth's poetry is ultimately a Kantian transcendental subject, "a feeling of existence without the least concept of it," then self-creation is the attempt to conceptualize or define it. *The Prelude* is indeed an autobiographical epic, but to invest this unconceptualized self with a character and a biography is to turn it into an object of thought, and thus an other, for its essence is, as it were, to remain undefined. Bevis writes that the "feeling that what is laughable may be akin to ourselves extends to a feeling for the self *as* other," and invokes Coleridge and Stern to argue that my earlier self, separated from me by time, is as estranged from me as my neighbor separated from me by space. Recollection may be the past "morphing into presentness," and while "*The Prelude* is a study in its maker's fabrication of the past as a means of holding himself together," "this process is subject to constant slippage"; and so the task of self-creation is always ongoing and incomplete, something to be constantly renewed. And the remarkable contention of *Wordsworth's Fun* is that this futility, far from being a source of frustration or despondency, is something in which he revels.

* * *

In developing his reading of Wordsworth, Bevis makes frequent allusions to modern and contemporary poets; and while Wordsworth's relation to modernism isn't one of his explicit subjects, his book seems to me to have implications for it, and I'll conclude by saying a little about what I think they are. As I indicated earlier, I agree with the Bloomian idea that modernism—at least the line of it that runs through Eliot and Stevens—is, in its fixation on subjectivity and the self, a continuation of romanticism (the idea is Edmund Wilson's too). But whereas romanticism celebrates and affirms them, by contrast with their objective setting in the natural world that threatens them with annihilation, modernism in its belatedness, disillusionment, and fragmentation acknowledges the temptations of the sublime and its affirmation of the self but is unable to succumb to them. This inability to embrace and find comfort in the consolations offered by high romanticism is most conspicuous in Stevens, whose work is marked by repeated oscillations between a movement towards the sublime and a withdrawal from and a disowning of it.

But in bringing out Wordsworth's ambivalence and uncertainty about the sublime and the self-creation it involves, Bevis undermines or at least complicates this conception of the contrast between romanticism and modernism. Or rather, he blurs the contrast between Wordsworth's poetry and modernist poetry, since I don't think a comparable case could be made for attributing the ambivalence Bevis sees in Wordsworth to, say, Keats or Shelley. The effect is to draw his work closer to that of many twentieth-century poets for which it is usually seen as a foil. As I've mentioned, Bevis often alludes to modern and contemporary poets, and I've noted what strikes me as an affinity between "Resolution and Independence" and Bishop's poem "The Moose."

But I want to end by sketching an affinity Bevis's reading suggests between Wordsworth and another twentieth-century poet, John Ashbery.

With the reader's indulgence, I'll take the liberty of quoting a favorite passage from a review of my own work, a review by Mark Jarman of *The Late Wisconsin Spring* published in the mid-1980s: "In his new book ... John Koethe completes the long task of turning John Ashbery into William Wordsworth. It is a worthwhile business, since Ashbery himself is loath to complete the assignment." Would that this were true, but no matter. Reading *Wordsworth's Fun* I often found myself entertaining the converse of Jarman's transformational conceit, for the unsettled qualities Bevis attributes to Wordsworth's work only heighten the similarities that have always been evident between it and Ashbery's. Childhood is central to both poets, and both are capable of writing with a combination of plainspokenness and tenderness that can be heartbreaking. Wordsworth's poems are more biographical of course, but the strong sense of self that informs the work of both is, I've argued here and elsewhere, that of a Kantian transcendental or metaphysical subject, rather than of a psychological self constituted by its experiences and biography. *The Prelude* is a mock-epic of self-creation that takes the form of a quest that has to be constantly renewed, while many of Ashbery's poems are quest poems (e.g., "Grand Galop"), and his entire corpus can be seen as a never quite completed and constantly renewed exercise in self-creation—not only in the explicit manner of poems like "Self-Portrait in a Convex Mirror," but in the sense that in creating poems like the late, meandering, and lesser-known "Tuesday Evening" he simultaneously creates the self from which the poem issues. Certainly one of the central poems of Ashbery's ongoing attempt at self-definition is "Soonest Mended," which even shares some of the characteristic preoccupations and reference points that Bevis identifies in Wordsworth:

> Barely tolerated, living on the margin
> In our technological society, we were always having to be rescued

On the brink of destruction, like heroines in *Orlando Furioso*
Before it was time to start all over again.
There would be thunder in the bushes, a rustling of coils,
And Angelica, in the Ingres painting, was considering
The colorful but small monster near her toe, as though wondering whether forgetting
The whole thing might not, in the end, be the only solution.

Reading *The Prelude*, one constantly has the sense of approaching a climax or conclusion, only to have it deferred and the journey towards it renewed, and of "morphing into presentness" as Bevis puts it. Similarly, in reading long Ashbery poems like *Three Poems*, one constantly has the sense of "cresting into the present in a standing wave of arrival" which never quite arrives. And while combining these similarities with the ambivalence, unsettledness, and uncertainty that Bevis attributes to Wordsworth and in which, he argues, the poet revels as much as Ashbery obviously does in his own bafflement and disorientation may not quite turn William Wordsworth into John Ashbery, it certainly brings them within hailing distance.

Philosophical Reflection on Poetry (2021)

In a series of essays and occasional pieces on poetry and philosophy written over the past forty years, I've gradually developed a conception of poetry and its relation to subjectivity, the self, and consciousness. I want to consider the metaphysical and epistemic status of this conception, but I'll begin by giving a rough characterization of it since, as I say, it has developed in a piecemeal fashion over the years, though some of its main features were laid out in my 1993 essay "Poetry and the Experience of Experience."[1] It sees poetry as basically an expression of human subjectivity and self-consciousness that takes the form of an interior soliloquy, a kind of talking to one's self. This isn't meant to be solipsistic, since one can talk to one's self about anything under the sun; rather, it's meant to be a form of reflection in which I address myself rather than an audience, and thereby portray what the uniquely human experience of self-consciousness is like. It has its roots in the Shakespearean soliloquy, and comes to fruition in romanticism in a very broad sense, in which subjectivity becomes not just the vehicle but the subject of the poem; and it continues in an often disillusioned and fragmented form in modernism and its aftermath. Its underlying impulse is a version of the Kantian experience of the sublime, which involves a conflict or tension between the subjective perspective of the individual consciousness and its objective situation in a natural world that threatens to overwhelm or annihilate it, and which in its high romantic form it tries to transcend—a transcendence that becomes increasingly problematic and unavailable as it continues through modernism and beyond. It's a fundamentally humanistic conception of poetry, since it seeks to give voice to the capacity for self-consciousness that makes us distinctively human and underlies our status as Kantian ends in themselves and the ultimate source of all value. Moreover, in its basis in the self or mind, individual experience and consciousness and their relations to the natural world, it shares many of the originating impulses of philosophy, though it acts on and develops those impulses in very different ways. In particular, philosophical explorations of the mind–body problem or of mental states aim to discover the truth about their nature, whereas poetry explores mental states by trying to portray or capture what it's like to inhabit them, or to see life and the world from a particular conscious viewpoint. Of course, this is an abstract characterization of the conception of poetry I have in mind, and leaves out the actual subjects of the interior conversations with one's self it enacts, something I've tried to flesh out in the philosophical reflections I've mentioned on such individual poets as Wordsworth, T. S. Eliot, Wallace Stevens, Elizabeth Bishop, and John Ashbery.

What might be the basis or justification for a conception of poetry like this, that ties it inherently to interiority and subjectivity? The claim that a particular poem ought to be read subjectively, rather than in a more public or impersonal way, is typically based on the methodology of literary criticism, rather than an appeal to an abstract philosophical conception of poetry. Consider the well-known example of Eliot's "The Waste Land." I think most would agree with Helen Vendler's characterization of it as a phantasmagoria, but what is the underlying impetus of its heightened fantasy? On the most widespread initial reading, it was regarded as a depiction of the deterioration and collapse of contemporary civilization, with the possibility of a partial refuge from this despair in resignation and acceptance. But thanks to critics like Randall Jarrell, it soon became common to read it in a much more personal way, as a portrayal of a psychological and spiritual crisis on the part of its author. And Eliot himself, while disavowing any claim to an authoritative reading of the poem, discouraged seeing it as a "criticism of the contemporary world" or "social criticism," describing it instead as a "relief of a personal and wholly insignificant grouse against life" and "a piece of rhythmical grumbling." My own inclination, influenced by some suggestions of Vijay Seshadri's in his introduction to his recent selection of Eliot's poems, is to see it as a visceral reaction to the carnage of the Great War (as attested to by a letter from his brother-in-law that Eliot forwarded to *The Nation*), combined with the personal crisis and breakdown brought on by Eliot's marriage.[2]

This is certainly a way of coming to a conclusion, however tentative, about how one thinks an individual poem ought to be read; but it can't account for the generality and normative character of the conception of poetry I've been trying to elaborate. In suggesting that poetry's importance lies in its ability to capture and portray human subjectivity, I seem to be making a claim about what the ultimate goal of poetry is, and about what poets should aim at in writing it. I've tried to suggest how this ostensible goal emerges historically out of Shakespeare and Wordsworth, romanticism and modernism, but what about alternative conceptions of poetry that locate its importance in something other than the portrayal of private interiority? What about the idea of modernism more associated with Pound, Williams, Zukofsky, and Charles Olson than Eliot, Stevens, and Ashbery, that stresses the accurate portrayal of the material world and an avoidance of interiority? What about poetry that seeks to be politically efficacious, which seems to require it to be addressed to an audience, rather than taking the form of an interior soliloquy? What about (what's mostly miscalled) "confessional" poetry, that serves as a dramatization of the self to be sure, but distorts it by exaggerating and valorizing it, rather than capturing the oscillation between the subjective and objective views we're able to take of ourselves that renders the individual human consciousness something both ordinary and miraculous? These are conceptions of poetry I find misguided or uninteresting, but how can one reject them without appealing to an essentialistic conception of what poetry is? And isn't one of the legacies of modernism a rejection of the idea that there's something poetry essentially has to be in order to qualify as poetry? Indeed, I've suggested that modernism represents a continuation of romanticism in an attenuated and fragmented form, but inherent in the experience of the individual subjective consciousness is a sense of a freedom from constraints that poetry (or anything else) might try to impose on it—which (as I noted in "The Metaphysical Subject of John Ashbery's Poetry"[3]) led Kant to posit the transcendental subject in the first place, as a way of reconciling our feeling of freedom with our subjugation to the laws of nature. Nothing has become more familiar in the wake of modernism than the idea (from Dada to Flarf) that there's nothing that poetry essentially excludes, and a suspicion of the idea that there are forms of expression that essentially *can't* be poetry. But in the absence of a conception of poetry that delimits it, it's hard to see how one might engage in philosophical reflection about poetry, and what is or isn't important about it. Consider, for example, philosophy of science in its received form, which seeks to describe, explain, and justify scientific practice. It certainly seems to presuppose a conception of what science is—say, a set of hypotheses or a theory possessing characteristics like generality and truth or empirical adequacy (a presupposition I'll return to more skeptically later). Wouldn't philosophical reflection on poetic practice have to presuppose a similarly settled conception of poetry? And if such a conception isn't possible, doesn't that mean that this kind of philosophical reflection on poetry isn't possible either?

    I think an answer to this question is suggested by the kinds of causal or historical accounts of reference put forward by Saul Kripke, Hilary Putnam, and others in the 1970s.[4] On traditional descriptive accounts of reference, what you refer to or talk about when you use a singular or general term is determined by a descriptive concept associated with the term, and you're talking about whatever satisfies that concept. "Aristotle," for instance, might be associated with the description "the student of Plato's who taught Alexander the Great," and when you use the name you refer to the person, if there is one, who satisfies that description. Or the natural kind term "water" might be associated with the concept of a transparent liquid that's a nearly universal solvent, and when you use "water," you're talking about anything that satisfies that concept. But given the shortcomings of descriptive accounts, they were superseded by so-called causal or historical accounts of reference, on which for many singular or general terms, what you refer to or talk about when you use the term is the object or kind of substance to which the term was originally applied, and to which your current use of it is related to or linked by a causal or historical chain of subsequent uses, even if the descriptive concept you associate with it no longer fits that thing or substance, if it ever did. What water is, on this account, isn't determined by a conceptual characterization that distinguished it from everything else and that you're prepared to give, but by the history of your and other people's applications of the term "water."

How might this help us in understanding what we're talking about when we talk about poetry, or what we're doing when we reflect on it philosophically? Since poetry is neither an individual thing nor a natural kind of physical substance, the application of this account of reference to it isn't straightforward, but here is what I have in mind. Poetry is best thought of as defined not conceptually but historically, a kind of generalization of Harold Bloom's idea of poems as responses to previous poems. In *The Anxiety of Influence*, Bloom proposed a basically Freudian account of poetic originality and of the psychological mechanisms whereby a "strong" poet manages to overcome the burden of his or her predecessors and their poems by misreading or revising them, so that the history of *important* poetry is constituted by a sequence of precursor and successor poems standing in certain internal relations to one another.[5] I don't want to endorse the details of this account, which underwent considerable revision at Bloom's own hands, and in any case was originally meant as an account of the psychological relations between individual poets and the poems of their predecessors, rather than between readers and poetry (though Bloom himself was evidence of its applicability to readers, as it clearly influenced how he saw the main lines of English poetry, though he wasn't a poet himself). What I do want to adopt is the idea that the normatively recognizable development of (what we call) poetry and poems is constituted by a sequence of responses of a certain kind to previous poems, which are themselves seen as appropriately related in this way to other, earlier poems and so on backwards. What's important is that this sequence of responses and responses to responses isn't conceptually constrained, or at least isn't completely determined by an articulatable concept of what poetry is or ought to be. Rather, it starts (or we pretend it starts) with certain forms of linguistic expression that engage us in certain ways, and that we feel compelled to continue to engage in. I've been arguing that the main line of poetry running through romanticism and modernism is centered on interiority, though obviously this isn't true of the earliest poetry (the poetry Plato banished from the *Republic* wasn't grounded in subjectivity). What changes over time is the character of the poems that engage us in the way poetry does, so that what makes certain linguistic expressions poetry is the way they engage us, rather than their character or content. Engage us in what ways though? Well, that's hard to say, though it's in ways we feel we can recognize, and that differ from the ways we're engaged by other forms of linguistic expression involved in science, philosophy, politics, or religion. What's important is that our attitude towards these forms of expression isn't a *disinterested* one of assessing them according to certain concepts or rules, and that we continue to be to be engaged in these ways by some forms of expression of this kind and not by others.

This picture of the historical development of poetry has an affinity with Wittgenstein's treatment of following a rule or continuing a series, especially in the form suggested by Kripke in his discussion of Wittgenstein's private language argument.[6] Suppose someone tries to write out the series of numbers that conforms to the order "+2" by writing down the numbers 0, 2, 4, 6, ... up to 1,000. What are the right numbers to write next? The obvious answer seems to be 1,002, 1,004, 1,006, ... But why is this the right continuation, rather than 1,004, 1,008, 1,012, ...? To appeal to the meaning of the order or an articulation of the rule he or she is supposed to be following doesn't help, because the order or rule can be interpreted in different ways that are compatible with either continuation; and other possible answers to the question seem upon examination to be equally unsatisfactory. Should we conclude then that there's simply no such thing as the "correct" way of continuing the series of numbers, and that we're free to go on in any way we feel like? Presumably not, and what seems to me the right way to avoid this conclusion is to appeal to a notion of what Hannah Ginsborg calls *primitive normativity*, which she introduces in an attempt to explain Kant's view of the normativity of aesthetic judgments.[7] The idea is that an acquaintance with the series 0, 2, 4, ... 998, 1,000 simply compels us to regard 1,002 (rather than 1,004) as the correct number to write next, without this judgment of correctness being based on a conception of the rule we think we're supposed to be following or the meaning of a formula we've been given—it's simply *primitive*, a normative judgment made directly in response to the numbers we've been given previously, without an appeal to a prior grasp or understanding of a concept or rule. Leaving aside the question of its plausibility for a moment, I think that the applicability of this answer to the problem of following a numerical rule or continuing a series to the idea of seeing poems as appropriate responses to previous poems is clear enough in a rough and general way, however it might be filled out in detail (though I don't think it can). The kind of direct, intimate engagement with poetry, whether through writing or reading, that I alluded to in the last paragraph can instill in us a conviction that some poems but not others are appropriate responses to it, or ways of continuing to create or identify poems that capture what's important about it, or capture what engaged us in the poems we previously found compelling. But this conviction isn't mediated by a prior conception of what's essential to poetry or what makes it important—it's ultimately just a direct response to it, though one that requires the kind of intimate engagement with it I've been emphasizing.

How plausible is this view of how poetry is constituted? I've been defending a view of poetry centered on interiority, but earlier I noted a range of alternative judgments about what's important in poems, judgments that engage other poets and those who reflect on poetry, ranging from an aversion to interiority and subjectivity, to politically efficacious forms of address directed towards an audience, to melodramatic valorizations of the self. Don't these alternative possibilities indicate that our normative judgments about how poetry should be pursued lack the certainty and determinacy of our judgments about how genuine rules should be followed or numerical series continued? And doesn't this make my proposed account of what philosophical reflection on poetry involves untenable? I don't think so, for it seems to me to represent a strength rather than a weakness of this account, in that it accommodates something important about poetry (and other arts) in the wake of modernism, namely that by their very nature they're inherently problematic. In my comments on Susan Wolf's Tanner Lectures, *Meaning in Life and Why It Matters*, I tried to argue that the fact that we're engaged in creating certain kinds of art can't be a source of comfort and satisfaction that this fact renders our lives meaningful, since the possibility of failure and delusion is inherent in modern art itself, and so our judgments about whether we've been successful in creating it are always tentative and revisable.[8] But if this is right, then the indeterminacy inherent in my proposed account of how poetry is recognized is a reflection of something inherent in modern poetry itself, rather than a weakness in this account of how important poetry is to be delimited from poetry that isn't as central. Our engagement with poetry can indeed instill in us primitive normative convictions and judgments about it. It's just that those convictions and judgments are in principle always open to challenge, and should such disagreements become widespread, persistent, and ineliminable, then the practice of poetry might survive in an attenuated form, but it would lose much of its point and its role in our lives. I don't think that this is the case, but to argue this would require a deeper exploration of the kind of engagement serious reflection on poetry requires than I'm prepared to give now, and I'm not going to pursue the matter here.

But even without a clearer understanding of what this kind of engagement with poetry amounts to, I think it's clear enough to suggest that philosophical reflection on poetry differs in important ways from the philosophical investigation of other issues and practices that matter to us, or at least differs from a familiar ideal of what philosophical inquiry is supposed to be. I've described my writings on poetry and philosophy as "occasional" pieces, written in response to invitations to reflect on them, rather than expressions of systematic views I'd formulated about the relations between the two disciplines; and initially I regarded this as a shortcoming, reflections offered in lieu of more considered and disinterested investigations into the nature of poetry. But I've come to feel that philosophical reflection on poetry is inherently occasional, in that it can only result from specific engagements with poetry, rather than from systematic views about it which might be formulated and defended independently of such practical engagements; and that the results of these occasional practical engagements are inherently tentative and revisable. I began this brief essay by using the example of debates over whether "The Waste Land" should be read as a cultural critique or as an enactment of an individual psychological crisis to illustrate the difference between criticism or interpretation of poetry and philosophical reflection on it, but I'll end by suggesting that the difference between the two isn't as clear as I may have made it seem at the outset. Philosophical reflection is characterized by generality and normativity, but so is the kind of reflective criticism practiced by such critics as James Longenbach and Matthew Bevis. Once we abandon essentialistic philosophizing about poetry and recognize the role of engagement and the occasional character it shares with reflective criticism, the difference between the two begins to seem more like a difference in emphases or areas of interest, rather than a difference in methodology. A familiar ideal of philosophical inquiry is of a conceptual inquiry that is disinterested and rigorous, grounded in a clear understanding of its subject matter and pursued in accordance with objective constraints of consistency and coherence. Wittgenstein's views about language and philosophy in the *Tractatus* were based on a view about the essence of language and thought, a detailed view of them as essentially representational; and much traditional philosophy of science rests on a picture of science as aiming at explanatory theories consisting of exceptionless generalizations and closed under consequence, what Mark Wilson calls the "theory T" view of science.[9] But whether this ideal of disinterested and objective philosophical rigor is tenable is another question. Wittgenstein certainly came to think that the investigation of language had to proceed in a piecemeal fashion based on actual engagements with the multitude of our linguistic practices; and Wilson himself has called into question, on broadly Wittgensteinian grounds, the unified "theory T" conception of science on which much received philosophy of science is based. For the most part I've deferred to the ideal model of rigorous and disinterested philosophical inquiry, at least for some of the core areas of philosophy, if only for the sake of bringing out what still seem to me to be genuine differences between philosophy and poetry itself—though just how clearly these differences can be characterized remains for me an open question. But in the course of writing and thinking about poetry, I've become convinced that the model of disinterested and rigorous investigation isn't a viable one for philosophical reflection about it.

Appendix: Metaphysics and the Mind–Body Problem (2019)

If this is all we need fear from spinach
Then I don't mind so much.[1]

—John Ashbery

1.

In its current form, the mind–body problem is largely an investigation into whether and how a materialist account of consciousness might be possible. Since dualism is regarded as prima facie unacceptable, views of consciousness and conscious states, events, and processes—for example, ones involving subjective first-person viewpoints and qualitative contents—that might encourage it are to be avoided, in pursuit of what might be called an "inside out" strategy of trying to treat mental phenomena as phenomena for which a materialist account doesn't seem implausible. One motivation, for example, for trying to treat conscious states as complex intentional states is that these might be treated in turn as computational or functional states, for which a materialist account seems unproblematic.

I want to propose instead what might be called an "outside in" approach to consciousness and the mind–body problem. Let's just assume that human beings and other higher life forms are, like most other things that uncontroversially exist, completely material entities, and then explore the consequences of the fact that these material entities have mental lives and are, whatever it might mean, subjects of conscious states, events, processes, and properties. I'll argue that while doing so should lead us to endorse a kind of metaphysical dualism, it's a harmless one that not only doesn't have the unacceptable consequences of traditional substance dualism, but even accords with reflective common sense, if we make what I'll also argue are sensible adjustments to our metaphysical and ontological views.

What does it mean to think of ourselves as complex but completely material entities? First, it means that we're made of parts composed of ordinary matter arranged in very complicated ways, and that we, both as a species and as individuals, came into existence as a result of physical or material events and processes (I'll usually prefer to speak of materialism rather than physicalism here because of the unsettled state of the ontological interpretation of contemporary physics). While we'll undoubtedly learn a lot more about the nature of these parts and their systems of arrangement as the sciences that study human organisms' progress, it's pretty certain that we're not going to learn things that will require us to revise our basic understanding of matter or the laws of nature, incomplete as that understanding is. Moreover, these complex material entities are the sites of all kinds of states, events, and processes, straightforwardly physical ones as well as mental ones, about which there's also much to be learned. While mental states, events, and processes have a lot to do with how our brains are structured and what goes on in them, our knowledge of that relationship is still quite limited, though that shouldn't lead us to regard mental phenomena with skepticism, or worry that they might be at odds with thinking of human beings as complex material entities. We're conscious, whatever that means exactly, as well as self-conscious; we're capable of thinking and reasoning in various ways including scientific and philosophical ones; of feeling, believing, understanding, possessing concepts, remembering, and imagining; of deliberating, intending, desiring, willing, and acting; and we're sentient, capable of experiencing sensations of a wide variety of kinds. While we may wonder about the range and nature of all these mental phenomena (or even, as I'll discuss later, whether they really have "natures"), we shouldn't worry at the outset that recognizing most of them as genuine might put the idea that we're entirely material beings at risk. After all, we're just stuff.

(Implicit in this attitude is a repudiation of what David Chalmers calls the "hard problem" of consciousness and the associated possibility of philosophical "zombies," which are supposed to be creatures physiologically identical to us but lacking consciousness.[2] The thought seems to be that in the absence of an explanation of how conscious mentality results from sufficiently complex neural mechanisms, it would be possible, in some sense, to construct, bit by bit, beings with all of our neurological structures and properties, but which nevertheless have no sensations or other conscious experiences at all. But while it's true that we currently lack such an explanation, it doesn't follow that zombies are possible in any sense that threatens materialism, and in fact we know that they aren't. We construct creatures physiologically identical to us bit by bit every day, and they're invariably conscious [barring certain birth defects]. The fact that this construction takes place in the womb rather than in the laboratory is irrelevant to the question of whether it's possible for beings so constructed to be philosophical zombies.)

In the next section, I'll begin by describing the central features of consciousness and conscious mental states that I want to focus on, and then try to defuse the prima facie threat they pose to materialism laid out in Frank Jackson's Knowledge Argument.[3] In the section after that I'll explore some of the metaphysical consequences of this idea of consciousness and explain why they do indeed lead to a kind of dualism. The arguments in this section are almost entirely Cartesian. Parts of the approach to the mind–body problem I'm trying to lay out here were inspired by some ideas of Rogers Albritton's contained in an unpublished paper on Wittgenstein, and in the following section I'll describe those ideas and indicate how I intend to use them. And in the final section, I'll combine the view of the mind and mental states I'm presenting with some metaphysical and ontological proposals to explain why the kind of dualism I'm committed to isn't something materialists should find troubling.

Two general comments. First, it's sometimes suggested that progress on the mind–body problem depends on the progress of neuroscience. Almost nothing I'll say here appeals to neuroscientific knowledge, and in fact I think that the question of the relation of the mind and the body is more a metaphysical than a neuroscientific one. Second, some of the elements of the overall picture I want to present are familiar and much discussed, and I often won't argue for them beyond noting their familiarity and initial plausibility. My aim is to rather to combine these elements into a package that hangs together in a natural way and does justice to consciousness, while rendering it less philosophically problematic than it often seems.

2.

There are two features of consciousness—human consciousness anyway—that I want to emphasize. The first is that it's inherently perspectival: being conscious involves having a subjective first-person point of view, a point of view from which one apprehends or is aware of the various phenomena of which one is aware. This is a familiar enough idea, though difficult to articulate clearly. This kind of viewpoint is what Kant calls a transcendental subject, likening it to "a feeling of existence without the least concept" that underlies the unity of apperception that makes one's various conscious feelings and experiences those of a single consciousness.[4] The early Wittgenstein calls it, after Schoepenhauer, a metaphysical subject, and compares the relation of it to its objects of awareness to the relation of the eye to the visual field.[5] And Thomas Nagel makes it the defining feature of consciousness, and contrasts it with the objective viewpoint of science, which doesn't really have a viewpoint at all, but rather a "view from nowhere."[6] But saying that consciousness is inherently perspectival isn't to say anything about the ontological status or nature of this subjective viewpoint, or even that it has a nature (things I'll discuss later); only that being conscious involves having one.

The second important feature of conscious mental states and processes is that many of them have qualitative contents, in the sense that being in them or experiencing them involves a phenomenal awareness of instances of various sensible qualities, which used to be called ideas of sensible primary and secondary qualities and are now called qualia. These include instantiations of visual, tactile, and auditory qualities or properties, as well as instances of kinds of sensations like pain (and to avoid confusion it's important to think of the qualia we're aware of as instantiations or instances of qualities or properties like redness, rather than of the properties or universals themselves, an awareness of which doesn't really make sense). That conscious states and processes have qualitative contents seems most obviously true of sensations and other vivid experiences, but it's also true to some extent of intentional states and processes like believing, desiring, remembering, intending, and understanding (though intentional states and processes are often largely devoid of qualitative contents, which commends them as models for conscious mental states generally to philosophers hostile to qualia).

These features of consciousness are familiar and plausible enough, though we're far from having an account of how complex material entities like human beings come to have it, an account neuroscience will probably eventually provide. Nevertheless, there are many philosophers, mostly notably Daniel Dennett, who reject them because of a suspicion that accepting them inevitably leads to dualism.[7] To Dennett's credit, I think he's correct in this suspicion, though I don't believe that's a reason to deny subjective viewpoints and qualitative contents. But before saying more about this, I want to consider a well-known argument that a phenomenal awareness of qualitative contents is directly at odds with materialism.

A quick summary of Frank Jackson's Knowledge Argument: Mary is a neuroscientist whose whole life has been spent in a black, gray, and white environment, in which she's acquired through reading all the physical information there is to know about what happens in the world and the brain when someone perceives, say, a red rose. She then leaves this environment and actually sees one. She comes to know something about the experience of seeing a red rose—namely, what redness looks or feels like—she didn't know before. But by hypothesis, she knew all the physical properties of the experience of seeing a red rose. So this new property of the experience of seeing a red rose that she learns about mustn't be a physical property, and so physicalism or materialism must be false.

A well-known objection to this argument, due to David Lewis and others, grants that Mary does acquire new knowledge when she sees a rose, but holds that it isn't propositional knowledge of a nonphysical property, but rather knowledge how, or new abilities she didn't previously have, abilities to recognize, remember, and imagine red things.[8] This response seems inadequate. First, while she may indeed acquire abilities like these, abilities don't generally have qualitative contents as her new experience does, and if she does acquire them, they would seem to be based on her knowledge of this new quale, rather than constitutive of it. Second, this proposal seems open to an empirical objection, for while many people (including myself) report that they can indeed remember and imagine, say, a red room, they can't remember or imagine the qualitative feeling of pain (which was something I first noticed when I was running track in high school: the pain in my legs at the end of a race was excruciating, but I couldn't remember it afterward or imagine experiencing it again in the next race). But if this is so, then our knowledge of what pain feels like can't be identified with an ability to remember or imagine it, since we can't.

I think the correct objection to Jackson's argument is due to Paul Churchland, at least as I read him (which may not be as he intended).[9] He suggests that the propositional physical knowledge of brain states and processes involved in seeing a rose that Mary learns in her black-and-white room is a certain kind of representation of those physical states and processes, but that what she acquires when she finally sees a rose is a different kind of representation of the same physical states and processes, rather than new factual knowledge of an additional nonphysical property of them. Those physical states and processes can be represented both propositionally, as Mary does in her room, or (we might say) phenomenologically, as she does when she sees a rose and actually has them. But they're the same physical states and processes.

Churchland says almost nothing about what he means by a representation, in the sense that both a body of propositions and a quale can count as representations of the same thing (the former obviously contains a lot more information than the latter), so I'll take the liberty of putting his point the way I'd like to understand it, whether or not this is what he has in mind. One familiar kind of representation of something is the appearance it presents to us; and since the most obvious fact about Mary when she leaves her black-and-white room is that she is now *in* the brain states she'd only read about before, it seems plausible to say that when Mary finally sees a rose she acquires, from her first-person subjective viewpoint (which she had even back in her room), a view of the physical brain states she'd learned about earlier, a view she now has by virtue of being in those states herself. In other words, the new representation of those brain states she acquires is the appearance they present to someone who's in them, and the redness of which she becomes aware is a property of that appearance rather than a property of the states themselves. From a third-person objective or scientific viewpoint (which isn't really a viewpoint at all), they have the physical properties that she acquired exhaustive knowledge of in her room. But when she enters into those states herself, she's able to take a subjective first-person view of them she didn't have before, and the view or appearance she apprehends from that subjective point of view instantiates redness.

Of course it's a commonplace that things present appearances to us and often don't have the properties they appear to have, like the trapezoidal appearance of a rectangular object when viewed from an angle. Yet one might be uneasy about extending this commonplace to things other than ordinary sensible objects, like complex physical brain states, and allow that they too can present appearances when "viewed from the inside," as it were, by someone who's in them. But we're already familiar with things other than sensible particulars that present phenomenal appearances when we're in or at them. Consider the physical property of heat, mean molecular kinetic energy. A certain degree of heat appears to us as, and is represented by, a sensation like warmth. While Berkeley was wrong about many things, he was certainly correct in denying that the sensible quality of warmth we feel when our hand is in a bowl of hot water is a property of the hot water it partially represents (though of course he doesn't think it does represent it). More dramatically (and more controversially), consider moments or temporal points, which feel or appear present to us when we're in or at them, and to which we can stand in demonstrative relations and refer to by means of indexicals like "now" or "the present." Some philosophers might deny that moments we're in or at appear to us via a qualitative feeling of, so to speak, *presentness*, and would explain the intuition that I and other philosophers have that they do by the indexicality of temporal terms like "now." But against this, note that spatial terms like "here" are similarly indexical, and yet we don't have the intuition that only one's present location is real, while we (or at least some of us) can least understand the intuition that only the present moment is real and that past and future moments aren't. The familiar feeling that time "flows" in the sense that there's a unique present moment that moves along the ordered sequence of objective temporal moments, whereas space doesn't flow in a comparable sense, can be explained if we allow that each objective moment can present a phenomenal appearance of presentness to us (or to our temporal stages) when we're at it, and that these moments are ordered in a way that each one can present such an appearance at most once to each conscious individual (whereas spatial locations, or their contents, aren't so ordered and can be experienced repeatedly). Of course the phenomenal quality of presentness is harder to describe than the red appearance her brain state presents to Mary when she's in it and which allows her to refer demonstratively to "this state," or "my present state" (for at least we have a vocabulary for that appearance); but it seems to me just as genuine, as genuine as the obvious difference between how 12:05 p.m. November 5, 2019 (when this is being written), appears to me and how 12:05 p.m. November 4, 2019, does. Yet just as the properties of the appearance Mary's brain states present to her when she's in them aren't additional properties of the brain states themselves, so the fact that temporal locations appear present to us when we're in or at them says nothing about the objective nature of time (an open question) and doesn't require us to posit an objective property of presentness to temporal locations in addition to their physical ones (though it's easy to understand the temptation to do so).[10]

If what I've said in this section is at all plausible, it might seem that we have at least a rough sketch of an unproblematic materialist view of consciousness and the mind. We're completely physical or material beings, and though neuroscience is still far from figuring out how we come to have them, we do have conscious mental states involving first-person points of view and qualitative contents, and this fact isn't at odds with the idea that our constitution is entirely material. But unfortunately, the relationship between metaphysics and what's real is more complicated than this sketch suggests.

3.

We're conscious and self-conscious human beings capable of thought and feeling, and in addition to sensations this includes the kinds of conscious thinking and reasoning involved in science, mathematics, philosophy, and psychology (not to mention politics, mythology, art, literature, music, and all our other mental endeavors). And once the genie of a thinking being is out of the bottle, it gets to figure out what's real. It's a perhaps underappreciated point that the question of what's real or what exists is a *question* to be answered by *us*, rather than something automatically settled by the nature of the universe of which we're parts. The fact that we're entirely material beings doesn't preclude us from conceiving of, thinking about, and even affirming the existence of things that aren't material. In a world devoid of conscious reasoning beings like us there wouldn't be any physics, mathematics, or metaphysics, though any truths we've established through them about such a world would still be true of it. But they wouldn't have been established by reasoning in it.

Descartes's *Meditations* is the locus classicus of the ontological status of minds and mental phenomena, and though his arguments there are usually dismissed, I think that when properly understood they're almost entirely correct, though exactly what they establish can easily be misunderstood, as it was by Descartes himself. I'll start with a summary of the reasoning of the cogito, and then turn to the subsequent arguments for the immateriality of the mind.

The cogito isn't so much an argument or proof as it is the outcome of a method for ascertaining which of one's beliefs could conceivably be mistaken. To apply this method to a particular belief of mine, I have to formulate a skeptical hypothesis to the effect that even though the belief is false, it seems to me for all the world that it's true, in the sense that I have all the subjective thoughts, feelings, sensations, and memories I would have if it were true, even though it isn't. I then ask myself if I can rule out this hypothesis, and if on reflection I have to admit that I can't, I have to conclude that I could be mistaken in my belief. This method seems prima facie effective when applied to objective beliefs about the external world, including beliefs about my physical body. But when I try to apply it to my belief in my own existence expressed by the proposition "I exist" it fails, since the skeptical hypothesis I have to formulate to call it into question is self-contradictory or incoherent (for it asserts both that *I* don't exist and that it seems to *me* that I do), and so can be ruled out immediately. This reasoning seems to me entirely correct, though it's important to emphasize it's not a deductive inference to the conclusion that I exist, but rather the realization that the most general rational method for showing how beliefs could be mistaken fails when applied to my belief in my own existence, so that the truth of this belief (assuming I have it) is undeniable.

The failure of this "method of doubt" also explains the second, less noticed part of the cogito, which establishes the undeniability of my subjective beliefs about my own thoughts and sensations. Consider my belief that I have a sensation of warmth. To call it into question I'd have to formulate a skeptical hypothesis that says that I don't actually have a sensation of warmth, though it seems to me that I do, in the sense that I have all the thoughts and sensations I'd have if I really did have a sensation of warmth. But this hypothesis is also self-contradictory, since the sensation I'd have if I did have a sensation of warmth is just the sensation of warmth itself. (Incidentally, the suggestion in the previous section that sensations can be thought of as appearances of brain states and processes supports this, since in general appearances don't have appearances distinct from themselves: the appearance of an appearance is just the appearance itself. And it also supports the familiar claim that if, for instance, it seems to you that you're in pain, i.e., it feels to you like you are, then you *are* in pain.)

Let me make a few observations about this reasoning before turning to the case for dualism. The first part of the cogito assumes that we do have a belief expressed by "I exist" and that "I" in this proposition is referential. And the second assumes that we do have subjective beliefs about our sensations, thoughts, and other states of mind (or what Descartes called ideas), and that the propositions expressing these beliefs are also referential. Various philosophers, including, many say, Wittgenstein, whom I'll discuss in the next section, have disputed both of these assumptions. But I think that even though their contents are obscure, the intuition that we do have such beliefs is strong enough that it shouldn't be abandoned unless it really does lead to absurdity, which I don't think it does. Kant's characterization of the transcendental subject as "a feeling of existence without the least concept" could just as well have used "conviction" instead of "feeling," and he equated it with the fact that "I think" can be prefaced to all of our judgments. What my belief in my own existence comes to, as far as the cogito goes (and never mind what Descartes goes on to say about the self), is a conviction or feeling of the perspectival character of conscious thought and experience, or the reality of my first-person point of view. And similarly, acknowledging the reality of qualitative subjective beliefs amounts to little more than acknowledging our self-conscious awareness of the qualitative character of conscious mental states and processes. Put another way, if consciousness involves an awareness of how things appear from a subjective point of view, then beliefs about our own sensations and existence are beliefs about those appearances and that viewpoint. And if they're referential, what the cogito establishes is that the truth of those beliefs in the reality of those appearances and that viewpoint is undeniable. Of course, some of our subjective beliefs—for example, beliefs about our own beliefs, desires, and memories—aren't necessarily qualitative, and while the second part of the cogito concerns them too, it's really the qualitative ones that are most important for our purposes here and figure in the most straightforward arguments for dualism.

Descartes gives four arguments for the immateriality of minds and mental phenomena. Three of them are somewhat tendentious, based on the essence or nature of the mind, our knowledge of the mind, and the possibility of a disembodied mind. But the main argument, based on Leibnitz's law, is so straightforward that it hardly seems like an "argument" in a deep sense at all: conscious viewpoints, and the things we apprehend from those viewpoints, are existing particulars, but there aren't any physical particulars in the brain (or anywhere else) to identify them with. Any physical particulars must have physical properties like mass, shape, location, and having parts, but it doesn't even make sense to attribute such properties to a first-person viewpoint or self. This argument is based on Leibniz's law only in a negative sense, since it doesn't attribute positive properties to conscious viewpoints and then argue that they aren't possessed by material entities, but only maintains that concepts applicable to material entities don't apply to them. Its real force lies in the absurdity of imagining that we might discover that a person's seat of consciousness or conscious viewpoint is really just a particular clump of cells in the brain, or something like the pineal gland. The reality is that when our brains are in certain very complex physical states we're conscious of having an undeniable particular subjective viewpoint, even though there's no physical entity in the brain that corresponds to it.

The argument for the immateriality of the qualitative mental phenomena we apprehend from that viewpoint is even more straightforward and obvious: this apprehension involves an awareness of the instantiation of sensible qualities like redness, and if qualities are instantiated, it must be by particulars of some sort; but since there aren't any physical particulars in the brain that possess qualities like this, they must be instantiated by immaterial particulars.[11] This argument only applies to mental phenomena that involve an awareness of sensible qualities, and not all mental phenomena do. Of course, there are other arguments for dualism, like the argument from the possibility of a disembodied mind, that apply to mental phenomena generally. But the arguments based on Leibniz's law seem to me sufficient to show that the conception of consciousness I've adopted here does indeed have immaterialist metaphysical consequences, and that philosophers like Dennett are correct in thinking that the admission of qualia and seats of consciousness is the first step down the (very short) garden path to dualism, which they find unacceptable. That it's such a short path makes these arguments seem sophistical, but once we accept viewpoints, qualia, and the reasoning of the cogito, I don't see how to get out of them. Of course, if dualism really is unacceptable then there must be something wrong with them. I don't think it is, but before trying to explain why, I want to look at some suggestions Rogers Albritton makes in the course of trying to figure out Wittgenstein's puzzling remarks about the reality of sensations like pain and other mental phenomena.

4.

"A Difficulty in Understanding Wittgenstein" is a circulated but unpublished paper by Rogers Albritton from 1982 in which he tries to make sense of *Philosophical Investigations* 304–8, sections in which Wittgenstein characterizes pain as "a grammatical fiction," "not a *something*, but not a *nothing* either," and suggests that "the physical problem about mental states and processes" arises because of a "decisive movement in the conjuring trick" in which we "talk about states and processes and leave their nature undecided," assuming that eventually we'll come to learn more about them and find out what their nature really is. Albritton's aim in the paper is to figure out what Wittgenstein's view of the ontological status of pains and other mental phenomena actually comes to, and in the course of it he considers and rejects a number of familiar suggestions about what he thinks the problem with them is. These include the suggestion that the problem is about pain in particular, rather than psychological phenomena generally; that psychological assertions don't convey thoughts; that there's no such thing as pain; that the problem is how to categorize them (as objects, states, processes, events, etc.); that concepts like pain or remembering are family resemblance concepts; that the problem is their inwardness or privacy, which makes ostensive definitions of terms for them impossible; and that psychological terms aren't referential and that their apparent reference can be paraphrased away (e.g., by treating them adverbially).

His positive suggestions are characteristically tentative and inconclusive, but they include at least these points. First, apparent psychological reference really is reference: when I talk about pain or use the word "pain," I really am referring to pain, and similarly for talk about remembering, intending, and even meaning—I'm really referring to them. But second, and (at least at first) paradoxically, what I'm referring to when I refer to pain (and the rest) isn't a "something," whatever that might mean. Yet rather than taking it to mean that

I'm not referring to anything, he proposes that we take it to mean that what I'm referring to is "metaphysically thin," in contrast with what I refer to when I talk about stars, digestion, or lightning. And what the metaphysical thinness of these objects of psychological reference seems to amount to is that they don't have "natures" that we can hope to learn something about, by contrast, presumably (and here I'm fleshing out and possibly going beyond what he says) with metaphysically robust phenomena, things "in the world," like lightning, about whose nature we reasonably speculated before discovering it's an electrical discharge. The decisive movement in the conjuring trick of *Investigations* 308 isn't the mere positing of processes like remembering (at least if denying them would mean denying, say, that we ever remember anything), but processes with natures to be investigated, discovered, and filled in by neuroscience or philosophy or whatever. If I ask myself what I actually know about what, say, happens when I remember something, the honest answer is next to nothing, for though I may be aware of some of the conscious accompaniments of remembering, they're not "the remembering itself." This isn't because of ignorance on my part, but because there isn't anything to know or find out about it. No doubt much happens in my brain when I'm in pain or remember something, but I know almost nothing about it; and as for the various conscious sensations I'm actually aware of, they don't add up to anything substantial, even if I'm mistakenly tempted to assume they do. The upshot is that pains and the rest are real all right, just not as real as a lot of other things. Albritton: "Pain a something after all, just metaphysically *thin*. Maybe as thin as a *number*, though *particular*."

Never mind whether this is a helpful way to read Wittgenstein (though I think it is). While it's offered as a view about psychological phenomena generally, not just conscious ones (as well as phenomena like meaning that aren't clearly psychological), I think applying it to conscious minds and mental phenomena helps both to make sense of them and their relation to the brain and body, and to explain why the dualism of the previous section isn't troubling. The three elements of the view Albritton sketches that I want to adopt are, first, that our talk about the aspects of consciousness I've described is referential; second, that our criteria for determining what's real are broadly Quinean, in that that we're ontologically committed to things the propositions we accept as true quantify over or refer to; and third, the very un-Quinean idea that the things we're ontologically committed to and have to regard as real aren't all on a metaphysical par, and that some (like minds, pains, and other sensations, and perhaps numbers and other things too) are less real than things like brains, bodies, stars, and the fundamental objects of physics (if only we could figure out what they were).

5.

Albritton likens the metaphysical thinness of mental particulars to that of numbers. Something that's always puzzled me is the difference between the attitudes philosophers take towards mathematical Platonism and dualism. While Platonism isn't enthusiastically embraced by many, it tends to be regarded as something we have to live with unless we can find a way out of the apparent ontological commitment of the physical sciences to numbers and other mathematical entities. Harty Field's attempt to do this didn't succeed,[12] Quine and Putnam are prepared to live with indispensability arguments for Platonism,[13] and while the espousal of mathematical-realism by most working mathematicians doesn't carry much positive weight, no one takes it as a reason to think of mathematics as an endeavor on an intellectual par with astrology. By contrast, an acceptance of dualism, even a grudging one, or a suspicion that, like Platonism, it's unavoidable, is extremely rare, and it's usually regarded instead as a kind of superstition on a par with believing in "Ghostbusters" or ectoplasm.

No doubt this difference in attitude is due to the fact that traditional Cartesian dualism treats mental entities as immaterial substances possessing essences and causal powers, which on the face of it seems incompatible with the settled laws of physics. Mathematical entities aren't saddled with this baggage, even if, as Paul Benacerraf has argued, this makes our knowledge of them problematic (arguments I don't think have found wide acceptance).[14] But dualism can be stripped of that baggage too, and while this may threaten to drive a wedge between our mental lives and our behavior, I don't think it has to.

For reasons I'll turn to in a minute, the idea that not all things that exist are on an ontological par, or that there might be degrees of being, isn't current in contemporary philosophy, and so it's worth pointing out that it's both venerable and intuitive. From Plato and Aristotle until the twentieth century, the thought that some of the things we recognize, talk, and think about aren't all equally real is a familiar one (remember primary vs. secondary substances), and examples of things whose existence doesn't seem as robust as that of ordinary material particulars are easy to think of—numbers and sets certainly (most of us know the sinking feeling you get when you first try to convince a roomful of beginning philosophy students that in addition to the tables and chairs in the room there's another thing called the set of them—not to mention the null set), but also fictional characters, possibilia, mereological sums, properties, countries, money, mental images, appearances, and so on. Mark Wilson has often written about the particularly interesting phenomena of rainbows, which we've all seen and typically believe to consist of droplets of water occupying a curved region of space located a certain distance from us and refracting light rays of different wavelengths.[15] But they aren't physical things of this sort at all: they're not hallucinations, yet they're "private" to observers in different locations, and unlike atmospheric phenomena like lightning, there's nothing to find out about what they really are. But it's hard to deny that there are rainbows—after all, we see them, and even agree about where they are.

Of course the reason the metaphysical idea of different degrees of being fell out of favor is that with the rise of analytic philosophy, philosophers attempted to replace traditional metaphysical disputes, which they came to think of as empty, with issues in the philosophy of language. Carnap proposed, for instance, that while a question like whether there's an odd perfect number is an "internal" one to be formulated and addressed using the language of mathematics, the apparently metaphysical question of whether numbers actually exist is an "external" question about whether we should choose to adopt the language of mathematics, and that this question isn't a factual one.[16] Similarly, Ayer maintained that the apparently metaphysical issue of the reality of material objects was really a question of whether to use a "material object language" or a "phenomenal language," and since the choice between them is a matter of convention and convenience, it's not a question with an objectively right or wrong answer.[17]

For various reasons these strategies proved unworkable. Their leading current incarnation is the idea, due to Eli Hirsch and others, of quantifier variance.[18] Quantifier variance maintains that the quantifiers aren't univocal, and that there's no fact of the matter as to which meanings we should assign to them. Someone who claims that there are entities like mereological sums uses an existential quantifier with a domain that includes them, while someone who denies that there are uses an existential quantifier with a domain that doesn't. But the difference between them isn't over the metaphysical question of whether mereological sums really exist, but over the choice between two equally legitimate readings of the existential quantifier. I'm persuaded though by arguments (sometimes called "collapse" arguments) by Bob Hale and Crispin Wright and others that quantifier variance isn't a coherent view, for it appears that someone using the quantifier with the supposedly smaller domain is committed to the domain of the quantifier with the larger one.[19] Also, though it isn't an objection to any of these linguistic strategies, it's worth remarking that they're all motivated by the intuition that some things are ontologically less robust than others, combined with a desire to account for this intuition nonmetaphysically. And since none of these strategies seem to me to succeed, I'm suggesting we just relax and accept the intuition that there are a lot of real things, but that some are more real than others, at face value as a metaphysical one.

Only a few current philosophers take the idea of degrees or ways of being seriously. Jody Azzouni, for instance (who also uses "thin" to characterize lesser existents), suggests ontological independence from us and causal powers as marks of "thick" existents, which I find plausible.[20] But it's Kris McDaniel's recent explorations of different ways of being that I find most helpful in fleshing out the kind of dualism I'm proposing.[21] He tries to explain the sense in which certain entities exist but are, intuitively, ontologically degenerate or second-rate, diminished beings he calls "almost nothings." He focuses on the example of holes, since the literature on them is extensive, but the account he offers can, he thinks, be extended to other entities that might have the diminished status of almost nothings too. Holes and other such entities enjoy what he calls "being by courtesy," which he characterizes as follows.[22] First, we're ontologically committed to them by virtue of accepting truths that quantify over or otherwise refer to them, references that can't, either in principle or in any practical sense, be paraphrased away. And second, "the existence and qualitative nature of almost nothings is completely determined by the existence and qualitative nature of positive entities,"[23] which almost nothings aren't. Holes, for example, aren't concrete material entities, but their existence and their properties and relations are determined by the properties of their metaphysically robust concrete material hosts.

McDaniel suggests that this account might be extended to other putative examples of almost nothings, and he discusses, among others, fictional entities and possibilia. But it seems to me to capture nicely the kind of metaphysical thinness I want to attribute to selves and qualia. First, cogito-like reasoning commits us to recognizing their existence, and arguments for dualism establish that they're immaterial. And second, we're metaphysically robust material beings with the kinds of mental lives and the abilities to reason about them that establish the truths about these metaphysically thin almost nothings, and so commit us to their existence. If selves and qualia are, as I've suggested, simply appearances of complex brain states apprehended from the inside, as it were, then they're completely determined by and dependent on the existence and natures of metaphysically robust material human beings, just as holes are determined by and dependent on the existence and natures of their material hosts, which is the mark of beings by courtesy.

If McDaniel's account of ontologically diminished beings is plausible, as I think it is, and can be extended in this way to selves and qualia, it helps clarify the kind of dualism I proposed earlier, which says that conscious "selves" or the occupants of first-person subjective viewpoints, as well as the qualitative mental phenomena they apprehend, are both real and that their reality isn't problematic, in the sense that their existence is compatible with the overall materialism about human beings I described at the outset, and is compatible with settled laws of science. Consider the self. The cogito establishes its undeniability (or the undeniability of the truth of my belief that I exist), but this undeniability is grounded in the perspectival nature of our conscious mental states, which are in turn grounded in our complex material brain states. But immediately after establishing its existence, Descartes says things about it that go beyond what the cogito establishes, which is just that "I" refers to something undeniably real. He attributes an essence or nature to it (namely, to think), which is the first step towards treating it as a "substance," or something metaphysically robust. And he completes this journey towards substantiality by attributing causal powers to it, maintaining that it causally interacts with the material body to which it's somehow "attached."

Neither of these claims about the self is justified. Its supposed nature or essence, the ability to think, isn't really an ability to do anything substantive at all. The "thoughts" it has aren't produced by it if, as I've suggested, they're metaphysically thin appearances of brain states and processes; and its even thinner reality consists in the fact that if these appearances or qualia are apprehended from a subjective point of view, then that viewpoint must be real and something must exist to apprehend them. But as Hume noted, we never apprehend this self, and as Kant said, we have no concept of it. It's rather, as Berkeley replied when asked to justify a belief in the existence of minds (which, like the material objects he denies, he admits are never perceived either), that their existence is implied by the existence of ideas, for if ideas exist and only exist when they're perceived, there must be something (let's call it a mind) to perceive them. But none of this entitles us to attribute a substantial essence or nature to the thing whose existence (or the undeniability of whose existence) is established by the cogito. As for the attribution of causal powers to it, not only does this go beyond the reasoning of the cogito; it also makes no sense if the self is insubstantial and incapable of doing anything but apprehend appearances. And of course it's also in tension with apparently settled aspects of physics.

But don't minds and thoughts obviously causally affect material bodies, in the sense that it seems that how we act and behave is largely the result of what we think and feel? And if immaterialism about minds and thoughts is incompatible with this, mustn't it be false? I don't think so, and to explain why let me return to the question of what we really know about the metaphysically thin sensations, feelings, intentions, beliefs, desires, and memories of which we're aware. I'll borrow Dennett's notion of what he calls "heterophenomenology," an imaginary narrative describing in detail all the phenomenal conscious states, events, and processes we're convinced we're aware of (of course his goal is to explain why we're convinced of it even though it isn't true, whereas I think it's largely true).[24] This narrative, Wittgenstein would point out, is spottier and less continuous than we assume it to be in positing mental states and processes, but it captures all we're phenomenally aware of regarding our own thoughts and sensations, and contains as well phenomenal representations of our environment and how we take ourselves to act and behave. What it doesn't contain is an awareness of any causal relations between our sensations and thoughts and our behavior. Rather, it ordinarily possesses a familiar feeling of continuity and coherence, even if it's somewhat fragmentary, a continuity and coherence that feel disrupted at times, when our thoughts and behavior feel out of whack with each other. Now suppose, as I've suggested, that what this heterophenomenological narrative is describing are the appearances our own brain states and processes present to us when we're in them or having them (along with phenomenal appearances of own behavior). The narrative's coherence would simply be a reflection of the fact that these brain states and process are causing our behavior as they ordinarily do and whose appearances we've become used to, and would be disrupted when this causal etiology is unusual or abnormal. But the causal powers underlying the coherence or incoherence of the narrative belong to the brain states and processes themselves, not to their appearances—which is a point about substances and their appearances generally. This is not an unfamiliar idea. Benjamin Libet's experiments about the causal antecedents of behavior are inconclusive and open to a variety of interpretations, but they're consonant with the idea that what causes our behavior is the brain activity underlying our phenomenal representations of it, rather than the conscious representations themselves.[25]

But doesn't this account simply dismiss out of hand familiar folk psychological causal explanations of behavior in terms of beliefs, desires, and intentions? I don't think it does, at least not in an objectionable way, for it leaves open the question of the truth of these models of explanation, versus various alternative eliminativist models. Remember that while our heterophenomenological narratives refer to some phenomenal representations of ostensible beliefs, desires, and intentions, they're fragmentary and discontinuous, and most of our purported beliefs and other intentional states aren't consciously represented in them. It seems to me that whether the causal explanatory models of folk psychology are true depends on whether the taxonomy of the intentional states they posit corresponds roughly to the taxonomy of the causal explanatory brain states and processes neuroscience eventually discovers. If it does, then they're largely true, and all my account does is attribute the causal powers to the underlying brain states rather than to their phenomenal appearances, something that isn't at odds with our conscious experience. If it doesn't, then they're not true anyway, so the fact that my account doesn't validate them is no objection to it. I myself find it hard to believe that they'll turn out to be entirely false, but that's another question.

All this sounds like epiphenomenalism, in which conscious phenomena are caused by physical goings-on in the brain but are themselves causally inert. And it almost is, but with the twist that the immaterial conscious phenomena aren't really caused by the brain states and processes of which they're appearances. At the beginning of this paper, I suggested that we're wholly material beings with brains of sufficient complexity that we have the kinds of mental lives we do. We don't know yet how our brains give rise to mentality, though as I said, I don't think it's the philosophically "hard" problem that Chalmers thinks it is. No doubt it involves brain states that represent and monitor, in a materialistically unproblematic way, themselves and other brain states (and the fact that our mentality is due to our physical complexity should dispel the suggestion that in order to allow for consciousness we might have to embrace panpsychism, a suggestion I've always found ridiculous). Having the kinds of mental capacities we do enables us to think and engage in scientific, mathematical, and philosophical reasoning in an attempt to describe and explain the world and ourselves; and when we reason metaphysically about our mental lives we find ourselves ontologically committed to the immaterial viewpoints and qualitative contents of conscious thoughts. But these immaterial mental entities aren't caused by the brain, an idea that makes no sense. Recall Albritton's comparison of metaphysically thin pains to numbers. Our mental capacities allow us to engage in scientific and mathematical reasoning, and when we reflect philosophically on the results of this reasoning we find ourselves ontologically committed to the existence of numbers and other mathematical objects. But of course it would be ridiculous to say that because our brains endow us with the ability to reason in ways that commit us to numbers, our brains somehow cause them, the way physiological processes in our heads cause hairs to grow on them.

If this makes sense, then the dualism I've offered here doesn't have the features that make dualism in its traditional form seem superstitious and prima facie unacceptable; while at the same time it does justice to conscious thoughts and experiences and doesn't force us to deny obvious facts about them in order to avoid it. It allows that our mentality is grounded in material facts about us, but acknowledges that our exercise of the reasoning powers that are part of that mentality leads us to conclusions about causally inefficacious immaterial entities. Some may complain that what I've said here does nothing to explain how our mentality *is* grounded in our physical nature; and indeed it doesn't. But that seems like a task for neuroscience rather than metaphysics, which only needs to show, if I'm right, that dualism isn't unreasonable and isn't incompatible with the completion of that task. It might also be complained that there's little that's original about the elements of and the arguments for the view of consciousness I've offered here, and that I've merely repackaged them in a way that may seem, as Russell said about postulating, to have the advantage of theft over honest toil. This is probably true too. All I've tried to show is that these elements and arguments hang together to form a coherent view of conscious mentality that's neither unreasonable in itself nor denies anything obvious. And I simply can't see what's wrong with it.

Notes

1 The Metaphysical Subject of John Ashbery's Poetry (1978)

1. In John Ashbery, *Houseboat Days* (New York: Viking, 1978).
2. Kenneth Koch is said to have once remarked that the paradigmatic Ashbery line would be "It wants to go to bed with us."
3. Ashbery, *Houseboat Days*.
4. David Kalstone, *Five Temperaments* (New York: Oxford University Press, 1977), 195.
5. Ashbery, *Houseboat Days*.
6. In John Ashbery, *The Double Dream of Spring* (New York: Dutton, 1970).
7. Ashbery, *Houseboat Days*.
8. In John Ashbery, *Self-Portrait in a Convex Mirror* (New York: Viking, 1975).
9. In John Ashbery, *Rivers and Mountains* (New York: Holt, Rinehart and Winston, 1965).
10. In John Ashbery, *Three Poems* (New York: Viking, 1972).
11. David Hume, *A Treatise of Human Nature* (1739), bk. 1, pt. 4, sec. 6.
12. Immanuel Kant, *Prolegomena to Any Future Metaphysics* (1785), pt. 3, sec. 46.
13. Immanuel Kant, *Critique of Pure Reason* (1781), A350.
14. Arthur Schopenhauer, *The World as Will and Representation* (1818), bk. 2, sec. 278.
15. Ludwig Wittgenstein, *Tractatus Logico-Philosophicus* (1921; London: Routledge and Kegan Paul, 1961), 5.63–6.41.
16. Kalstone, *Five Temperaments*, 187.
17. Kant, *Prolegomena*, pt. 3, sec. 46.
18. Ashbery, *The Double Dream of Spring*.
19. Marjorie Perloff, *Frank O'Hara: Poet among Painters* (New York: Braziller, 1977), 135–6.
20. Hume, *Treatise*, bk. 1, pt. 4, sec. 6.
21. In Frank O'Hara, *Collected Poems* (New York: Alfred A. Knopf, 1971).
22. Kalstone, *Five Temperaments*, 195.
23. Perloff, *Frank O'Hara*, 136.
24. Ashbery, *Three Poems*.
25. John Ashbery, "Art" column, *New York* 11, no. 35 (August 28, 1978), 104.
26. Ibid.

2 Contrary Impulses: The Tension between Poetry and Theory (1990)

1 Helen Vendler, "Married to Hurry and Grim Song," *New Yorker*, July 27, 1987.
2 Rene Wellek and Austin Warren, *Theory of Literature*, 3rd ed. (New York: Harcourt Brace Jovanovich, 1977), 37.
3 For a reading of Derrida's arguments in *Limited Inc* along these lines, together with an interesting comparison of his views with those of philosophers like W. V. Quine and Donald Davidson, see Samuel T. Wheeler III, "Indeterminacy of French Interpretation: Derrida and Davidson," in *Truth and Interpretation: Perspectives on the Philosophy of Donald Davidson*, ed. Ernest LePore (Oxford: Oxford University Press, 1986), 477–94.
4 J. Hillis Miller, *The Linguistic Moment* (Princeton, NJ: Princeton University Press, 1985), 4.
5 Miller, *Linguistic Moment*, 45, 55.
6 "On Kitsch: A Symposium," *Salmagundi* 85–6 (Winter–Spring 1990), 279.
7 Ibid., 282, 306.
8 Ludwig Wittgenstein, *Philosophical Investigations*, 3rd ed., trans. G. E. M. Anscombe (New York: Macmillan, 1968), 223.
9 For a useful exposition of Cavell's views, especially regarding their relation to literature and deconstruction, see Michael Fischer, *Stanley Cavell and Literary Skepticism* (Chicago: University of Chicago Press, 1989).
10 See Thomas Nagel, *The View from Nowhere* (Oxford: Oxford University Press, 1986).
11 John Ashbery, "Fantasia on 'The Nut-Brown Maid,'" *Houseboat Days* (New York: Viking, 1977).
12 See Allen Grossman, "Summa Lyrica: A Primer of the Commonplaces in Speculative Poetics," *Western Humanities Review* 44 (Spring 1990), 5–138; and *Against Our Vanishing* (Boston, MA: Rowan Tree Press, 1981), 14–15.

3 Poetry and the Experience of Experience (1993)

1 Pierre Bourdieu, *The Field of Cultural Production: Essays on Art and Literature* (New York: Columbia University Press), 34.
2 Samuel Johnson, *Preface to Shakespeare* (1765), in *Selected Poetry and Prose*, ed. Frank Brady and W. K. Wimsatt (Berkeley: University of California Press, 1977), 301, 303.
3 Mary Kinzie, *The Cure of Poetry in an Age of Prose* (Chicago: University of Chicago Press, 1993), 1.
4 John Locke, *An Essay Concerning Human Understanding* (1690), bk. 2, chap. 8, sec. 8.
5 George Berkeley, *Three Dialogues between Hylas and Philonous* (1713), First Dialogue.
6 Descartes, *The Passions of the Soul* (1649).

7 T. S. Elliot, a talk on "Tradition and the Practice of Poetry" (1936), *Southern Review*, ed. A Walton Litz, 21, no. 4 (October 1985): 883.
8 Harry Frankfurt, *The Importance of What We Care About* (New York: Cambridge University Press, 1988).
9 David Hume, *A Treatise on Human Nature* (1739), bk. 1, pt. 4, sec. 6.
10 Immanuel Kant, *Prolegomena to Any Future Metaphysics* (1783), pt. 3, sec. 46.
11 Thomas Nagel, *The View from Nowhere* (New York: Oxford University Press, 1986); and *Mortal Questions* (New York: Cambridge University Press, 1979).
12 Paul Churchland, *Scientific Realism and the Plasticity of Mind* (New York: Cambridge University Press, 1979); Daniel Dennett, *Consciousness Explained* (Boston, MA: Little, Brown, 1991).
13 Richard Rorty, *Objectivity, Relativism, and Truth* (New York: Cambridge University Press, 1991).
14 Rorty, "Putnam and the Relativist Menace," *Journal of Philosophy* 90, no. 9 (September 1993): 457.
15 Gilles Deleuze and Felix Guattari, *Anti-Oedepius: Capitalism and Schizophrenia* (Minneapolis: University of Minnesota Press, 1983), 17, 19.
16 Nagel, *View from Nowhere*, 86. But Nagel is ambivalent with regard to "property dualism," which merely adds qualitative properties to the world's real properties.
17 The quotations in this paragraph are from Allen Grossman, *The Sighted Singer* (Baltimore, MD: Johns Hopkins University Press, 1992), 6, 306. The third quotation is Grossman's own citation from Kant's *Foundations of the Metaphysics of Morals* (1785), sec. 2.
18 The quotations in this paragraph are from Kant, *Critique of Judgment* (1790), bk. 2, sec. 28.
19 Nagel, "The Absurd," *Mortal Questions*.
20 Ibid., 23.
21 In John Ashbery, *Rivers and Mountains* (New York: Holt, Rinehart and Winston, 1966).
22 Ludwig Wittgenstein, *Tractatus Logico-Philosophicus* (1921; London: Routledge and Kegan Paul, 1961), 6.45.
23 All quotations are from the 1805 version of *The Prelude*. Neil Hertz discusses some of the following passages in chapters 3 and 10 of *The End of the Line: Essays on Psychoanalysis and the Sublime* (New York: Columbia University Press, 1985).
24 In John Ashbery, *Self-Portrait in a Convex Mirror* (New York: Viking, 1975).

4 The Romance of Realism (1996)

1 I. A. Richards, *Coleridge on Imagination* (New York: Norton, 1950), 145.
2 Ibid., 147.

3 Steven Knapp, *Personification and the Sublime* (Cambridge, MA: Harvard University Press, 1985), 3.
4 Stanley Cavell, *In Quest of the Ordinary* (Chicago: University of Chicago Press, 1988), 4.
5 Ibid., 154–5.
6 Cavell, "Knowing and Acknowledging," in *Must We Mean What We Say* (New York: Scribner's, 1969).
7 Cavell, *In Quest of the Ordinary*, 4.
8 Ibid., 44–5.
9 Harold Bloom, "The Internalization of Quest-Romance," in *Romanticism and Consciousness*, ed. Harold Bloom (New York: Norton, 1970), 9.
10 Ibid., 8.
11 Ibid., 16.
12 Paul de Man, "Intentional Structure of the Romantic Image," in Bloom, *Romanticism and Consciousness*, 70.
13 Ibid.
14 Ibid., 75.
15 Ibid., 76–7.
16 Michael Dummett, *Truth and Other Enigmas* (Cambridge, MA: Harvard University Press, 1978), xxxix.
17 In Elizabeth Bishop, *The Complete Poems, 1927–1979* (New York: Farrar, Straus and Giroux, 1983).
18 Ibid.
19 Ibid.
20 David Kalstone, *Becoming a Poet* (New York: Farrar, Straus and Giroux, 1989), 67.
21 Helen Vendler, "Apollo's Harsher Songs," *Part of Nature, Part of Us* (Cambridge, MA: Harvard University Press, 1980).

5 Poetry at One Remove (1998)

1 Quoted without reference by Steven Knapp in *Personification and the Sublime* (Cambridge, MA: Harvard University Press, 1985), 3.
2 Immanuel Kant, *Critique of Judgement*, trans. Werner S. Pluhar (Indianapolis: Hackett, 1987), pt.1, bk. 2, secs. 28–9.
3 Christine Korsgaard, *The Sources of Normativity* (Cambridge, MA: Cambridge University Press, 1996), chap. 3.
4 Ibid., 118.
5 Bernard Williams, "Persons, Character and Morality," *Moral Luck* (Cambridge, MA: Cambridge University Press, 1981), 18.
6 Ludwig Wittgenstein, *Philosophical Investigations*, 3rd. ed., trans. G. E. M. Anscombe (New York: Macmillan, 1968), sec. 109.

7 Ibid., sec. 133.
8 T. S. Eliot "East Coker," in *The Complete Poems and Plays, 1909–1950* (New York: Harcourt, Brace and World, 1952), 11, 71–2.
9 Quoted without reference by Roger Kimball in "A Metaphysical Loss Adjuster," *TLS*, no. 4946 (January 16, 1998): 29.

6 Thought and Poetry (2000)

* This paper was written for a nonphilosophical audience and presented as part of a panel, "Poetry and the Curriculum," organized by Willard Spiegelman at the meeting of the Association of Literary Scholars and Critics in Chicago in October 2000.
1 These have been collected in *Poetry at One Remove* (Ann Arbor: University of Michigan Press, 2000).
2 See "The Metaphysical Subject of John Ashbery's Poetry" in *Poetry at One Remove*.
3 See "The Romance of Realism" in *Poetry at One Remove*.
4 Rene Descartes, *Meditations on First Philosophy* (1641), Meditation VI.
5 Immanuel Kant, *Prolegomena to Any Future Metaphysics* (1783), pt. 3, sec. 46.
6 Immanuel Kant, *Critique of Pure Reason* (1781), A350.
7 David Hume, *A Treatise of Human Nature* (1789), bk. 1, pt. 4, sec. 6.
8 Daniel Dennett, *Consciousness Explained* (Boston, MA: Little, Brown, 1991).
9 E.g., in "What Is It Like to Be a Bat," *Philosophical Review* 83 (1974): 435–50.
10 The example is taken from W. D. Hart, *The Engines of the Soul* (Cambridge, MA: Cambridge University Press, 1988).
11 David Kalstone, *Becoming a Poet* (New York: Farrar, Straus and Giroux, 1989), 67.
12 In Elizabeth Bishop, *The Complete Poems, 1927–1979* (New York: Farrar, Straus and Giroux, 1983).

7 Styles of Temptation and Refusal in Wittgenstein and Stevens (2003)

* This was originally presented at a symposium of the Modernist Studies Association in 2002.

8 On John Ashbery's "Definition of Blue" (2007)

* This was originally presented at a conference on John Ashbery at The New School in 2007.

9 Wittgenstein and Lyric Subjectivity (2007)

* This was originally presented at a symposium of the Association of Literary Scholars and Critics in 2007.

10 Comments on Susan Wolf's *Meaning in Life and Why It Matters* (2007)

1 I am grateful to Carla Bagnoli, Tom Bamberger, William Bristow, John Godfrey, Edward Hinchman, James Longenbach, Charles North, Susan Stewart, Arthur Szathmary, and Susan Wolf for discussions and suggestions.

11 Poetry and Truth (2009)

* This is an edited and somewhat revised transcript of a lecture I gave to a general audience when I served as the Elliston Poet in Residence at the University of Cincinnati in May 2008.
1 "Poetry and Abstract Thought." As I was preparing this transcript I learned to my pleasant surprise that Lamarque's paper is contained in this volume of *Midwest Studies in Philosophy*.
2 In "Poetry and the Experience of Experience," in my *Poetry at One Remove: Essays* (Ann Arbor: University of Michigan Press, 2000).
3 See my "Knowledge and the Norms of Assertion," *Australasian Journal of Philosophy* (forthcoming).
4 See Alexander Nehamas's paper "Plato and the Mass Media" in his *Virtues of Authenticity: Essays on Plato and Socrates* (Princeton, NJ: Princeton University Press, 1998).
5 See Cora Diamond's paper "Throwing Away the Ladder" in her *The Realistic Spirit* (Cambridge, MA: MIT Press, 1991).
6 See my paper "Thought and Poetry," *Midwest Studies in Philosophy* 25 (2001): 5–11.
7 Harry Frankfurt, *On Bullshit* (Princeton, NJ: Princeton University Press, 2005).

12 Poetry, Philosophy, and the Syntax of Reflection

1 See my essays "Thought and Poetry," *Midwest Studies in Philosophy*, 2002, and "Poetry and the Experience of Experience" and "The Romance of Realism," both in other essays in the collection.

2 See "Contrary Impulses: The Tension between Theory and Poetry" and "The Romance of Realism," both in *Poetry at One Remove*.
3 Thomas Nagel, "The Absurd," in *Mortal Questions* (Cambridge, MA: Cambridge University Press, 1979). I have described his generalization of the experience of the sublime in "Poetry and the Experience of Experience."
4 Charles Olson, "Projective Verse," in Donald M. Allen, ed., *The New American Poetry 1945–1960* (New York: Grove Press, 1960).
5 See my "Introduction: Poetry and the Structure of Speculation" in *Poetry at One Remove* and "Thought and Poetry."
6 In "Poetry and Truth," *Midwest Studies in Philosophy*, 2009.
7 If memory serves, I've adapted this example from W. D. Hart's *The Engines of the Soul* (Cambridge, MA: Cambridge University Press, 1988).
8 Kenneth Winkler, "Causal Realism and Hume's Revisions of the *Enquiry*," in *Matters of Reason: Essays in Early Modern British Philosophy* (Oxford University Press, forthcoming).
9 Anthony Grafton, *The Footnote: A Curious History* (Cambridge, MA: Harvard University Press, 1997).
10 Marjorie Perloff, *Wittgenstein's Ladder* (Chicago: University of Chicago Press, 1996).
11 In "Wittgenstein and Lyric Subjectivity," in *Literary Imagination*, 2007; see also my "Styles of Temptation and Refusal in Wittgenstein and Stevens," *Fulcrum*, 2003.
12 Rogers Albritton, "A Difficulty in Understanding Wittgenstein," unpublished typescript, 1982. Underlining in the original.

15 On Helen Vendler's Wallace Stevens (2014)

* This was originally presented at a panel of the Modern Language Association in 2014.

18 Philosophical Reflection on Poetry (2021)

1 John Koethe, "Poetry and the Experience of Experience," in *Thought and Poetry: Essays on Poetry and Philosophy* (London: Bloomsbury, 2022).
2 Vijay Seshadri, *The Essential T. S. Eliot* (New York: Ecco, 2020).
3 John Koethe, "The Metaphysical Subject of John Ashbery's Poetry," in *Thought and Poetry*.
4 Saul Kripke, *Naming and Necessity* (Cambridge, MA: Harvard University Press, 1980); Hilary Putnam, "The Meaning of 'Meaning,'" in *Philosophical Papers Vol. 2* (Cambridge, MA: Cambridge University Press, 1975).

5 Harold Bloom, *The Anxiety of Influence* (New York: Oxford University Press, 1973).
6 Saul Kripke, *Wittgenstein on Rules and Private Language* (Cambridge, MA: Harvard University Press, 1982).
7 Hannah Ginsborg, *The Normativity of Nature: Essays on Kant's Critique of Judgement* (New York: Oxford University Press, 2015).
8 Susan Wolf, *Meaning in Life and Why It Matters* (Princeton, NJ: Princeton University Press, 2010).
9 Mark Wilson, *Wandering Significance* (New York: Oxford University Press, 2008).

Appendix: Metaphysics and the Mind–Body Problem (2019)

1 John Ashbery's "Farm Implements and Rutabagas in a Landscape" from *The Double Dream of Spring*.
2 David Chalmers, *The Conscious Mind* (New York: Oxford University Press, 1996).
3 Frank Jackson, "Epiphenomenal Qualia," *Philosophical Quarterly* 22, no. 127 (April 1982): 127–36.
4 Immanuel Kant, *Prolegomena for Any Future Metaphysics*, sec. 46.
5 Ludwig Wittgenstein, *Tractatus Logico-Philosophicus*, 5.641.
6 Thomas Nagel, *The View from Nowhere* (New York: Oxford University Press, 1986).
7 Daniel Dennett, *Consciousness Explained* (New York: Little, Brown, 1991). Dennett doesn't explicitly argue that an acceptance of qualia and seats of consciousness inevitably leads to dualism, but his rejection of anything that smacks of immaterialism is so strong that it seems clear that he thinks it does.
8 David Lewis, "What Experience Teaches," *Proceedings of the Russellian Society (University of Sydney)* 13 (1985): 29–57.
9 Paul Churchland, "Reduction, Qualia, and the Direct Introspection of Brain States," *Journal of Philosophy* 82, no. 1 (January 1985): 8–28.
10 Craig Callender, in What Makes Time Special (New York: Oxford University Press, 2017), discusses the parallel between the idea that we have a phenomenal experience of the present and Jackson's Knowledge Argument. He's skeptical of the comparison, both because he thinks that the intuition that there is such a phenomenal quality might be accounted for by indexicality, and because he doubts that moments might possess an objective property of presentness. He doesn't, as far as I can see, consider the possibility that presentness might be a phenomenal property of how moments appear to us, rather than of moments themselves.
11 The reader may suspect that an extension of this argument would lead to an endorsement of sense-data. I think that given some plausible assumptions about the structure of the mental states involved in perceptual experiences, this suspicion is correct. But I hasten to add that such sense-data would be as metaphysically

harmless as the kind of dualism I'm endorsing, and that they needn't have the central role in epistemology that traditional foundationalism assigns to them.
12 Hartry Field, *Science without Numbers: A Defence of Nominalsim* (Princeton, NJ: Princeton University Press, 1980).
13 W. V. Quine, "Carnap and Logical Truth," in *The Ways of Paradox and Other Essays* (Cambridge, MA: Harvard University Press, 1976); Hilary Putnam, "Philosophy of Logic," in *Mathematics Matter and Method* (New York: Cambridge University Press, 1979).
14 Paul Benacerraf, "Mathematical Truth," *Journal of Philosophy* 70, no. 19 (1973): 661–79.
15 Mark Wilson, *Wandering Significance: An Essay on Conceptual Behavior* (Oxford: Oxford University Press, 2006).
16 Rudolf Carnap, "Empiricism, Semantics, and Ontology," *Revue Internationale de Philosophie* 4 (1950): 40–50.
17 A. J. Ayer, *Language, Truth, and Logic* (London: Victor Gollancz, 1936).
18 Eli Hirsch, *Quantifier Variance and Realism* (New York: Oxford University Press, 2011).
19 Bob Hale and Crispin Wright, "The Metaontology of Abstraction," in David Chalmers and David Manley (eds.), *Metametaphysics* (New York: Oxford University Press, 2009).
20 Jody Azzouni, *Deflating Existential Consequence: A Case for Nominalism* (New York: Oxford University Press, 2004).
21 Kris McDaniel, "Degrees of Being," *Philosophers' Imprint* 13 (2013); McDaniel, *The Fragmentation of Being* (Oxford: Oxford University Press, 2017).
22 McDaniel, *The Fragmentation of Being*, chapter 5. McDaniel develops his account in a framework involving fundamental "natural" restricted existential quantifiers that range over only metaphysically robust or fully real entities. For various reasons I'm uneasy with this framework and have tried to abstract his account of being by courtesy from it.
23 McDaniel, *The Fragmentation of Being*, p. 143.
24 Dennett, *Consciousness Explained*, 72–9.
25 Benjamin Libet et al., "Unconscious Cerebral Initiative and the Role of Conscious Will," *Behavioral and Brain Sciences* 8 (1985): 529–66.

Bibliography

Albritton, Rogers, "A Difficulty in Understanding Wittgenstein" (unpublished), 1982.
Ayer, Alfred Jules, *Language, Truth, and Logic*, London: Victor Gollanez, 1936.
Azzouni, Jody, *Deflating Existential Consequence: A Case for Nominalism*, New York: Oxford Univ. Press, 2004.
Benacerraf, Paul, "Mathematical Truth," *Journal of Philosophy*, Vol. 70, No. 19 (1973), 661–79.
Callender, Craig, *What Makes Time Special*, New York: Oxford Univ. Press, 2017.
Caranap, Rudolf, "Empiricism, Semantics, and Ontology," *Revue Internattionale de Philosophie*, Vol. 4 (1950), 40–50.
Chalmers, David, *The Conscious Mind*, New York: Oxford Univ. Press, 1996.
Churchland, Paul, "Reduction, Qualia, and the Direct Introspection of Brain States," *Journal of Philosophy*, Vol. 82, No. 1 (January 1985), 8–28.
Dennett, Daniel, *Consciousness Explained*, New York: Little, Brown, 1991.
Field, Hartry, *Science without Numbers: A Defence of Nominalism*, Princeton, NJ: Princeton Univ. Press, 1980.
Hale, Bob, and Wright, Crispin, "The Metaontology of Abstraction," in Chalmers, David, and Manley, David, eds., *Metamataphysics*, New York: Oxford Univ. Press, 2009.
Hirsch, Eli, *Quantifier Variance and Realism*, New York: Oxford Univ. Press, 2011.
Jackson, Frank, "Epiphenomenal Qualia," *Philosophical Quarterly*, Vol. 22, No. 127 (April 1982), 127–36.
Kant, Immanuel, *Prolegomena for Any Future Metaphysics*, Cambridge: Cambridge University Press, 2004.
Lewis, David, "What Experience Teaches," *Proceedings of the Russellian Society (Univ. of Sydney)*, Vol. 13 (1985), 29–57.
Libet, Benjamin, et al., "Unconscious Cerebral Initiative and the Role of Conscious Will," *Behavioral and Brain Sciences*, Vol. 8 (1985), 529–66.
McDaniel, Kris, "Degrees of Being," *Philosophers Imprint*, Vol. 13 (2013).
Nagel, Thomas, *The View from Nowhere*, New York: Oxford Univ. Press, 1986.
Putnam, Hilary, "Philosophy of Logic," in *Mathematics Matter and Method*, New York: Cambridge Univ. Press, 1979.
Quine, Willard Van Orman, "Carnap and Logical Truth," in *The Ways of Paradox and Other Essays*, Cambridge, MA: Harvard Univ. Press, 1976.
Wilson, Mark, *Wandering Significance: An Essay on Conceptual Behavior*, Oxford: Oxford Univ. Press, 2006.
Wittgenstein, Ludwig, *Tractatus Logico-Philosophicus*, London: Routeledge and Keegan Paul, 1961.

Index

abstractness 48
academic writing 22
affinity 95, 98, 153, 159
   with antirealism 56
   between consciousness and world 53
   O'Hara with Hume 18
   of philosophical doctrine 58
   between poetry and philosophy 1
   in poets of consciousness 58
   with realism 51, 58, 74
affirmation 44, 54, 152
   of interiority 60
   ontological 42
   problematic 52
   of subjective consciousness 62
   of subjectivity 52, 55–7, 65, 68, 73, 118
Albritton, Rogers 83, 127, 165, 173, 180
   "Difficulty in Understanding Wittgenstein, A" 99, 173
Alighieri, Dante 103
Allen, Donald
   New American Poetry 21
Alone with America (Howard) 21
American transcendentalism 53. *See also* transcendentalism
Anglo-American philosophy 133
animism 52–3
antirealism 51, 53, 56–8, 61. *See also* realism
anxiety 33, 40, 53, 97, 120
Anxiety of Influence, The (Bloom) 158
Apollinaire, Guillaume 102
Appiah, Anthony 138
"Archaic Torso of Apollo" (Rilke) 135
Ariosto, Ludovico
   Orlando Furioso 151
Aristophanes
   Clouds, The 117
Aristotle 40, 158, 175
Art and Literature 129
Ashbery, John 5–7, 9–19, 103, 142, 144, 153, 156–7

"As I pursued my bodily functions" 92
"As One Put Drunk into the Packet Boat" 91
"Blue Sonata" 13
"Chateau Hardware, The" 92
"Clepsydra" 13, 94, 124, 129–33
conception of self in poetry 10
"Daffy Duck in Hollywood" 10–11
"Definition of Blue" 13, 91–2
Double Dream of Spring, The 91–2
"Fantasia on 'The Nut-Brown Maid'" 11–12, 30
Girls on the Run 103
"Grand Galop" 131, 153
"It was always November there" 92
"Little birds/Used to collect along the fence, The" 92
"Recital, The" 14
on religions 102
Rivers and Mountains 91
"Self-Portrait: and "Flow Chart" 47
"Self-Portrait in a Convex Mirror" 13, 46, 91, 153
"Skaters, The" 45
"Soonest Mended" 131, 153
"Sortes Vergilianae" 105
Tennis Court Oath, The 91, 129
Three Poems 5, 47, 125, 154
"Time is sorting us all out" 12
transcendental subject 74
"Tuesday Evening" 153
"Wet Casements" 13
Where Shall I Wander 91
"Wolf Ridge" 91
"As I pursued my bodily functions" (Ashbery) 92
"As One Put Drunk into the Packet Boat" (Ashbery) 91
assertion 24, 111–12
assessment 25, 56, 103, 126, 128
   philosophical argument 49
   standard of 39

Asylum (Morrel) 19
"As You Leave the Room" (Stevens) 88
"At Pleasure Bay" (Pinsky) 47
"At the Fishhouses" (Bishop) 111–12
attitudes 50, 53, 56, 82, 95–6, 142, 159, 164, 175
　propositional 39, 48
　reorientation 28
　representation of experience 33
　towards human communicative practices 30
　towards one's experience 44
　towards subjectivity 40, 45
　unselfconscious 29
Auden, W. H. 5
"Auroras of Autumn, The" (Stevens) 47, 87–8
Austin, J. L. 53
　dismissal of skepticism 82
autobiographical poem 17
Ayer, A. J. 50–1, 176
Azzouni, Jody 177

Bachmann, Ingborg 93
Banquet Years, The (Shattuck) 102
"Beauty is truth, truth beauty" (Keats) 122
Beckett, Samuel 93, 126
beliefs
　about the natural order 36
　and concepts 56
　desires and 36
　illusory 36
　and imagination 35
　objective 170
　ostensible 180
　subjective 170–1
　and thoughts 51
　unintelligibility 30
Benacerraf, Paul 175
Berkeley, George 168, 178
Bernhard, Thomas 93, 126
Bernstein, Charles 126
Berrigan, Ted 105
Berryman, John 9
Beryl of the Biplane 91
Bevis, Matthew 161
　Wordsworth's Fun 147–54
Bishop, Elizabeth 6, 11, 47, 63, 79, 136, 144, 156

"At the Fishhouses" 111–12
"Branches of the date-palms look like files, The" 58
"First Death in Nova Scotia" 58
"Fish, The" 58
"In the Waiting Room" 77–8, 100, 114, 118, 122, 136
"Moose, The" 153
"Over 2,000 Illustrations and a Complete Concordance" 58–9, 120, 136
"Quai d'Orleans" 59
Black Mountain School 141
Blackmur, R. P. 63
Blade Runner 92
Bloom, Harold 4, 54, 57, 97, 116
　Anxiety of Influence, The 158
　idea of poetry 113
　Shakespeare: The Invention of the Human 4, 95, 110
"Blue Sonata" (Ashbery) 13
Bradley, F. H. 7
"Branches of the date-palms look like files, The" (Bishop) 58
Brooke, Rupert
　"Soldier, The" 26
Brooks, Cleanth
　Well-Wrought Urn, The 111
"Burnt Norton" (Eliot) 105

Callender, Craig
　What Makes Time Special 188 n.10
Captive, The (Proust) 109
Carnap, Rudolf 176
Cartesian 16, 24, 28, 70
　conception of mentality 98
　dualism 74, 118, 119, 122, 135
　immateriality 150
causation 42, 119, 134, 136
Cavell, Stanley 28, 53–4, 104, 138
Chalmers, David 164, 180
"Chateau Hardware, The" (Ashbery) 92
Churchland, Paul 167
Civil War 145
"Clepsydra" (Ashbery) 13, 94, 124, 129–32
Clouds, The (Aristophanes) 117
Cocteau, Jean 103
Coleridge, Samuel Taylor 2, 50, 53

Coleridge on Imagination (Richards) 50
"Comedian as the Letter C, The"
    (Stevens) 84–5
"confessional" poetry 109, 157
conscious/consciousness 15, 165
    awareness 61
    experience 6, 8, 15, 39, 155, 164–5
    "hard problem" of 164
    immaterial 179
    mental states/mentality 23, 75, 164–6,
        180–1
    with realism 57
    reasoning 170
    reflection 37
    reflexive 45
    and self-conscious 169
    self excluded 77
    self-reflective 67
    sensations 174
    subjective 6, 34, 52–3, 58, 62, 68, 144
    thought/thinking 38, 169, 180
    transcendental subject of 57
    unitary 11
    unproblematic materialist view of 169
Consciousness Explained (Dennett) 75
"Constructor, The" (Koethe) 126, 144
contemporary poetics/poetry 21, 34,
    38, 63–4, 107, 125–6, 141, 148,
    152–3
contemporary theory 22, 34, 40
contrary impulses 21–31
    contemporary theory 22
    institutionalization of poetry 26–7
    logocentrism 25
Creeley, Robert 93, 126
critical theory 23
Critique of Judgment, The (Kant) 65, 149
Critique of Pure Reason (Kant) 43
Crito (Socrates) 49
cultural studies 21, 23
Culture and Value (Wittgenstein) 97

"Daffy Duck in Hollywood"
    (Ashbery) 10–11
Darger, Henry
    *Story of the Vivian Girls, in What Is Known
        as the Realms of the Unreal, The* 103
Davidson, Donald 23
"Day Lady Died, The" (O'Hara) 109

deconstruction 23
    antiphilosophical rhetoric of 25
    critique of metaphysics 25
    impulse 25
    philosophical 23–4, 82
    poetry and 23
    protophilosophical 30
deconstructive theory 27
"Definition of Blue" (Ashbery) 13,
    91–2
deflationism 95
de Man, Paul 55–7
Dennett, Daniel 38, 166, 172, 179,
    188 n.7
    Consciousness Explained 75
depiction 1, 24, 33–4, 43, 58, 156
Derrida, Jacques 23, 31
Descartes, Renè 14–15, 35, 74, 118,
    171, 178
    immateriality 172
    Meditations 170
    Second Meditation 34
    views on emotions as internal
        perceptions 48
"desires wordlessness" 134
detrimental effects 65
Diamond, Cora 82, 113
Dickenson, Emily
    "I Heard a Fly Buzz When I Died" 77
"Difficulty in Understanding Wittgenstein,
    A" (Albritton) 99, 173
Dionysian 38
discursive philosophy 138–9
distinctness of the self 76, 118, 122
Don Quixote 70
Double Dream of Spring, The
    (Ashbery) 91–2
dualism 8, 71, 75
    arguments 100, 114, 172
    Cartesian 74, 98, 118–19, 122, 135,
        150, 175
    metaphysical 163
    mind–body 84
    philosophical 7, 70, 114, 122
    Platonism and 175
    substance 163
Duchamp, Marcel 103
Dummett, Michael 58
Duncan, Robert 144

"East Coker" (Eliot) 70
Edmonds, David
   Wittgenstein's Poker 82
Eidinow, John
   Wittgenstein's Poker 82
Eliot, T. S. 5–7, 22, 35, 48, 110, 117, 144, 156–7
   "Burnt Norton" 105
   "East Coker" 70
   Four Quartets 142
   "Gerontion" 141
   "Little Gidding" 108
   "Waste Land, The" 141–2, 156, 161
   "We had the experience but missed the meaning" 125
emotion 150
   abstract 48
   and experience 100
   and personality 100
   prelinguistic cognitive and 24
   propositional attitudes 48
   resonance 64
   and sensation 35
   visceral 36
End of Beauty, The (Graham) 21
England 22
epistemological skepticism 53
ethics 71, 82
eudaimonia ("flourishing") 40
evocation 43, 86
excitement and fear 36
experience 33–48
   conscious/consciousness 6, 8, 15, 39, 155, 164–5
   and emotion 100
   representation 42–8
   scope of 34–40
   subjective 40–2
expression 42
   of emotion and personality 100
   of human subjectivity 155
   and interpretation 25
   language and 30
   linguistic 159
   in poetry 3
   of romantic futility 96
   of subjectivity 66
   of thought/experience 23–4, 26, 29

"Falling Water" (Koethe) 145
fanaticism 52, 65
"Fantasia on 'The Nut-Brown Maid'" (Ashbery) 11–12, 30
fear 1, 8, 36, 78, 87, 131
feeling 2–3
   abstract 48
   of astonishment 136
   of being threatened 6
   of continuity and coherence 179
   of diminution 135, 149–50
   experience of 7
   of freedom 157
   of pain 167
   and perception 35
   perception and 35
   unmediated expression 24
feminist criticism 23
Fermat's Last Theorem 48
Field, Harty 175
"First Death in Nova Scotia" (Bishop) 58
"Fish, The" (Bishop) 58
folk psychology 38, 179
Forbidden Planet 92
Foucault, Michel 103
Four Quartets (Eliot) 142
Frankfurt, Harry 36, 138
   On Bullshit 115

"Gerontion" (Eliot) 141
Gide, Andrè 103
Ginsborg, Hannah
   primitive normativity 159
Girls on the Run (Ashbery) 103
Goldbert, Mike 109
Goodman, Nelson 57
Grafton, Anthony 125
Graham, Jorie 91
   End of Beauty, The 21
Grand Canyon 43
"Grand Galop" (Ashbery) 131, 153
Great War 156
Grossman, Allen 31, 42, 91
Guermantes' way of social circulation 10

Hale, Bob 176
Hart, Kevin 147
Hass, Robert
   "Meditation at Lagunitas" 124

Heidegger, Martin 3
Hemingway, Ernest 145
heterophenomenology 38, 179
Hirsch, Eli 176
Howard, Richard
  Alone with America 21
human consciousness 143, 157, 165. *See also* conscious/consciousness
humanism 5, 143–5
human subjectivity 155–6
Hume, David 14–15, 17–18, 36–7, 41, 74, 126–7, 178
  analysis of causation 119, 136
"Hymn to Life" (Schuyler) 47

I am the world (The microcosm) (Wittgenstein) 143
idealism 57
  philosophical 50, 82
  and realism 50
identity
  limited 67
  poetic 67–8, 70–1
  practical 66–7, 69–70
  professional 71
  sexual 67
"I do this/I do that" (O'Hara) 119
"I have wasted my life" (Wright) 134–5
"I Heard a Fly Buzz When I Died" (Dickenson) 77
illusory beliefs 36. *See also* beliefs
immaterialism 179, 188 n.7
incidental effects 65
"Inconceivable idea of the sun, The" (Stevens) 86
individualism 5, 52
infinite magnitude 43
institutional explanations 22
institutionalization of poetry 26–7
instrumental poetry 29
"In the Waiting Room" (Bishop) 77–8, 100, 114, 118, 122, 136
intrinsic explanations 22
It Must Be Abstract (Stevens) 86
It Must Change (Stevens) 86
It Must Give Pleasure (Stevens) 86
"It was always November there" (Ashbery) 92

Jackson, Frank 165–6, 188 n.10
James, Henry 125
Jarman, Mark
  Late Wisconsin Spring, The 153
Jarrell, Randall 26, 63, 141, 156
John, Berryman 63
Johns, Jasper 93
Johnson, Samuel
  Preface to Shakespeare 33
Jollimore, Troy 117

Kalstone, David 16, 59, 77, 144
Kant, I. 6, 15, 17, 19, 34–5, 37, 41, 44, 47–8, 73–5, 87, 96, 143, 149, 155, 159, 178
  condition of rational raving 58
  Critique of Judgment, The 65, 149
  Critique of Pure Reason 43
  dualism 122
  dynamical sublime 52, 65, 67, 119, 150
  ethics 71
  fanaticism 52, 65
  rational raving 65
  transcendental subject 165
Keats, John
  "Beauty is truth, truth beauty" 122
Kinzie, Mary 34, 124, 134–5
Knapp, Steven 52
Korsgaard, Christine 66, 138
  Sources of Normativity, The 66
Kripke, Saul 23, 94, 157

"*La Duree*" (Koethe) 145
Lamarque, Peter 107, 111, 113–14
Language Poetry 27, 29, 93
Language Poets 120, 126
Late Wisconsin Spring, The (Jarman) 153
Laurencin, Marie 102
"Lecture on Ethics, A" (Wittgenstein) 82, 97, 136
Leibnitz's law 172
Levinas, Emmanuel 31
Lewis, David 167
Life Studies (Lowell) 17
linguistic construction 26
linguistic moment 24
Linguistic Moment, The (Miller) 24
literary criticism 6, 156
"Little birds/Used to collect along the fence, The" (Ashbery) 92

"Little Gidding" (Eliot) 108
Locke, John 35, 134
logical positivism/positivists 43, 50
logocentrism 25
Longenbach, James 129, 161
Lowell, Robert 9, 58, 63, 109–10
  Life Studies 17
Ludwig Wittgenstein: The Duty of Genius (Monk) 97
"Lying in a Hammock at William Duffy's Farm in Pine Island, Minnesota" (Wright) 123–4, 134
Lyrical Ballads (Wordsworth) 54
lyric philosophy 134–5, 137–9
lyric subjectivity 93–100
lyric thought 137

Marxist analysis 23
materialism 8, 75, 164–7. *See also* immaterialism
materialization 79
McDaniel, Kris 177
Meaning in Life and Why It Matters (Wolf) 101–5, 160
meditation
  abstract 5, 145
  romantic poetic 95
  social 145
  and speculation 65
"Meditation at Lagunitas" (Hass) 124
Meditations (Descartes) 170
meditative individualism 5
meditative poets 7
Menard, Pierre 70
mentality
  and agency 34
  conscious 23, 75, 164–6, 180–1
  and language 24
  physical complexity 180
  self and 93
metaphysical dualism 163. *See also* dualism
metaphysical subject 16, 18–19
"Metaphysical Subject of John Ashbery's Poetry, The" (Koethe) 157
metaphysical theory 83
metaphysicians 138
metaphysics 163–81
metonomy 43

microcosm 143–5
Miller, J. Hillis
  Linguistic Moment, The 24
Milton, John
  Paradise Lost 52
mind-body problem 163–81
modernism 5–6, 22, 89, 156
modernist poetry 21–2, 153
Molesworth, Charles 26
Monk, Ray
  Ludwig Wittgenstein: The Duty of Genius 97
"Mont Blanc" (Shelley) 61
Moore, Marianne 6
  "Octopus, An" 47, 130
"Moose, The" (Bishop) 153
moral deliberation 67
moral obligations 66
"Morning of the Poem, The" (Schuyler) 47
Morrel, Owen
  Asylum 19
"Music" (O'Hara) 17
mysteries of animism 53

Nagel, Thomas 6, 28, 37, 42, 44–5, 75, 138, 166
narrative voice 27
National Geographic 77
Nauman, Bruce 93
Nehamas, Alexander 112
Nemerov, Howard 117
neopragmatism 34, 39
neuroscience 165–6, 169, 174, 180
New American Poetry (Allen) 21
New Criticism 22–3, 26, 43, 63
New York 64, 81
New York School 64, 105
nine-to-five philosophy 121, 133
Ninety-Fifth Street (Koethe) 145
nonpsychological subject/self 10–11
North, Charles 117
"Notes toward a Supreme Fiction" (Stevens) 125

objectification 42, 55, 61, 65
Objectivists 141
obligation 66–8, 73, 97, 100

"Octopus, An" (Moore) 47, 130
O'Hara, Frank 14, 18, 123, 144
    "Day Lady Died, The" 109
    "I do this/I do that" 119
    "Music" 17
Olson, Charles 5, 115, 119, 144, 157
    "Projective Verse" 120
"'O mercy!' to myself I cried, /'If Lucy should be dead!'" (Wordsworth) 148
On Bullshit (Frankfurt) 115
On Extended Wings (Vendler) 141
Orlando Furioso (Ariosto) 151
Oulipo 93, 121
"Over 2,000 Illustrations and a Complete Concordance" (Bishop) 58–9, 120, 136

panpsychism 180
pantheism 54
Panza, Sancho 151
Paradise Lost (Milton) 52
Parfit, Derek 138
Paris Review, The 97
Part of Nature, Part of Us (Vendler) 142
Pasternak, Boris
    Safe Conduct: An Autobiography, and Other Writings 17
pathetic fallacy 52–3
perception 15
    commotions 35
    and feeling 34–5
    internal 48
    of passion 15
    phenomenology 117
    representation and 115
Perloff, Marjorie 17, 94–5
    Wittgenstein's Ladder 93, 126
perplexity 133–9
personality 9–11, 13–14, 16–17, 19, 69, 98, 100
personification risks 52
Phaedo (Plato) 1
philosophical deconstruction 24
philosophical dualism 7, 70, 114, 122. *See also* dualism
Philosophical Investigations (Wittgenstein) 81, 109, 173
philosophical poetry 7, 117, 122. *See also* poetry

philosophical realism 5, 30, 49, 51, 56, 58, 74
philosophical reflection 155–62
philosophy
    Anglo-American 133
    discursive 138
    lyric 134–5, 137–9
    nine-to-five 121, 133
    and poetry 1–6, 117–18, 120, 135
physicalism 167
Picasso, Pablo 102–3
Pinsky, Robert
    "At Pleasure Bay" 47
Plath, Sylvia 112
Plato 97, 134, 175
    and dualism 175
    opposition to poetry 1–2, 50
    Phaedo 1
    Republic 112, 117, 159
plausibility 133–9
poetic identity 68, 71
Poetry at One Remove 63–72
Popper, Karl 81
positivism, logical 50
possibility of the self 76
postmodernism 5
Pound, Ezra 5, 157
practical identity 66–7
pragmatists 39
Preface to Shakespeare (Johnson) 33
prejudice about poetry 5
Prelude, The (Wordsworth) 46, 62, 77, 119, 135–6, 148, 150–4
presentness 152, 154, 168–9, 188 n.10
primitive normativity 159
professional identity 71. *See also* identity
"Projective Verse" (Olson) 120
Proust, Marcel 35, 109, 145
    Captive, The 109
    Remembrance of Things Past 9, 109
    Sweet Cheat Gone, The 109
psychoanalysis 23
psychological ego 10–11
Putnam, Hilary 157
    trivial semantic conventionalism 121

"Quai d'Orleans" (Bishop) 59
qualia 166, 172, 177–8, 188 n.7

Quine, W. V. 23
Quixote, Don 151

Rawls, John 138
realism 49–62
　critics of 58
　critique of 57
　denial of 51–2
　extreme 61
　first doctrine 50
　and idealism 50
　philosophical 5, 30, 49, 51, 56, 58, 74
　and romanticism 50, 52, 57
reception theory 23
"Recital, The" (Ashbery) 14
Remembrance of Things Past (Proust) 9, 109
renunciation 87
representation of experience 33, 42–8. *See also* experience
Republic (Plato) 112, 117, 159
resemblance 15, 41–2, 99, 138, 173
"Resolution and Independence" (Wordsworth) 153
rhapsodic fallacy 34–5, 39, 45, 124, 134–5
Rhie, Bernie 94
Richards, I. A. 51
　Coleridge on Imagination 50
Rilke, Rainer Maria
　"Archaic Torso of Apollo" 135
　"You must change your life" 135
Rivers and Mountains (Ashbery) 91, 129
Robbe-Grillet, Alain 103
Rock, The (Vendler) 59–61, 142
romanticism 5–6, 28–9, 34
　central impulse of 52
　and lyric philosophy 134
　and modernism 156
　poetry 33
　and realism 50, 52, 57
　valorization of consciousness with realism 57
　Wordsworthian 67
romantic lyricism 96, 127
Rorty, Richard 39, 57, 98
Rosenthal, M. L. 58
ROTC Kills (Koethe) 145
Rousseau, Henri 102–3

Roussel, Raymond 103, 120
Russell, Bertrand 82

Safe Conduct: An Autobiography, and Other Writings (Pasternak) 17
Sally's Hair (Koethe) 145
Scanlon, Thomas 138
Schopenhauer, Arthur 15, 74, 165
Schuyler, James 144
　"Hymn to Life" 47
　"Morning of the Poem, The" 47
Schwartz, Delmore 63
Second Meditation (Descartes) 34
"Secret Amplitude, The" (Koethe) 107, 114, 144
self-consciousness 22, 37, 39, 113, 143, 150, 152, 155, 169
selfless self 55
"Self-Portrait: and "Flow Chart" (Ashbery) 47
"Self-Portrait in a Convex Mirror" (Ashbery) 13, 46, 91, 153
semantic theory 83
Seshadri, Vijay 156
Sexton, Anne 112
Shakespeare, William 5, 33, 103, 156
Shakespeare: The Invention of the Human (Bloom) 4, 95, 110
Shattuck, Roger
　Banquet Years, The 102
Shelley, Percy Bysshe 153
　"Mont Blanc" 61
simulation 42
Sixth Meditation 118
"Skaters, The" (Ashbery) 45
skepticism
　epistemological 53
　and mind/body problem 49
　overcoming 56
　philosophical 104
　realism and 139
"Slumber Did My Spirit Seal, A" (Wordsworth) 60
social construction 26–8
social criticism 156
social identity 114
Socrates 1
　Crito 49
"Soldier, The" (Brooke) 26

"Soonest Mended" (Ashbery) 131, 153
"Sortes Vergilianae" (Ashbery) 105
Sources of Normativity, The
  (Korsgaard) 66
Stein, Gertrude 92, 93, 102, 126
Stein, Leo 102
Stevens, Wallace 5–7, 24, 60, 64, 71, 81–9, 110, 117, 141–2, 156–7
  "As You Leave the Room" 88
  "Auroras of Autumn, The" 47, 87–8
  "Comedian as the Letter C, The" 84–5
  "Inconceivable idea of the sun, The" 86
  It Must Be Abstract 86
  It Must Change 86
  It Must Give Pleasure 86
  "Notes toward a Supreme Fiction" 125
  poetry 81, 84
  soliloquy 143
  "Sunday Morning" 107–8
  "World as Meditation, The" 88
St. Louis Arch 43
Stonborough-Wittgenstein, Margaret "Gretl" 93
Story of the Vivian Girls, in What Is Known as the Realms of the Unreal, The (Darger) 103
Strand, Mark 149
subjective consciousness 6, 34, 52–3, 58, 62, 68, 144. *See also* conscious/consciousness
subjective experience 40–2. *See also* experience
subjectivity
  affirmation of 52, 55–7, 65, 68
  demands 31
  fixation on 152
  individual 5
  moral appeal 41
  pure 67
  representation 44
  risks 52
  self-conscious 4
  simpliciter 69
  transcendent 54, 58, 67, 70
sublime
  attenuated 61
  dynamical 52, 55, 65, 67, 73, 119, 150
  Kantian 6, 34, 45, 47–8, 95–6, 119, 135, 143, 147, 150

representation 42–8
romanticism and 7, 150
self-unimportance 151
temptation 87, 99, 149, 152
transcendence 60
sub specie aeternitatis 44, 119
"Sunday Morning" (Stevens) 107–8
Swann's way of domesticity 10
Sweet Cheat Gone, The (Proust) 109
Swimmer, The (Koethe) 145

Tennis Court Oath, The (Ashbery) 91, 129
theism 58
Three Poems (Ashbery) 5, 47, 125, 154
"Time is sorting us all out" (Ashbery) 12
Times Literary Supplement 91
Toklas, Alice 102
Tractatus Logico-Philosophicus
  (Wittgenstein) 15, 30, 37, 82–4, 94, 96–8, 113–14, 136–9, 162
transcendentalism, American 53
transcendental self 75, 136
transcendental subject 16–17, 74, 149
transcendent subjectivity 54, 57–8, 67, 70
trivial semantic conventionalism 121
truism 33
truth and poetry 107–16
  abstract thought 107–8
  "confessional" poetry 109
  issues 109
"Tuesday Evening" (Ashbery) 153
Tyson, Ann 151

Ulysses 88
unbounded magnitude 43
unselfconscious attitude 29
utilitarianism 41

vapidity 52
Vendler, Helen 6, 21, 141–2
  On Extended Wings 141
  Part of Nature, Part of Us 142
  Rock, The 59–61, 142
viewpoint dependence 41, 104

"Waste Land, The" (Eliot) 141–2, 156, 161
Wegner, Peter 93
"We had the experience but missed the meaning" (Eliot) 125

Well-Wrought Urn, The (Brooks) 111
"Wet Casements" (Ashbery) 13
What Makes Time Special (Callender) 188 n.10
Where Shall I Wander (Ashbery) 91
Why It Matters (Wolf) 101–5
Wilbur, Richard 117
Williams, Bernard 67, 102, 138
Williams, William Carlos 5, 157
Wilson, Mark 162, 176
Winkler, Kenneth 125
Wittgenstein, Ludwig 3, 23, 43, 49, 53, 59, 74–5, 81–9, 113, 126, 131, 162, 165, 171, 173–4
  anti-philosophical tendencies 81–2
  Culture and Value 97
  deflationist attitude 95
  I am the world (The microcosm) 143
  inner soliloquy 96
  interiority 100
  "Lecture on Ethics, A" 82, 97, 136
  and lyric subjectivity 93–100
  Philosophical Investigations 81, 109
  temptation of philosophy 84
  Tractatus Logico-Philosophicus 15, 30, 37, 82–4, 94, 96–8, 113–14, 136–9, 162
  views on mentality 99
Wittgenstein's Ladder (Perloff) 93, 126
Wittgenstein's Poker (Edmonds and Eidinow) 82

Wolf, Susan 138, 144
  Meaning in Life and Why It Matters 101–5, 160
"Wolf Ridge" (Ashbery) 91
Wordsworth, William 5–6, 50, 53–4, 87, 147, 156
  characterization of nature 55
  Lyrical Ballads 54
  "'O mercy!' to myself I cried, /'If Lucy should be dead!'" 148
  Prelude, The 46, 62, 77, 119, 135–6, 148, 150–4
  "Resolution and Independence" 153
  romanticism 67
  "Slumber Did My Spirit Seal, A" 60
Wordsworth's Fun (Bevis) 147–54
World as I found it, The 15–16
"World as Meditation, The" (Stevens) 88
Wright, Crispin 84–5, 176
Wright, James
  "I have wasted my life" 134–5
  "Lying in a Hammock at William Duffy's Farm in Pine Island, Minnesota" 123–4, 134

"You must change your life" (Rilke) 135

Zukofsky, Louis 5, 157
Zwicky, Jan 133, 135, 137–8

www.ingramcontent.com/pod-product-compliance
Lightning Source LLC
Chambersburg PA
CBHW061829300426
44115CB00013B/2304